Exploring
Physical
Mediumship

Exploring Physical Mediumship

Psychic Photos, Spirit Voices, & Materializations

Elaine M. Kuzmeskus

REDFeather™
MIND | BODY | SPIRIT

4880 Lower Valley Road, Atglen, PA 19310

ISBN: 978-0-7643-6376-4
Printed in India
Published by REDFeather Mind, Body, Spirit
An imprint of Schiffer Publishing, Ltd.
4880 Lower Valley Road
Atglen, PA 19310
Phone: (610) 593-1777; Fax: (610) 593-2002
Email: Info@redfeatherpub.com
Web: www.redfeatherpub.com
For our complete selection of fine books on this and
related subjects, please visit our website at
www.redfeatherpub.com. You may also write for a
free catalog.
REDFeather Mind, Body, Spirit's titles are available at
special discounts for bulk purchases for sales promotions
or premiums. Special editions, including personalized
covers, corporate imprints, and excerpts, can be
created in large quantities for special needs. For more
information, contact the publisher.
We are always looking for people to write books on new
and related subjects. If you have an idea for a book,
please contact us at proposals@schifferbooks.com.

Other REDFeather Titles by the Author:

Séance 101: Physical Links to the Other Side, ISBN 978-0-7643-2717-9

The Art of Mediumship: Psychic Investigation, Clairvoyance, and Channeling,
ISBN 978-0-7643-4016-1

Healing with Spirit: Health Intuition, Clairvoyance, and Afterlife Communication,
ISBN 978-0-7643-5638-4

Other REDFeather Titles on Related Subjects:

Light the Way: A Guide to Becoming a Rescue Medium, Amy Major,
ISBN 978-0-7643-5508-0

Life after Death: An Analysis of the Evidence, Robert Davis, PhD,
ISBN 978-0-7643-5438-0

Acknowledgments

During the course of investigating physical phenomena, I read extensive literature on the subject. I conducted my own research on table tipping, the spirit cabinet, and psychic photography. Also I attended over forty séances. Without witnessing the physical phenomena of the world's top mediums, this book would not be possible. Only a handful of physical mediums are alive today, and Hoyt Robinette, Kai Muegge, Warren Caylor, Mychael Shane, and David Thompson are among the best in the world. My thanks to these great souls for sharing their talent.

Rev. Hoyt Robinette created amazing spirit cards filled with names of my deceased relatives—the cards all written while placed in a closed basket! Several of his séances were conducted in my living room in full view and daylight. English medium Warren Caylor also gave unique séances at my home, so I can assure readers that there was no hidden microphone, wires, or hocus-pocus—yet, Warren levitated two trumpets, moved objects, and contacted the spirit of Winston Churchill, who spoke directly to sitters.

I also made it a point to attend the séances of German medium Kai Muegge when he was in Lily Dale, New York. He was the first medium that I saw produce sheets of ectoplasm. The medium levitated ping-pong balls, demonstrated trumpet mediumship, and gave a table-tipping session to remember!

Kai Muegge, Warren Caylor, and Seattle medium Mychael Shane are known for their apports. Without a doubt, they possess that rare ability to materialize objects. I have witnessed a 3-inch faceted crystal materialize in Caylor's mouth and literally fifty crystal apports pour out from Mychael Shane's mouth, as well as watched closely as a 3-inch Hindu religious medal appeared from thin air at a Kai Muegge séance.

New Zealand medium David Thompson's séance is perhaps the best known of the materialization mediums. I attended six of his séances over a two-year period. Not only do the spirits materialize in his séance room, but spirits such as Louie Armstrong also speak directly so everyone one can hear them. The spirits who materialize gave their names as well as touched sitters with spirit and leaving a lasting impression with their messages.

My list of acknowledgments would not be complete without thanking Dr. Neal Rzepkowski for hosting Kai Muegge, Warren Caylor, and Mychael Shane at his home in Lily Dale, New York. He has traveled the world at his expense to observe physical mediums firsthand. I also wish to thank Rev. Thomas Newman for graciously hosting David Thompson, as well as Rev. Gail Hicks, Theresa Howard, Sylvia Molta, and Ronald Kuzmeskus for organizing Hoyt Robinette's séances.

Camp Chesterfield also deserves a note of thanks. I was allowed free access to the Hett Art Gallery and Museum. It was a privilege to view their large collection of precipitated portraits of the Bangs sisters and other physical phenomena. Rev. Suzanne Greer, Rev. Patricia Kennedy, Rev. Glenda Cadarette, and Rev. Vickie Corkell were most helpful.

Ron Nagy, curator of the Lily Dale Museum, was most generous with his assistance. The author of *Precipitated Spirit Paintings* patiently answered my many questions regarding spirit art of the Bangs sisters and the Campbell Brothers, which hang on the walls of the Lily Dale Museum.

So many people have made this book possible by sharing their expertise: Rev. Gladys Custance; Rev. Kenneth Custance; Tom and Lisa Butler, directors of the Association TransCommunication; Rev. Muriel Tenant, a tutor at the Arthur Findlay College; Rev. Brian Kent; Rev. Lynn Kent; and spirit artist Rev. Rita Berkowitz. Over the years I have received great encouragement from sessions with Rev. William Ellis, Jean Crown, Elwood Babbitt, Rev. Carl Hewitt, Rev. Dorothy Smith, and Kevin Ryerson.

Finally, I wish to thank my editors. Dr. Susan Roberts has worked with me on all ten of my books. Not only does she excel in checking punctuation and quotes, but she also gives the candid feedback so necessary when tackling an esoteric subject such as physical mediumship. It is always a pleasure to work with a friend. I also wish to thank Peggy Kellar, developmental editor at Schiffer Publishing, for her insightful comments and detailed final edit of the book. Thanks also to Schiffer editor James Young for giving the book a last look and an expert polish.

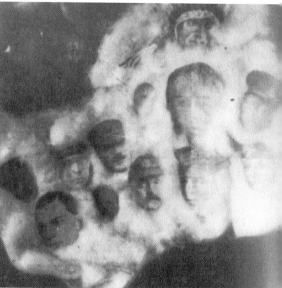

Contents

Spirit Plays the Harp!

There is no death and there are no dead.

—Spiritualist tenet

Pundits in the East note, "When the student is ready, the teacher appears." At twenty-two, I was ready for my first spiritual teacher, Rev. Bill Ellis. It happened unexpectedly during a weekend trip to Maine. While I was perusing a local Bangor newspaper, I spotted a small announcement at the back of the paper: "Opening services for the First Spiritualist Camp of Etna Maine Sunday at 2:00 PM." As I felt every hair on my arm lift, I knew that I had to go!

Since I had never met a medium, I did not know quite what to do when I arrived at the camp. The first person I spied was a short, gray-haired lady out for a walk. "Do you know any mediums?" I asked. "Yes," she replied. "If you want an honest reading, go to Bill Ellis." The woman then directed me to a cottage across the way. As I started toward the Ellis cottage, I had second thoughts and asked the stranger, "How do you know that Bill Ellis is an honest medium?" "I am Mrs. Ellis," she smiled sweetly.

With this recommendation, I gingerly knocked on Rev. Ellis's door. He kindly gave me my first reading for a fee of five dollars. The Spiritualist medium tuned into many aspects of my life. For example, he said, "You have a lot of yellow [my favorite color] in your aura," "An older, taller lady was in back of you and is guiding you" [my grandmother], and "You are not going to marry the man you are seeing" His words turned out to be true! While all his comments seemed plausible, I shrugged as Rev. Ellis said: "I know you don't believe me, but someday you will be doing this work." Twelve years later I ran into Rev. Ellis at Camp Temple Heights, in Northport, Maine, where I was the resident medium. When I told him how skeptical I had been when he had prophesized I would become a medium, we both had a hearty laugh.

After my reading at Camp Etna, I was sufficiently intrigued by spirit communication to enroll in a Boston Spiritualist circle presided over by Rev. Gladys Custance and her husband, Rev. Kenneth Custance. In 1969, their Boston group had expanded to about forty sitters, including housewives, secretaries, retirees, teachers, a rabbi, a dentist, and a professor from Massachusetts Institute of Technology.

The psychic professor proudly told the group how he had prophesized in the 1940s that the United States would have a man on the moon. When his colleagues expressed skepticism, he pounded his desk, declaring, "In twenty-five years, I'll have a piece of moon on my desk!" Sure enough, his prediction came true in 1969, when one of the astronauts brought a moon rock as a gift to the MIT researcher.

We were all in awe of the instructor, Rev. Gladys Custance, who gave lessons while in trance. Her guide was a Hindu spirit dubbed "the Professor." Mrs. Custance stressed three rules for mediumship: (1) "Tension shuts the door," (2) "Give impressions as they come to you," and (3) "Speak up when you are given a message." The last rule was because Mrs. Custance often required the voice of the sitter, so she could continue the message from spirit. She explained, "Spirit works off voice vibration."

During the meditation portion of our mediumship training, Rev. Kenneth Custance turned out the lights, so the spirits could do their work. Soon we were experiencing clairvoyance as blue and purple lights swirled around the room, clairaudience as many heard messages from spirit, and clairguisience as we caught the scent of lilacs, roses, and cherry tobacco. These fragrances would permeate the room as different spirits made their appearances. Almost everyone experienced a heaviness like a helmet over their head. It seemed as if the spirits were opening the crown chakras and third eyes of fledging clairvoyants.

After all the messages were given for the evening, Mrs. Custance would ask, "Did anyone feel a change of forces?," indicating that the energy was going down as the spirits departed for the evening. While it is hard to explain, it just seemed like a "dead zone"—no lights, energy, or fragrance remained after the spirits departed.

Their mutual interest in mediumship brought the Custances to several Spiritualist locations such as the Church of the Golden Gate in San Francisco, Lily Dale Assembly in New York, and Camp Chesterfield in Indiana. It was at Chesterfield that Gladys and Kenneth Custance attended a materialization séance. According to Mrs. Custance, the medium sat down on a chair, and the curtains to the black-cloth cabinet were closed. The medium then went into trance. Within minutes, a materialized form of Mrs. Custance's grandmother stepped out from behind the curtains. Not only did the spirit appear to look like her grandmother, but also she sounded like her grandmother, who was Gladys's first harp teacher.

Even so, Gladys was surprised to hear the spirit even offer to play a song on her grand-daughter's harp. Kenneth hastily fetched Gladys's Irish harp from their car. He obligingly placed the harp in front of the materialized grandmother, who always played a full-sized concert harp. When the spirit looked at the Irish harp, she quipped, "My but the harp has shrunk." Next, Grandmother asked, "What do you want me to play, dear?" Gladys sagely replied, "Our favorite song." The spirit then proceeded to play "Brahms Lullaby," the song she and her granddaughter played every night before bedtime!

Rev. Gladys Custance and Rev. Kenneth Custance, with artist Meroe Morse in the center. *Author's collection*

CHAPTER 1:

Camp Chesterfield

Before our eyes we saw the form of a violin and bow assemble. As the bow was drawn across the gauze-like strings, we heard music . . . violin music . . . only sweeter . . . more heavenly than an earthly instrument could produce. The selection played was "Sweet Mystery of Life."
How appropriate!

—Grace P. Schafer

Grace P. Schafer, feature writer for the *Psychic Observer*, described a séance in which the spirit of a teenage boy materialized to play the violin for his mother. The medium was Lulu Taber, and the séance took place at Camp Chesterfield on August 4, 1941. Coleen Owen Britt, the lad's mother, was anxious to contact her sixteen-year-old son, Bryon, who had passed to spirit in 1939. Mrs. Britt was pleased beyond words at the sight of her son, a budding violinist, emerge from the cabinet to play the violin. According to Grace P. Schafer:

What I like about Mrs. Taber's materializations is there is no question about the spirits who come through. When they make an entrée they announce their full names and the names of the ones they have come to visit. I was deeply impressed by the spirit who announced his name, "Byron Britt." He called for his parents. They asked him if he could play something on the violin for them. Before our eyes we saw the form of a violin and bow assemble. As the bow was drawn across the gauze-like strings, we heard music . . . violin music . . . only sweeter, more heavenly than an earthly instrument could produce. The selection played was "Sweet Mystery of Life." How appropriate![1]

For those who are open to the power of spirit, physical phenomena are possible. Since 1885, Camp Chesterfield in Chesterfield, Indiana, has been home to Spiritualists who sought to practice their faith away from the prying eyes of nonbelievers. Originally, it was a place for ardent Spiritualists to pitch a tent, attend gatherings, listen to lectures on mediumship, and hold séances in peace and privacy. Simple tents and wooden cottages built around its meetinghouse were used at Camp Chesterfield's beginning. Later, the camp added a dining hall, lodging house, tent auditorium, and two séance cabins. By 1914, a two-story hotel, the Sun Flower, was constructed. In 1945 the Western Hotel was added. The Western Hotel, with its art deco check-in counter, is similar to the many roadside inns of the day. In 1954, the Cathedral in the Woods was added as an avenue for large gatherings.

The Hett Gallery, financed by Dr. J. E. Hett in 1958, was the last building to be constructed at Camp Chesterfield, about an hour from Indianapolis. The massive task of acquiring objects for the space was entrusted to Mrs. Mable Riffle and her assistant, Juliet Ewing Pressing. The two soon acquired artifacts for the museum from Spiritualist communities in the United States and all over the world. The museum houses artifacts ranging from 3-inch medallions, apported by Boston medium Margery to a life-size bust of an Egyptian queen.

The Hett Gallery also has a vast number of precipitated portraits done by sisters May and Lizzie Bangs. The Chicago mediums were known for their portraits produced by invisible hands. The likenesses were often made for grief-stricken relatives, such as a precipitated portrait of Bernal Tobias, a blonde lad dressed in a frilly white blouse. Sadly, the four-year-old diabetic son of Addie and Henry Tobias died on Christmas Eve. When the Bangs sisters did his precipitated portrait, a cloud appeared and then the picture took form. According to those present, the child's eyes were shut; then they opened and closed several times before they finally remained open.[2]

The Bangs sisters precipitated another unusual portrait for Dr. Daughtery, who lost his wife and two twin daughters in an accident in the 1920s. He asked Lizzie and May Bangs for a painting of his family. When he sat for the portrait, only his wife appeared—not the twins, Mary and Christina. The disappointed father placed the picture in a closet, with the intention of returning it the next day. When he went to fetch it, Dr. Daughtery was amazed to see the likeness of his twins on the precipitated painting.

Another famous precipitated painting is that of Rose Carson, the second wife of Dr. Carson, of Kansas City, Missouri. The portrait was precipitated in 1894, the same year as another picture was produced of Dr. Carson's late first wife, Emily. Over the years, the portraits have maintained their supernatural quality. Seminary students at Camp Chesterfield like to visit the gallery just to count the number of roses in the precipitated portrait of Rose Carson. Sometimes there are twelve; other times, eleven or thirteen.

Camp Chesterfield is also known the world over for its trumpet séances. The most noted of its trumpet mediums were John Bunker, Clifford Bias, James Laughton, and Bill English. John Bunker began to sit for development with the medium Margaret Bright after the death of his ten-year-old daughter, Eva. When his little girl came through, he was delighted at the prospect of having her back in his life as a spirit messenger.

According to John Bunker, "Much of your mediumship will be gained in direct proportion to your ability to relax at the time the demonstration takes place."[3] He also stressed the importance of controlling the mind and emotions, along with meditation and breathing exercises. He believed that by controlling the breath and focusing energy on the spine, that it was possible to raise psychic energy from the base of the spine to the fifth psychic center at the top of the spine.

Rev. Bunker also recommended that students sitting for physical mediumship sit in a straight-back chair without touching the back of the chair. When mentally ready, the student should inhale to the count of seven heartbeats. "As you do this, mentally direct the Cosmic energy which is in the air to the base of your spine or first psychic center. Hold the energy at this point for a count of three heartbeats. Then draw it up your spine to the root of your neck and exhale through the mouth for seven beats. Pause for three heartbeats, then begin the inhalations again."[4] Bunker suggested up to seven inhalations—but no more.

John Bunker soon became a sought-after trumpet medium. As his reputation grew, he was consulted by many well-known figures, including the "veiled lady" who was known to visit Rudolf Valentino's grave each year. On the anniversary of Valentino's death, a beautiful lady arrived for a trumpet mediumship session in which spirit spoke through the trumpet so the sitter could talk with the deceased. "A man spoke through the trumpet and suddenly Mr. Bunker realized it was Rudolf Valentino. Only then did the medium realize that he was talking to the fabled '"veiled lady!'"[5]

Reverend Clifford Bias was so adept at physical phenomena that he wrote a book on the subject. In *Trumpet Mediumship and Its Development*, he gave this advice: "If you are sitting for the enfoldment of the mental phases of mediumship, you must acquire the ability to receive, translate, and transmit information from the spirit places of life to the dwellers of the earth plane. If you are developing any of the physical phases of mediumship, you are attempting to act as a center into which energy can be accumulated and then used for the production of physical phenomena."[6]

Rev. Robert G. Chaney, author of *Mediums and Their Development*, also explained the dynamics of physical communication. His first evidence of spirit survival came from his psychic great-grandmother. After sitting for six weeks of trumpet mediumship and psychic photography, he heard a male voice say, "Grandmother Holcolm."[7] Eventually Chaney developed trumpet mediumship and psychic photography. He received instructions for solar plexus photography from spirit at another trumpet séance. The male voice coming from the levitating trumpet requested that he take a handkerchief from his pocket, then hold it, unfolded over his solar plexus for a minute. Chaney did as directed by spirit. When the séance was over, there was a picture of a young man on the handkerchief.[8]

Camp Chesterfield remains much the same since the 1940s, when Robert Chaney was resident medium. Even as late as the 1950s, genuine materializations were taking place. When Indiana medium Don Kemp attended a séance at the camp, he received five materializations: "I felt the first three visitations weren't authentic but then my brother materialized followed by my Grandma. I knew they were authentic." Kemp's convincing detail was his brother's reference to Don's actual birth date, which had always been in dispute with the date printed on his birth certificate.[9]

Later, in 1960, psychic investigators Andrija Puharich and Tom O'Neill uncovered fraud with the aid of infrared photography and a snooperscope—a device developed by the United States Army to enhance night vision of the battlefield. Noted medium Edith Stillwell agreed to conduct a materialization séance. Camp president Mable Riffle acted as her cabinet attendant. The film clearly revealed "spirits" merging from trap doors to produce fraudulent materialization. "Peering through the snooperscope in the dark, Puharich saw that what were supposed to be spirit forms materializing out of thin air were actually figures wrapped in chiffon entering the séance room through a hidden door from an adjacent apartment."[10] When Dr. Puharich later examined the infrared motion picture, his eyewitness observation was confirmed. "There, etched unmistakably on the film, were the familiar faces of camp mediums, dressed up in gauze, impersonating departed spirits."[11] The July 10, 1960, issue of the *Psychic Observer* bore the headline "We Are in Mourning: The Tragic Deceptions in Materialization."

Since then, materialization mediumship at Camp Chesterfield has all but disappeared. Trumpet séances, however, have continued unabated. One of the last of the great trumpet mediums was Rev. Bill English. According to Rev. Suzanne Greer, "Bill had four trumpets up in the air at the same time." She was quick to add that Rev. English ran a strict séance room—requiring people to sign up in advance. "Once, when an uninvited woman knocked on his cottage door, telling the medium, 'My guide says I am to attend your séance,' Bill quipped, 'Well, he didn't tell me,' and closed the door."

In 2005, the camp was still sponsoring trumpet séances. I attended Reverend Suzanne Greer's "Introduction to the Séance Room." Rev. Greer, of Hungarian ancestry, has been a medium for over thirty years. She recommended that students read *101 Questions and Answers* by Peggy Barnes to familiarize themselves with physical mediumship. A stickler for accuracy would never accept a weak excuse such as "Well, spirit told me." "Remember," Greer reminded her pupils, "you are in control of spirit."

Before our group of twelve students descended the stairs to the medium's séance room, she explained that the room had to be pitch black. "If there is even a tiny speck of light, it can disturb the séance," she added. The sitters were warned not to leave the room since that would end the séance. Under no circumstances was anyone allowed to touch the medium or the trumpet. Then Rev. Greer took her seat inside a small cabinet about the size of a telephone booth. Once the lights were turned off, the room was pitch dark. As instructed beforehand, everyone sang cheerful tunes such as "Jingle Bells" to bring up the vibration for about five minutes. Soon the trumpet lifted and acted as a megaphone to the spirit world. The first spirit to come through was the medium's spirit guide, Penny. We could all hear Penny's voice. Next, each person received a message from a spirit loved one. While many students could see the trumpet float around the room, some had to squint a bit. The medium obligingly lowered the trumpet, so we could all feel the trumpet tap us on our toes!

Rev. Louise Irvine's Ascended Master Séance was also held in pitch darkness. For over an hour, the Ascended Masters spoke through two trumpets that were held in midair by an invisible force. One, El Morya, described his ashram in India. The participants were impressed with the séance, although one gentleman wondered if the gemstone apports we received supposedly from spirit had been purchased instead at the local crystal shop. However, everyone agreed that the two trumpets did float around the room, emanating voices from distinguished spirits. For instance, Morya came through the levitated trumpet and announced his presence in a male voice. He chatted about his ashram, located in the etheric sphere just above Darjeeling, India.

Another Camp Chesterfield resident, Rev. Hoyt Robinette, is one of the few mediums who can precipitate spirit drawing. He sat in a circle with his mentor Rev. Bill English for seventeen years to develop his gift of trumpet and spirit card mediumship. The premier physical medium now travels the word to demonstrate his precipitated cards, which he produced with the aid of spirit and his own spirit control, Dr. Kenner. Robinette was born in Tennessee earned a master's degree in clinical psychology from the University of

Kentucky. He first became aware of his gifts at the age of thirteen, when the spirit of a very recently departed friend contacted him. Later, at twenty-one years old, he met Reverend Bill D. English, a veteran trumpet medium. He eventually developed the gifts of trumpet mediumship and spirit card writing under English's tutorage.

When I visited Camp Chesterfield in the summer of 2005, Rev. Hoyt Robinette agreed to do a spirit card séance for eight sitters. The séance began with Rev. Robinette holding his cobra basket upside down to show it was completely empty. Then he opened a new pack of 3-by-5-inch index cards, which he placed in the basket with a variety of colored pens and pencils with their caps on. Minutes later, the medium opened the basket and handed each of us our spirit card. I was thrilled to see the names of my teachers, Gladys and Kenneth Custance; grandmother Katherine Brickett; guides Bright Star, Yogananda, Dr. Cathart, and Chief Kiokee; and Rev. Arthur Ford with a heart next to his name.

Then on the back were two figures who resembled the Rev. Carl Hewitt, a Connecticut medium who had passed to spirit, and the late physical medium Rev. Clifford Bias. The card was created in an unusual choice of colors—rust and green. The uncommon choice of colors did not make much sense until my book *Connecticut Ghosts* came out. The cover, chosen by the publishers, was in rust and lime green with two puffs of clouds!

Spirit card precipitated by Rev. Hoyt Robinette at Camp Chesterfield, Chesterfield, Indiana

Rev. Carl Hewitt. *Author's collection*

CHAPTER 2

Spirit Guides

Spirit guides can and do preform kindly offices for those on earth, but benefit can only be received on the condition that we allow them to become our teachers, not our masters, that we accept them as companions, but not Gods to be worshipped.

—Rev. Andrew Jackson Davis

Mediums such as those at Camp Chesterfield develop with the assistance of spirit guides. Two spirit guides played a vital role in the development of medium Rev. Andrew Jackson Davis. The first was the spirit of the Greek physician Marcus Galen, and the second that of the famous seer Emanuel Swedenborg. The pioneer of Spiritualism made contact with his guides while he was in this out-of-body state. After the Roman physician Galen delivered a discourse on the healing power of nature, Emanuel Swedenborg stepped forward to encourage the young clairvoyant to become a vessel for spirit. Davis took the advice of both guides and became a trance medium, well known for his medical clairvoyance. The young medium was able to accurately diagnose medical disorders by peering clairvoyantly into the human body: "Each organ stood out clearly with a special luminosity of its own which greatly diminished in cases of disease."[1]

Davis was left a legacy of over thirty books. In *The Penetralia*, written in 1856, the channeler described the automobile—a good twenty years before German inventor Karl Benz built the first car: "Look out about these days for carriages and travelling saloons on country—without horses, without steam, without any visible motive power—moving with greater speed and far more safety than at present. Carriages will be moved by a strange and beautiful and simple admixture of aqueous and atmospheric gases—so easily condensed, so simply ignited, and so imparted by a machine somewhat resembling fire engines as to be entirely concealed and manageable between the forward wheels."[2] His guides also foretold the invention of the typewriter and the discovery of more planets in the solar system. In March 1846, Andrew Jackson Davis said that there were nine planets in our solar system. At that time, astronomers knew of only seven (Mercury, Venus, Earth, Mars, Jupiter, Saturn, and Uranus)—Neptune and Pluto had yet to be discovered. "He wrote about The Theory of Evolution a decade before Darwin published *On the Origin of Species* and discovered many other scientific laws before their discovery."[3]

In the late 1930s, Maurice Barbanell, founder of *Psychic News* magazine, worked with a guide named Silver Birch. The North American Indian was quick to explain that he was only acting as translator. "I am but a humble servant," he said. "An interpreter for those who have sent me to expound forgotten laws that must be revived as part of the new world that is gradually dawning. Think of me always as a mouthpiece."[4] According to Silver Birch, "Life is not chance, accident or even coincidence. The whole of life is governed by immutable natural law."[5]

A contemporary of Barbanell's, trance medium Grace Cooke, also had an American Indian as a guide, named White Eagle. As the spirit explained, "We have worked for many incarnations in the personality we take on when we come into physical conditions, to bring to men and women an understanding of the brotherhood of all life, so that the kingdom of God shall come upon earth. But this can only happen when men and women have discovered that within their own souls is the light of the spirit of Christ, the Christ light which is the seed given to every one of them"[6] Sir Arthur Conan Doyle and British prime minister Ramsay MacDonald vouched for the truth of White Eagle's readings.

Professional mediums such as Grace Cooke often attract five guides: a personal guide, a master teacher, a master chemist, an American Indian, and a joy guide. Sometimes a deceased medium will step in to assist. For example, Glenda Cadarette, the popular Camp Chesterfield medium, has the spirits of two deceased mediums from the camp— trumpet medium Rev. Clifford Bias and departed materialization medium Pansy Cox. Rev. Hoyt Robinette, on the other hand, has Doctor Kenner as his control. However, his mentor, Reverend Bill English, occasionally makes his presence known in the séance room, along with Rev. Bias. When Rev. Robinette does spirit photographs on silk, the spirit of Charles Swann, a Chesterfield medium known for spirit photography, likes to make an appearance.

Camp Chesterfield honors mediums past and present by proclaiming, "Spirit lives," chiseled over the archway of the church platform. Spirit guides are equally important as the messenger. When mediums work on the platform, they make it a point to introduce their guides to the audience. For example, Rev. Suzanne Greer began her art program with "Hello, I am Rev. Suzanne Greer, and I will be working with my guide Penny today." Then the veteran medium tuned into spirits to do sketches of the faces of departed loved ones.

Another spirit artist, Rev. Phyllis Davis, did a portrait of my spirit guide in the spring of 2007. After a few minutes of conversation, the gray-haired medium went quietly to work. She tuned in to a Tibetan guide with her clairvoyance. She simply shut her eyes, remained silent, and then opened her eyes to pick up a brown pastel crayon to begin to draw. Within an hour's time, the elderly clairvoyant drew a portrait of the Tibetan lama.

In January 2013, Rev. Glenda Cadarette conducted a trance mediumship seminar at Camp Chesterfield. She stressed the importance of developing personal relationship with guides. For instance, her joy guide, Poppy, is a close connection. Her guide even helps her medium pick out the flowers for flower séances. One December, Poppy wanted Glenda to purchase a miniature Christmas tree that did not appeal to Glenda's sensibilities—it just seemed tacky. Somehow, the tree ended up in her shopping cart and in the basket of flowers slated for Camp Chesterfield. During the flower séance, Glenda was drawn to the tiny Christmas tree as she heard a voice claiming to be the father of a man sitting in a church pew. Glenda handed the gentleman the Christmas tree, with the message "Your father, James, is here and he wants you to have this Christmas tree. He wishes you a 'Merry Christmas' and says it will bring back many memories." The elderly man was overcome with emotion—he and his father owned a Christmas tree farm.[7]

Spirit guides often know best, since they can easily view past and present. However, they vary considerably in wisdom, from the personal recollections given by joy guides such as Poppy, to the lofty teachings of the ascended masters. Helena Petrovna Blavatsky (HPB) communicated with two ascended masters—Morya and Koot Hoomi. While accustomed to messages from them, she was still surprised to see Morya in London. Apparently, the master had materialized and was seen walking down Bond Street when Madame Blavatsky spied his familiar image.

She had a strong tie to Morya, who was known to be a formidable taskmaster. Even so, HPB never doubted his advice. Once when the medium was living in poverty in a Paris apartment, she was given a very large sum of money, 23,000 French francs. The ascended master came to her and told her to take the money and give it to a man at a specific location in Buffalo, New York. When she returned to the United States, she did as the master requested, and gave the sum to a most grateful man. The gentleman was just about to commit suicide due to a financial crisis.[8]

In 1875 Madame Blavatsky and Henry Steele Olcutt formed the Theosophical Society. Her psychic powers—telepathy, clairvoyance, and physical phenomena—were always evident. She was known to have the ability to access documents in faraway libraries she had never visited in her physical body. Colonel Olcutt described her pen flying over the page, "when she would suddenly stop, look out into space with the vacant eye of a clairvoyant seer, shorten her vision as though to look at something held invisible in the air before her, and begin copying on her paper what she saw."[9] Her efforts produced two occult masterpieces—*Isis Unveiled* in 1877 and *The Secret Doctrine* in 1888. Even Albert Einstein was known to keep a copy of *The Secret Doctrine* on his desk.[10]

Morya also materialized to reassure Madame Blavatsky's editor, Henry Olcutt. One evening as he was reading quietly in his room, he spied the master's tall turbaned head with long raven hair, black beard, and fiery eyes. Then as Colonel Olcutt was wondering how he could prove that the materialization was real, the spirit read his thoughts: "The Master smiled kindly as if reading my thought, untwisted the fehta [turban] from his head, benignantly saluted me in farewell and—was gone: his chair was empty; I was alone with my emotions."[11]

Psychic Edgar Cayce frequently received visitations of a spiritual nature. He met his first angel as a child, when a beautiful lady asked what he would like to do with his life. The young Cayce replied, "I would like to help others—especially children."[12] He did not become aware of his channeling ability, however, until he was an adult and lost his ability to speak. He consulted a local hypnotist, Al Layne, to help restore his voice. Not only did the hypnosis restore Cayce's speech, but it also led to contact with Cayce's guide known as "the Source." He also had a spirit guide that was a doctor from the turn of the century, who dispensed medical advice in Victorian prose. It wasn't long before Edgar Cayce became known as the "Sleeping Prophet."

Occasionally the archangel Michael came through the "Sleeping Prophet." Hugh Lynn Cayce, the prophet's son, was present on one such occasion: "[Archangel] Michael's message was given with such force that I could hear the windows rattling in their frames in our home. I could even hear the cups rattling in the dish drainer in the kitchen. The vibrations nearly knocked us all out of our chairs."[13]

Michael came through during a reading for four-year-old Faith Harding, known as "the Little Prophetess." Her mother was told that Faith was "a chosen channel of love which the Father hath bestowed upon the children of men."[14] According to Cayce, Faith was an incarnation of Saint Cecilia, the patron saint of music. Her parents were advised to foster "patience, in love, in kindness, in gentleness, in those things that bring constructive, hopeful, helpful forces into the experiences of others."[15] Unfortunately, Faith's father paid little heed to the reading. All too soon the gifted child was a pawn in a bitter custody battle. Her father, a nonbeliever, gained custody of Faith. Sadly, the child "oracle" of 1941 who had prophesized the Japanese attack on Pearl Harbor never developed her healing and psychic abilities.

During the 1920s Edgar Cayce was relatively unknown. The two most famous mediums of the period were Margery Crandon and Eileen Garrett. "Margery the Medium" was truly the last of the great physical mediums. Her deceased brother, Walter Stinson, loved to come through with a signature whistle and a few wisecracks. With her guide Walter's assistance, the Boston medium was able to produce psychic music, direct voice, and trumpet séances. She moved objects about the room and also produced apports—objects materialized by spirit forces.

Even Harry Houdini could not duplicate her feats. One of Walter's signature feats was to ring a bell box that was placed several feet away from the medium. Ever protective of his sister, Walter was incensed when Harry Houdini tried to put one over on his sister. Walter saw an eraser placed between the contact boards, which would make it difficult to ring the bell. The spirit, speaking in a voice that everyone in the séance room could hear, accused Houdini of cheating. "Houdini, have you got the mark just right?" When Dr. Daniel Comstock, one of the experts on the *Scientific American* prize committee, demanded to know what the spirit meant, Walter replied: "Comstock, you take that box into white light and examine it, and report back. You'll see fast enough what I mean." Sure enough, there the researcher found an eraser jammed in the bell box. His good-natured sister would never have known this if not for her spirit brother.[16]

While Margery Crandon's guide was a relative, her contemporary Eileen Garrett had several ancient spirit guides. The Irish-born medium's guides included her control, Uvani, a fourteenth-century Arab soldier, and three other guides. While Uvani remained in charge, Abdul Latif, a seventeenth-century Persian physician, would give advice on healing, and Tahotah and Ramah, who professed no prior earthly incarnations, spoke occasionally on philosophical matters.[17]

In the 1920s, the Irish-born medium studied with J. Hewat McKenzie, founder of the British College of Psychic Science in London. Eileen had the gift of second sight and often saw spirits as a child in Ireland. Under McKenzie's careful guidance, Mrs. Garret became one of the top trance mediums at the college, so much so that she was asked to hold a séance after the recent death of Sir Arthur Conan Doyle.

On October 7, 1930, the medium complied with the request for a trance session. To everyone's surprise, Uvani brought through instead the spirit of Flight Lieutenant H. Carmichael Irwin, the captain of the English airship R101, which exploded on a hillside in France on the evening of October 4, 1930. He wanted to set the record straight. No one had expected the luxurious airship equipped with two decks, fifty passenger cabins, and even an asbestos-lined smoking room to go down.[18]

Speaking in an agitated voice, Lieutenant Irwin was anxious to describe the accident that claimed the lives of forty-eight of its fifty-four passengers. Lord Thomson, secretary of state for air, and Sir Sefton Brancker, director of civil aviation, were listed among the dead.[19] During the séance (as well as six more sessions, in which other alleged deceased members of the crew spoke out), Irwin provided technical knowledge concerning the crash that no one else could have known at the time. Months later, the results of the official investigation confirmed everything that Irwin and the other crew members had revealed.[20] With her reputation as a trance medium firmly established, Eileen Garrett settled in New York City the following year, where she started Creative Age Press in 1941 and the Parapsychology Foundation in 1951. She continued as director of the foundation until her death in 1970. Two years before her 1970 death, she published her autobiography, *Many Voices.*

While Mrs. Garrett started her mediumship development through clairvoyant episodes, Arthur Ford realized his psychic abilities through clairaudience. During World War I, he heard the names of soldiers several days before they were written on the morning's casualty list.[21] In 1924 he made contact with the spirit of Fletcher, a childhood acquaintance who had met his death during World War II. With Fletcher's assistance, Arthur Ford became well known for his ability to provide first and last names of the deceased. When Sir Arthur Conan Doyle saw him work on the podium in 1927, he gave the medium high praise. "One of the most amazing things I have ever seen in 41 years of psychic experience was the demonstration of Arthur Ford."[22]

Two years later, Rev. Arthur Ford became famous after he contacted the spirit of Harry Houdini at a January 8, 1929, séance. Houdini spelled out the word "believe," using a code known only to him and his wife, Bess. Later, on February 9, 1929, Bess Houdini verified that the séance had been a success. "Regardless of any statement made to the contrary: I wish to declare that the message, in its entirety, and in the agreed[-]upon sequence, given to me by Arthur Ford, is the correct message prearranged between Mr. Houdini and myself."[23] In 1967, Rev. Ford made headlines again when he conducted the first televised séance for Episcopal bishop James Pike from his son who had been found dead. According to the *New York Times*, "Dr. Pike said he believed messages received in a taped séance, shown on a Toronto television station in 1967, were authentic."[24]

Few mediums receive the recognition of the late Arthur Ford. While Elwood Babbitt was not as well known as Ford, he was one of the nation's premier trance mediums. He had two main controls—Dr. Fisher, a physician from centuries ago, and Jim Cole, who helped adjust vibrations between spirit and Elwood's body. On occasion, Babbitt channeled the spirits of Mark Twain, Mahatma Gandhi, and Dr. Wilhelm Reich, among others. When Babbitt channeled his first book, *Talks with Christ*, the energy of the Christ consciousness was so high that the trance medium became ill for two weeks. His guide Doctor Fisher stepped in as an intermediary to buffer the intense Christ energy. Babbitt also channeled Vishnu in *God Within* and *Perfect Health*. In his last book, *Perfect Health*, Babbitt brought through distinguished doctors including Wilhelm Reich, the controversial Austrian psychiatrist who attributed diseases to emotional blocks. Reich was ahead of his times. He understood the mind-body connection in the 1930s, when most physicians scoffed at the idea of an energy medicine. Dr. Reich proposed the idea of orgone energy, a concept similar to Dr. Franz Anton Mesmer's animal magnetism or Dr. Carl Reichenbach's odic force. He believed that deficits or constrictions in orgone were responsible for disease, and he invented "orgone accumulators" to collect this energy and improve health.

Apparently, Dr. Reich still practices medicine from the other side of life. When one of Elwood Babbitt's clients asked the spirit psychiatrist about depression, the gentleman was told that his depression emanated from "fears and uncertainties of life" and "from those intimately associated with your life" as well as "thought pollution that surrounds you."[25] For those seeking relief from depression, Reich advised color and music therapy, as well as maintaining a positive attitude.

While Elwood Babbitt channeled Doctor Fisher, a guide from a few centuries ago, J. Z. Knight, brought through the spirit of a 35,000-year-old warrior from Lemuria. Ramtha literally stepped into her life in 1977, when Knight placed a replica of the Great Pyramid on her head in jest. She was balancing the paper pyramid when she looked up to see a very tall man standing in the doorway. Spirit announced, "I am Ramtha the Enlightened One. I have come to help you over the ditch."[26]

During the next seven years, Ramtha trained his protégé to be a trance medium. Eventually J. Z. channeled *The White Book*, which is filled with Ramtha's philosophy. In it, Ramtha explained that people have unlimited and largely untapped potentials: "The more you desire to love what you are and to live in knowingness, the more your brain is opened up by the God that surrounds your being, greater and greater and greater."[27]

Jean Loomis was just as surprised to be psychic as J. Z. Knight was. In the late 1970s, the high school English teacher suffered a cardiac-induced heart attack during a routine operation. She described her near-death experience to a group at the Phenix Society: "I floated above my body. I could see my doctor working frantically on my chest. Finally after a few minutes, he gave up and put the sheet over my head. 'She's gone,' he said. Then the intern—a young man with his hair in a pony tail—put the sheet off and started doing CPR." Immediately, Jean, who been watching the scene from above, was back in her pain-wrecked body. When Jeannie recovered, she told friends, "I am alive today all because of that intern with a pony tail!" In 1981, she opened the Aquarian Center in Branford, where she dispensed psychic advice along with astrology charts and hypnosis until her death in 2016.

A bout with ill health also increased Rosemary Brown's psychic abilities. When the spirit of Franz Liszt had contacted Rosemary Browne as a child, she did not pay much attention. As an adult, she began sitting at the piano while she was homebound due to a car accident. To her surprise, she found herself playing quite expertly—even with just a rudimentary knowledge of music. In her autobiography, *Unfinished Symphonies*, she stated that the spirit of Franz Liszt was guiding her fingers at the piano. She was now ready to channel his music.

Likewise, it took time for physical medium Mychael Shane to be ready for his guides. At the age of seven, he could produce apports of precious gems while playing in the backyard. However, as a young man he had no interest in psychic phenomena. Instead he pursued a variety of careers—including a stint in the military and being in a rock band—before he was ready to channel Ascended Being of Shamballah.

The Seattle medium has an affinity for Master Kuthumi (Koot Hoomi) and Ascended Master Saint Germaine, who watches over the United States. Rev. Shane has since been a certified physical medium of the ASSMPI organization (American Society for Standards in Mediumship & Physical Investigation). While he is known for his prodigious production of apports, he dedicates a considerable amount of his time bringing forth the teachings and principles of the ascended masters into the world with his channeling. As Rev. Mychael Shane affirms, "I believe everything that has been taught to me can be taught to others if they are willing to learn."[27]

British physical medium Warren Caylor has also been tested by the ASSMPI. The direct-voice medium has channeled Sir Winston Churchill, who sounds much like he did in life. When a voice analysis was performed using old newsreel clips of Churchill's speeches, there was a 94 percent match between the two voice prints. All of Warren Caylor's guides, by the way, have distinct voices and personalities. For instance, Luther, a tall Nubian, has a deep baritone voice. He often likes to joke with the ladies present in the séance room, telling them, "I still have room for one more wife." Little Tommy, on the other hand, has a high-pitched voice that sounds like a seven-year-old boy. Everyone in the room can hear Tommy's voice and infectious giggle.

Warren Caylor's main control is a Native American named Yellow Feather. In fact, many mediums attract Native American guides. For example, English medium Estelle Robert had a guide named Red Cloud, and Maurice Barbanell channeled Silver Birch until his death in 1981. Typical of Silver Birch's guidance was the guide's response to a question about death: "Similarly there is weeping when people die in your world, but there is rejoicing in ours. Death means that the life has served its purpose, or should have done, and the individual is ready to enjoy all the tremendous richness and beauty that the spirit life has to offer."[28]

Spirit guides even have a sense of humor about death. For example, Professor Hans Bender, the spirit control of physical medium Kai Muegge, gave this advice in a séance: "Don't worry about your dead relatives; they have just taken an early exit off the highway. You will catch up with them later."[29]

TYPES OF GUIDES

Angels: Loving and positive spiritual beings who have never incarnated

Ascendant Masters: Highly evolved masters such as Jesus, Saint Germaine, or Morya who look to encourage the good for all humanity

Gatekeepers: Spirits who come to keep order and help organize the séance

Joy guides: Spirit beings, often youngsters, who come to lighten the mood in the séance room

Loved ones: Spirit of parents, grandparents, children, aunts, uncles, cousins and departed friends

Master chemists: Deceased chemists and doctors who help to adjust the chemistry of the medium for spirit communication

Master teachers: Highly evolved master souls, often philosophers who wish to teach higher knowledge

Protectors: Strong spirits that come in for strength and protection. Mediums often attract Native Americans.

Spirit workers: Guides attracted by choice of work

Temporary guides: Spirits who wish to help in an emergency, such as a departed mechanic when a car breaks down

MEET YOUR GUIDE MEDITATION

The first step in developing any form of mediumship is to make contact with a spirit teacher or guide. Do the exercise in a quiet place when you have an hour to yourself. Be sure to turn off the phone, and place a pen and a notebook at your side. Have another person slowly read this exercise to you. If you do not have another person with you, then read it into a recorder and play it back.

Take three deep breaths—in through the nose, out through the mouth. In your mind's eye, go to your favorite place to relax. This may be the beach or your own backyard. See yourself in your favorite place to relax.

Visualize every detail of the place: sight, sound, touch, even the taste. You are totally relaxed. Very, very relaxed.

Imagine a white light just above your head. Visualize this white light shining above your head and gently coming down over your face, shoulders, chest, arms, hips, legs, and feet. Feel the protective warmth gently go down your body from your head to your shoulders; to your chest, hips, and legs; to the bottoms of your feet. You are totally surrounded by brilliant protective white light.

In a moment—at the count of three—your guide will join you.

One—You are filled with peace, and you are happy to see your guide.

Two—Send the thought out: "I am ready to meet my spiritual guide."

On the count of three but not before, you will see your guide.

Three—Your guide is right in front.

Take a moment and look down at the guide's feet. What do the feet look like?

Slowly go up the body. What type of clothes does the guide have on?

See or feel every detail of your guide. Take a moment to tune in.

Now describe your guide in detail. What does your guide look like?

Does the guide have a name or symbol to give to you?

Pause

Your guide has a message for you—a very important message. Take the next three minutes to tune into this message, which will help you at this time in your journey here on the earth plane.

(At this point, play some soft, New Age music for three minutes.)

Pause three minutes.

Now that you have received the guidance, thank the guide for being with you today. Send love from your heart to the guide.

On the count of seven you will awaken and remember every detail of your session. You will be able to write all the details clearly and easily. The more you write, the more you remember.

One—You feel refreshed and at peace.

Two—You are beginning to wake up.

Three—Your eyes are wide open.

For best results, practice this exercise every day for twenty-eight days at the same time and place.

Author's Tibetan guide, artist Rev. Phyllis Kennedy. *Author's collection*

CHAPTER 3

Psychometry, Billets, and Flame Cards

On such things as matter we have all been wrong; what we have called matter is energy, whose vibrations have been so lowered as to be perceptible to the senses. There is no matter.

—Albert Einstein

Spirit guides often bring through messages that go beyond everyday knowledge. For example, I gave a psychometry reading for Nora, who was visiting her Connecticut daughter. During the session, a man came through to give a message to "Ruth." The client appeared puzzled. "Well," she said, "the only Ruth I can think of is my neighbor across the street from me in Florida, and I barely know her." However, the spirit of Ruth's husband persisted and said if she told her neighbor that "Bill" had come through to say hello from the other side, his wife would be grateful.

When Nora returned to Florida the following week, she saw Ruth going out to fetch the mail. She bravely approached her neighbor to relay the message. Far from being upset, Ruth was delighted, and asked, "Was that psychic named 'Elaine'?" "Yes," answered Nora. "I know her well. Bill and I took classes with her when we lived in Connecticut!"

How exactly does a psychic pick up a neighbor's vibration from a personal item such as a ring? The information comes though psychometry. The word "psychometry" comes from the Greek word for soul—*psyche*—and *metron*—the Greek word for measure. The term was coined by Dr. Joseph Rhodes Buchanan, an American physician and professor of physiology at the Eclectic Medical Institute in Covington, Kentucky. He believed that every object, scene, or event that has occurred has left a psychic imprint: "Just as a photograph may be taken on film or plate and remain invisible until it has been developed, so may those psychometric photographs remain impalpable until the developing process has been applied. That which can bring them to light is the psychic faculty and mind of the medium."[1]

Dr. Buchanan understood psychometry to be primarily a psychic faculty. "However, Mrs. L. A. Coffin, in her preface to Dr. Buchanan's *Manual of Psychometry* [Boston, 1889], states that she was often impressed by spirits while performing psychometry."[2] Indeed, many mediums do make a connection with the spirit world through psychometry—for good or ill. If a psychometrist receives an object from a musician, he or she may hear classical music. However, if the object is from someone who recently died of illness, the psychic may suffer short-term symptoms of that same illness. It is interesting to note as well that "Buchanan experimented with some students from Cincinnati medical school and found that when certain students were given an unmarked bottle of medicine they had the same reaction as if they had taken the medicine."[3]

Professional mediums use psychometry to make a quick connection to the sitter when doing a reading. Fortunately, jewelry does not have to be worn for a long period of time in order to be psychometrized. As a Spiritualist medium, Elizabeth Owens, explains in her book *Spiritualism for Beginners*, "One misconception people have is that they sometimes assume that when they psychometrize an article such as a necklace, the necklace needs to be worn for a long time prior to it being psychometrized so that the energy is more intense. However, energy can be absorbed very quickly."[4]

It is also important that the article used for psychometry belongs only to the sitter. Personal items such as a ring or a watch carry an imprint similar to a fingerprint. This energy is filled with the owner's information, such as emotional state, physical traits, or hobbies. If more people handle an object, it may carry imprints of each owner, so it is important to use an object that solely belongs to the sitter. If a client hands over a ring that belongs to Grandma, then Grandma, not the client, will get the psychic reading.

A psychometrist can even read the past as well as the present from an object. Joan Grant found this to be true when she placed a stone from the Great Pyramid of Giza on her forehead. She was surprised to receive impressions of her life as Sekeeta, daughter of the pharaoh, who lived in Memphis, Egypt. She later fashioned her past life memories into a book, *Winged Pharaoh* (1937). In the course of the narrative, Sekeeta becomes co-pharaoh with her brother Neyah during the First Dynasty. The book became a surprise-success bestseller. According to the *New York Times*, *Winged Pharaoh* is "a book of fine idealism, deep compassion, and a spiritual quality pure and bright as flame."[5] What her readers were not privy to for almost another twenty years was the method the author used to obtain her story. Joan Grant claimed to have recalled the events in *Winged Pharaoh* while in a hypnotic or trancelike state, dictating piecemeal the lifetime that she believed herself to have lived.

Psychometry is also useful in missing objects and people. Stefan Ossowiecki was one of the world's most famous psychometrists. The chemical engineer was able to locate both lost objects and missing people with his psychic ability. When he was tested by French and Polish researchers in the 1920s and 1930s, he was able to reveal the contents of sealed envelopes. He amazed Baron Schrenck-Notzing at the 1923 International Psychical Research Congress in Warsaw. "Ossowiecki was asked to read the contents of a note sent by the Society for Psychical Research [SPR] and carefully sealed by Dr. Dingwall in an envelope after having been wrapped in several folds of paper of various colours. The note contained the sketch of a flag, a bottle, and in a corner, the date of Aug. 22, 1923. Ossowiecki reproduced correctly the flag and the bottle, and wrote the date like this: 19-2-23."[6] Baron Schrenck-Notzing thanked Stefan Ossowiecki in the name of science.

Later in 1935, the psychic was asked to describe the contents of a package that Hungarian businessman Dionizy Jonky had sealed before his death. "Ossowiecki touched the package and concentrated, 'Volcanic minerals,' he said. 'There is something here that pulls me to other worlds, to another planet.' Oddly, he also sensed sugar. Inside the package was a meteorite encased in a candy wrapper."[7]

In the spring of 1939, Marshal Edward Rydz-Śmigły, Polish supreme commander, asked about the future of Poland. Ossowiecki tearfully replied, "Poland would face a total disaster from Germans at the beginning and at the end of the war. The main winner would be Russia." He added that his country would return on the map of Europe, but in a completely different view and for a terrible price.[8] The marshal would not allow the psychic to give such news to the public. Instead, Ossowiecki was forced to lie and say that he saw a good future for his country.

The psychometrist's services were even more in demand than usual during World War II. After the Nazis invaded Poland, hundreds of people came to his apartment with photographs of family members and friends who had disappeared. "Ossowiecki would hold each photograph and try to help people find out what happened to their loved ones, always refusing payment for his services."[9] Ossowiecki even prophesized his own death. In July 1944, he told his wife, Zofia, that he would soon suffer a horrible death—but added, "I have had a wonderful life." Less than a month later, he was one of the ten thousand Polish men killed by the Nazis in a two-day massacre.[10]

While some such as Ossowiecki are born with the gift, others such as Beverly Jaegers did not have any childhood psychic experiences. Jaegers, who grew up in a police family, considers herself a "hard-nose investigator." She turned to the topic of psychic investigations when she was looking for an intriguing subject about which to write. In 1962–63, while at the library, she encountered in the science press some information about the USSR program in psi and their psi research. She learned remote-viewing using methods by borrowing from the Russian techniques, but she met with little success until she met a "world-class remote viewer" in 1965 who agreed to train her. She later became well known for stock market predictions as well as psychic detective work. She organized a group of her students into the U.S. Psi Squad to assist the police with unsolved cases. When the U.S. Psi Squad was successful in locating the body of a missing woman in 1971, Bev Jaegers became a famous psychic detective. She later wrote several books, including *Psychometry: The Science of Touch*.[11]

Noreen Renier also developed her psychic gift as an adult. Growing up in Greenfield, Massachusetts, she did not have any psychic experiences. Medium Rev. Anne Gehman introduced Renier to psychometry. When Rev. Gehman requested a room to do readings, Noreen, the hotel manager, felt uneasy. However, she accepted the medium's offer to do a session for her. Not only did she rent the medium a room for space, but Noreen Renier began taking classes with the talented medium. Anne Gehman was also skilled in the art of reading auras, mediumship, and psychometry.

For example, when Gehman was handed an object from missing person Vivian "June" Ritter, the medium foretold the location where the car and body were found. According to an April 26, 1968, article in the *Orlando Sentinel*, the Cassadaga medium "not only described the scene with accuracy, but drew a map showing the Treasure Island road, forking off State Road 44, although she had never visited the area and could not name the road." The story continued, "The young medium said the car could not be seen from the air, but was easy to see from the road, and this proved to be the case, when the vehicle was found Wednesday."[12]

Several years later, Rev. Gehman's student, Noreen Renier, became known for her work as a psychic detective. She often uses psychometry to solve cases. For instance, Lois Duncan asked the psychic to do a reading on her deceased daughter, Caitlin. Renier got an impression while holding a cross that the teenager was wearing when she was shot. Her mother wanted to know why someone had shot her daughter once in the temple and once in the cheek at a railway crossing on July 17, 1989, in Albuquerque, New Mexico. The psychic detective immediately sensed the motive for the shooting: "Oh, my God; it was a setup! He killed her because she knew too much! I think she accidentally knew too much. She got involved in something way over her head before she knew she was in over her head. I think they overestimated what she knew. She was someplace when something happened, and saw too much and saw too many people."[13] Duncan later found out that Kaitlyn's Vietnamese boyfriend, who later committed suicide, was allegedly causing car accidents in fraudulent scams. Lois Duncan suspects that Kaitlyn knew about the deception and was murdered to keep from testifying.

Noreen Renier was successful in solving another murder, that of Jake and Dora Cohn, an elderly New York couple. Dora was on the phone talking to her daughter when she screamed that her husband had been shot. Sadly, Dora too was murdered. Two years later, Dora's daughter consulted Renier regarding the unsolved case. She told the police that Dora had been talking to her mother on the phone, and then described how Jake had been shot as he ran down a hallway. The psychic sensed that Jake had known his killers and that one of the killers had a last name beginning with the letter "S." Renier said that Jake realized who the killers were, and then was shot. She felt pain in her face in the same area where he had been shot.

The medium then used photographs that the police brought to solve crimes. She closed her eyes and went through the pictures that the police gave her. She picked out three pictures; the first had nothing to do with the case, the second was Robert Skinner, and the third was James Mariani, the couple's grandson. The police soon determined that James Mariani had teamed up with Skinner to murder his grandparents.[14]

Not only can photographs be used as a tool for psychometry, but it is also possible to receive psychic impressions by looking at a photograph. While psychologists pay attention to facial expression, attire, and body language, a trained psychic can give deeper, more authentic impressions. It is possible to learn psychometry. First, take a moment to relax. Begin with a prayer of protection. Then ask for guidance. You may immediately sense the personality and interests of the person in the picture. Intuition will seem like imagination at first, so just let it come. You can sort out the details later. With practice, you can even scan a picture of the physical traits, such as scars, as well as emotional traits. With additional training, a psychic can be taught to read a person's past, present, and future from a photograph.

After you become adept at psychometry and photograph reading, you may wish to try your hand at billet reading. Turn-of-the-century Spiritualists would "mind-read" information on slips of paper called billets as a test for mediumship and clairvoyance. The word "billet" comes from the French for ticket. The technique is a simple one: The client writes his or her questions on a small slip of paper. The billet is then folded or placed in an envelope, so the psychic cannot see the contents. The psychic then reads the billet by holding it and psychometrizing the slip or the envelope. Sometimes a psychic will dramatically place the billet on his or her forehead. Even though billet reading is a relatively simple procedure, it does take a fair amount of practice to be accurate. One way to become adept is to practice with a group of friends. Be careful to weed out skeptics, since even one in the group can pull down the vibrations. Begin with a brief discussion of billet reading to warm up your audience. Then pass out small slips of paper.

Instruct each person to write the names of deceased relatives and friends that they wish to contact. They may also write one question. When they finish, each sitter signs his or her billet. Now collect the billets. It is important that no one touches the billet except the owner, so do not pass them around hand to hand as they place billets in a basket. Instead, have each person fold the billet and place it in a sealed envelope directly in the basket.

The medium must be securely blindfolded. Usually a member of the group will do this. The billet reader then opens each of the envelopes and holds the billet to gain rapport. At this point, spirit will come in for identification. It is important for the reader to gain rapport sufficient to see or hear the spirit in order to give an accurate description of deceased loved ones.

Then the skilled billet reader will tune in to the answer to the sitter's question. After the medium holds the envelope for the billet reading, he or she then pushes aside the blindfold and opens the envelope to confirm the accuracy of the message. However, this practice is discouraged. Instead, select a member of the audience to read the billet, and let the audience determine if the medium was accurate—and honest.

Since the paper is so small, it can be manipulated by fake psychics who peer out of their blindfold or even use the "one-ahead" method. Magician Joseph Dunninger managed to fool a number of people into believing he was a genuine psychic with this technique. He took the topmost envelope on the stack and pretended to mind-read the billet inside by holding it to his forehead. As he read a memorized statement, a plant in the audience jumped up and accepted the "message." The magician then opened the envelope to "make sure they got it right" and tossed it aside. The act continued as the magician picked up a second envelope and pretended to mind-read it, but he actually read aloud the statement from the envelope previously opened. The audience was amazed by the psychic's accurate message—which was, in fact, a magician's trick!

However, there many honest psychics such as Rev. Hoyt Robinette who do a superb job of billet reading. When Lisa and Tom Butler, directors of the American Association of Electronic Voice Phenomena (EVP), attended a billet reading with Robinette, they both were impressed by the Indiana medium. Lisa wrote the name "Konstantin Raudive," and her husband, Tom, wrote his father's name and that of Erland Babcock, a deceased member of the EVP association. Hoyt picked up on the fact that there were two gentlemen with the last name of "Babcock" in spirit that belonged to Tom Butler: one was his friend Erland Babcock and the other was his stepfather, Max Babcock. According to Lisa, "Hoyt had given the name of Tom's father as written on the paper, and then he said he was confused after saying Erland Babcock. He said something about being confused with fathers."[15] The remark made the reading even more evidential.

I've attended several billet readings from Rev. Robinette in Connecticut, Massachusetts, New York, and Maryland. One particularly memorable one occurred in 2014. As usual, Hoyt applied several strips of adhesive tape to each eye so there was no possibility of his peeking out. Then he put on a black blindfold over his bandaged eyes. While his eyes were completely useless, he fumbled a bit before he picked up a billet from the pile on the tray in front of him, my billet request: "Please give specific names of guides who are helping me with my next book." When Hoyt picked up my billet, he gave this answer to my query: "One Walter Prince."

At the time, I was working on *The Medium Who Baffled Houdini*—the biography of Boston medium Margery Crandon. Hoyt's answer, "Walter Prince," sent chills down my spine. Dr. Walter Franklin Prince was on the committee of *Scientific American* magazine and had assembled to investigate Margery Crandon in 1924. Under his direction, the Boston Society for Psychic Research also investigated Margery Crandon. He was so sure that Margery was a fake that he sent his secretary, Eleanor Hoffman, to spy on her. While Eleanor did not discover anything unusual about Margery, Prince still came to the conclusion that Margery Crandon's case was "the most ingenious, persistent, and fantastic complex of fraud in the history of psychic research."[16] Apparently, Dr. Prince now wished to set the record straight—to affirm that Margery Crandon really was a genuine physical medium!

Last but not least, spirit flame cards are an excellent way to begin physical mediumship. The method is fairly simple, since spirit does the work. First, tune in to your spirit guide. When you feel his or her presence, take a blank, 3-by-5-inch white index card and place it over a candle flame several times. Be careful to place the card close enough to form a picture but not so close as to catch the index card on fire. Generally it is good to do the passes quickly. However, your guide will impress on you how many times to pass the card over the flame, as well as the speed.

As spirit directs your hand to pass over a flame, recognizable images and faces may appear before your very eyes. At first, you may receive ambiguous markings; however, with practice, symbols, faces, and even names will appear. Many of these cards are very evidential. Often, spirit wishes to encourage students in developing physical mediumship. Such was the case when I did a workshop in the fall of 2009 at the First Spiritualist Church in Quincy, Massachusetts. Three people received spirit flame cards with trumpets to indicate their ability for trumpet mediumship.

INSTRUCTIONS FOR PSYCHOMETRY

Owner:

Date:

Psychometry

1. Obtain a small object such as a watch or a ring from a person you do not know. You can also use keys if only one person uses them.
2. Hold the object to gain rapport. Allow time to gain rapport and receive impressions. Start with basic impressions. Is the owner male or female, old or young, living or dead, shy or outgoing?
3. Now go deeper. What does the owner of the object look like? Describe the person's style of dress, hair, and eye color. What are his or her personality traits and hobbies?
4. Check to see if there is any more information. At this point, the sitter may ask a question.
5. Now ask the owner to give you some feedback. What percentage did you get right? A good psychic is usually about 85 percent correct.

Notes

INSTRUCTIONS FOR A BILLET READING

1. Write the names of three people in the spirit world that you would like to contact, and one question for spirit on the billet. Then sign the billet and date it.
2. Hold the folded billet in your hand to gain rapport. Allow time to gain rapport and receive impressions. Start with basic impressions. Describe spirits coming through.
3. Now go deeper. What questions need to be answered? Give information as you receive it.

4. Check to see if there is any more information from the spirit world.
5. Now ask the owner to give you some feedback. What percentage did you get right? A good psychic is usually about 85 percent correct.

Notes

Billet

Name:

_____

Question 1:

_____

_____

_____

Question 2:

_____

_____

_____

Question 3:

_____

_____

_____

Signature:

_____

Date:

_____

Once you sign your name, spirit will receive your questions automatically. Now fold the billet so that you cannot see the questions. Hold it between your hands or over your heart to give the billet extra energy. Hand it directly to the reader. In a group reading, the billet can be placed in a basket and the reader selects it. It is important that only you and the reader touch the billet, so do not pass billets around to the medium.

Stefan Ossowiecki at home, 1932, unknown photographer. *Source: Wikipedia Commons*

Daniel Dunglas Home

Example of slate writing of Fred P. Evans, 1885, *Psychography- Marvellous Manifestations of Psychic Power through Fred Paeans* by J.J. Owen

CHAPTER 4

Table Tipping and Levitation

On one occasion, as a heavy table shook and vibrated, the crashing sound of waves filled the room, together with the creaking of a ship's timbers. The "spirit" spelled out its name with the use of an alphabet and was immediately recognized by someone present as a friend who had drowned in a gale in the

Gulf of Mexico.

—Colin Wilson on Daniel Dunglas Home

Nandor Fodor described table tipping, or table turning, as "the crudest form of communication with the subconscious self or with extraneous intelligences."[1] However, Spiritualism began with raps and table tipping of the Fox sisters in 1848. By 1853 the movement and the practice of table tipping had spread to England, where it quickly became an acceptable method of contacting the spirit world.

One of the most evidential mediums was Daniel Dunglas Home. His array of phenomena was nothing short of amazing: "On one occasion, as a heavy table shook and vibrated, the crashing sound of waves filled the room, together with the creaking of a ship's timbers. The 'spirit' spelled out its name with the use of an alphabet and was immediately recognized by someone present as a friend who had drowned in a gale in the Gulf of Mexico."[2]

Home was best known for his ability to levitate. He was observed levitating over a hundred people. On occasion, he even levitated in daylight before a group of Hartford reporters in South Manchester, Connecticut. In August 1852, the young medium was observed rising up to the ceiling, by a reporter from the *Hartford Times*: "Suddenly, no one expected the group, Home rose into the air. I was holding his hand and examined his feet—were 30 cm above the ground. All of Home's body throbbed, a confusion of emotions ranging from joy to fear, choking his words. Again and again he levitated. In the third, he climbed to the roof of the apartment, where touched hands and feet."[3]

Several years later Home was observed flying 85 feet above the ground. On December 13, 1868, Lord Adare and his friend Lord Lindsay heard Home go into the next room and open the window. In a few minutes, "Home appeared upright standing outside the window. Daniel then opened the window and walked in, sat down and laughed."[4]

D. D. Home was tested by Sir William Crookes between 1870 and 1873. The physicist even designed a special cage, one with an opening large enough for just one hand. When Crookes placed an accordion (which would require two hands to play) inside the case, D. D. Home was able to play a tune such as "Home Sweet Home." To everyone's surprise, the accordion continued to play after Home let go of his thumb and middle finger, with no person touching it: after a materialization was heard to join the circle and touched Mrs. Crookes, the accordion was played and Crookes recorded that "we had a beautiful accompaniment, the chirping and singing of the birds being heard along with the accordion." Raps were heard and a luminous cloud appeared: 'Immediately the white luminous cloud was seen to travel . . . to Mrs. Wm. C.'s hand, and a small sprig of the plant was put into it. She had her hand then patted by a delicate female hand. The table was now heard to be moving, and it was seen to glide slowly."[5] Sir William Crookes concluded that Home did produce genuine phenomena; in his report *Researches into the Phenomena of Spiritualism*, published in 1874, Crookes stated that Home had proven "beyond doubt" the existence of a "psychic force."[6]

British medium William Eglinton also levitated in plain view. His first levitation was described by Archdeacon Colley in *The Spiritualist*, from June 2, 1876: "The medium was next entranced and carried by invisible power over the table several times, the heels of his boots being made to touch the head of our medical friend (Dr. Malcolm). Then he was taken to the further end of the dining room, and finally, after being tilted about as a thing of no weight whatever, was deposited quietly in his chair."[7]

In 1882, Eglinton amazed Harry Kellar with his physical mediumship. The magician, who made a good living exposing fake mediums, challenged the medium to levitate. The British medium performed a feat the conjurer could not duplicate: "Eglinton levitated, carrying Kellar holding his foot, into the air—an achievement Kellar had to admit he could not account for."[8] While Kellar could not account for the levitation, most Spiritualists such as Home and Eglinton gave credit to the spirits. For instance, when asked how then were his levitations accomplished, Home claimed not to know himself. He stated that an "unseen power" simply came over him and lifted him into the air.

Spiritualists generally concur that invisible spirit hands are also responsible for the movement of the table. For best results, table tipping should be done with a circle of believers. When skeptics are present, the results can be nil. In a good circle with a capable medium, tables will not only tip but levitate as well.

Such was the case for Boston medium Fanny Conant in 1873. She requested that the spirit of an African American by the name of "Big Dick" assist when a gentleman asked her to raise the table to the ceiling. Big Dick indicated he would—providing the medium sat on the table. "She did so and the table at once began to gradually ascend. Four of the party laid hands on it and exerted themselves to the upmost to keep it down, but it easily broke from their grasp and reached the top of the apartment, so that the medium was able to write her name upon the ceiling above her head."[9]

Very few mediums possess the ability to levitate; however, many physical mediums begin their careers with table tipping. In the 1920s, Margery Crandon started with table tipping. She soon produced extraordinary results: "The table followed Caldwell out through the corridor, into the bedroom, rumpling all the mats in transits. Then, on request for more, the table started downstairs after him, when we stopped it to save the wall plaster."[10] Margery eventually progressed to trance mediumship and was able to produce ectoplasmic rods and even a hand to a small table. On November 13, 1931, scientists using a low red light photographed the large materialized hand lifting the table under laboratory conditions.

In his book *Life after Death*, Smith College professor S. Ralph Harlow documented several of Margery Crandon's séances, including one that involved levitation. Walter, Margery's spirit guide, requested that wooden blocks embossed with letters of the alphabet be placed in the center of the spirit circle one evening. While members of the circle sat in total darkness, the spirit managed to move the blocks to spell out messages. Everyone heard the thumps of four blocks that were deposited at Professor Harlow's feet. Walter had brought through a message from Harlow's sister Anna, who had recently passed away. When the lights were turned on, much to Harlow's delight, there on the floor near his chair were "four blocks perfectly aligned, spelling 'Anna.'"[11]

Many physical mediums such as Margery Crandon begin their physical mediumship with table tipping. It is the easiest form of physical phenomena to demonstrate. If you wish to do the same, start with a small, wooden, three-legged table, about 30 inches in height and 18 to 30 inches in diameter. Make sure that it is real wood—not pressboard.

Then cleanse the table and dedicate it to spirit. This is important, since objects pick up vibrations from their surroundings. Cleansing is easily done by lightly spraying salt water on the table. For those who do not live near the ocean, a solution of sea salt and a quart of water will do the trick. Place a half cup of sea salt (not table salt) in a spray bottle with a quart of water. Gently spray the mixture on the table. Then as you wipe the water off, send the thought "This table is cleansed and dedicated to the highest and best spirits."

Start your table tipping with a prayer, such as "The Lord's Prayer." Then have each member of the group place his or her fingers palms down lightly on the table. You can do table tipping with as many as twelve or as few as two—four to six is an ideal number. Some mediums prefer that the thumb of one participant touch the little finger of the next person, but this is not necessary. Also, while some mediums insist on table tipping in a dark room, others do not require this.

Regardless of lighting, the group needs to raise the vibration in the room. This can easily be done by singing happy songs such as "Row, Row, Row Your Boat" or "You Are My Sunshine" or even "Jingle Bells." Rev. Suzanne Greer likes to improvise. The Camp Chesterfield medium has her students sing a chorus of "Raise the table," followed by "Raise it higher" to the tune of "Oh My Darling Clementine."

As you practice, your fingers will begin to feel sticky, as if they are melting into the table. This is a sign that you are making progress. As soon as you sense that the table is ready, try to send energy from one sitter to another across the table. At first the table will move a little bit, but with practice it will move back and forth.

Often, sitters like to establish a code at this point—such as movement means "yes" and no movement means "no." If you wish, you could also try a code for "yes"—moving to the back of the room, and "no"—moving to the front of the room. At first you will need to confine yourself to yes-and-no questions. Start with obvious ones such as "Was George Washington the first president of the United States?" Later try working with the alphabet: one tilt for A, two tilts for B, and so on. Sometimes a three-legged table may get up on one leg or even spin around on its own. Some advanced mediums such as Kai Muegge have even gotten the table to levitate several feet in the air. At first, he used wooden tables, but he broke so many of his mother's fine tables that he had to switch to plastic ones.

Kai works in the tradition of Rudi and Willi Schneider, the famous Austrian mediums of the 1920s who were discovered by Baron Schrenck-Notzing. "Between December 3, 1921, and July 1, 1922, around one hundred scientists witnessed his (Willi's) telekinetic and ectoplasmic phenomena and were completely convinced of their reality."[12] Rudi was tested in London from April 12 to 22, 1929, and then from November 14, 1929, to January 20, 1930. During all three séances, he exhibited unusual physical phenomena, including cold breezes felt by everyone; an occasional fall in the temperature of the cabinet; violent movements of the pair of curtains; movements and levitations of the luminous waste paper basket and the coffee table; the ringing of the bells and the twanging of the toy zither; even in midair, the emergence from and withdrawal into the cabinet of a handkerchief, afterward found in a far corner, tied into a tight knot; the touchings and brushings of the sitters at the wonderful thirteenth, fifteenth, twenty-first, and other séances; the intelligent knocking of the table when it was resting against a sitter's leg near the end of the circle farthest from the medium; the tugs-of-war with Olga [spirit guide]; and finally the emergence from and withdrawal into the cabinet of hands, arms, and tubes, some perfectly formed.[13] Harry Price came to this conclusion in his book *Rudi Schneider*: "The fact remains that Rudi has been subjected to the most merciless triple control ever imposed upon a medium in this or any other country and has come through the ordeal with flying colours."[14]

Rudi Schneider began his trance mediumship at eleven: One night when his older brother Willi was doing a séance, his guide Olga came through and asked that the sleeping Rudi assist. His parents objected to waking the child. "A few minutes later, however, the door opened and Rudi, in deep trance, entered, and joined the circle."[15] The petulant spirit of Olga Lintner, who in life was the mistress of Ludiwg L. the old King of Bavaria, became Rudi's permanent guide.

Kai Muegge has a team of spirits who work with him, including the spirit of German parapsychology researcher Hans Bender, who died in 1991. Dr. Bender demands strict control during all séances, including the table-tipping one given the evening of July 29, 2015, in the Cassadaga, New York, home of Dr. Neal Rzepkowski. Well educated with a background in filmmaking and sociality, the forty-three-year-old medium explained the rules:

- One: It is important to observe strict boundaries. During the table-tipping séance, half would remain seated at the table, and the other half would remain in the back of the room to observe.
- Two: Everyone was to stay in their respective seats.
- Three: When his wife and assistant, Julia, said "Chain," we were to link hands.
- Four: When she said "Silence," we were to cease talking.
- Five: It is important that everyone participate in singing to raise the energy. If you can't sing, then hum to the tune.

After Kai explained the rules, we were instructed to remove all jewelry and belts with metal buckles. Neal's kitchen vibrated with psychic anticipation as we prepared to enter the séance room—a good-sized space about 16 by 24 feet. The room had been specially prepared—wooden floors swept clean and eight chairs around a square, white plastic table. Eight more chairs were placed in the back for observers. There was also a candle and a CD player for music. In the corner of the room was a spirit cabinet—a black tent to be used for another séance. The spirit cabinet had a wooden chair ready for use.

Naturally, everyone was excited as they entered the darkened room. I was present at the first table session. During the séance I felt the plastic table abruptly rise about 3 feet in the air, with such force that I had to stand up. Then the table remained about thirty seconds in the air and crashed to the ground. It felt like the invisible hands that were holding the table just let go. "Now I realize why Kai uses a plastic table, because he has ruined so many wooden ones," I thought.

I was not surprised that the table levitated, since I had witnessed other levitations. For example, a glowing white handkerchief moved around the room as if carried by an invisible hand, rattles shook, ping-pong balls floated in the air, and a trumpet zigzagged across the room—all were proof positive that spirit was present. It was more the actual force that surprised me. There was no doubt the plastic table was being lifted up by an outside force.

On the evening of July 29 the spirits went a little further. During the table-tipping session, which like the first séance was held in darkness, we heard a loud thump on the table. Everyone became concerned. We were worried that something had gone wrong in the séance. Perhaps Kai had fallen ill? When Julia switched the red light on, there was a wooden chair in the middle of the plastic table. Julia abruptly ended the séance by switching on the light. To the group's surprise, the spirits had floated the wooden chair in the corner of the room—a good 6 feet away—and deposited in the middle of the table. In order to accomplish this feat, they had to levitate it and float the chair over the heads of the medium and sitters—yet no one felt it go by!

Few people will develop physical mediumship to the degree of Kai Muegge; however, most students can master basic table tipping with some time and patience. Even Kai had to spend many evenings practicing in his mother's basement. At first, his mother, a teacher, was uncertain about her son spending so much time on mediumship. Later she joined the group named for Kai's grandfather and spirit guide—the Felix Circle. Even if your friends and family have their doubts, do not allow their skepticism to influence you. It is essential to maintain a positive, even cheerful attitude. It is also important to make a date with spirit. For optimal results, practice with like-minded friends at the same time and place.

British medium Colin Evans levitating 1938, Courtesy *Wikimedia Commons*

CHAPTER 5

Talking Boards and Children's Slates

We come to you Sir because we see you are spreading the truth in the right way. I understood this phenomenon while in earth life, and had I lived, should have proclaimed it to the world. Press fo[r]ward My Brother. Never let thy step stray from the path of progress and truth. Your Friend, Abraham Lincoln.

—Spirit message written on slate of medium
Pierre Louie Ormand Augustus Keeler

Nineteenth-century mediums not only used table tipping to communicate with spirit but also experimented with "talking boards" and children's slates to receive messages from the other side. The talking board, or Ouija board as it later became known, is a flat board marked with the alphabet, numbers 0–9, and the words "yes" or "no." The communicator places his or her hand on the heart-shaped piece of wood called a planchette, and then patiently waits for it to move.

Victorians such as Isabella Beecher Hooker spent hours communicating with spirts on the talking board. Her lawyer husband, John Hooker, even wrote down the names of the spirits in alphabetical order. Most of her messages from spirit centered on family and friends. Occasionally, she became a fanatic with her predictions. According to her diary entries from May 1876 to January 1877, the spirits told her she would be forming a new government. Immediately, Isabella decided to have her husband, John, along with her nephew Fred Perkins and her daughter Mary in her cabinet.[1]

It is just as easy to be misguided as well as guided by the talking board, as Susy Smith pointed out in her 1971 book, *Confessions of a Psychic*: "Warn people away from Ouija and automatic writing until you have learned how to be fully protected."[2] As with any communication, it is important to find out the source—even more so with the unseen.

Still, there are many cases of spectacular Ouija board communication. One in particular comes to mind—that of Pearl Curran. The St. Louis housewife, with her neighbor, began experimenting with the Ouija board on July 12, 1912. A year later, July 8, 1913, the board seemed to be possessed by an unusually strong force who called herself Patience Worth. According to the spirit, she was born in 1649 near Dorsetshire in England. Patience's work, which included poems, novels, and a play, was comparable to that of Shakespeare, Chaucer, and Spenser. "Her most celebrated work, *The Sorry Tale*, a 644-page, 325,000-word novel about the last days of Jesus, was released in June 1917. The *New York Globe* stated that it exceeded Ben Hur and Quo Vadis as 'a quaint realistic narrative.'"[4] All this from a woman who dropped out of school at fourteen. Furthermore, Pearl Curran had no knowledge of life in the 1600s or Roman times, yet there was not a single anachronism in her text.[5]

Not only have talking boards been employed to contact spirts, but children's slates have been utilized as well. In the 1950s, slate writing was still practiced at Camp Chesterfield in Indiana. When Reverend Gladys Custance; her husband, Kenneth; and close friend Mrs. Morse attended a slate séance at the camp in the 1950s, they were not sure what to expect. However, they were each given two slates and a bit of chalk to be placed in the center between the two slates. Then the sitters tied their pair of slates together with a string and placed them carefully on the table in the center of the room. The medium asked the group of twelve to hold hands as she entered a trance state. In a few minutes, Gladys could hear scratching on the slates. When the scratching stopped, the medium came out of trance and told everyone that they could now open their slates. Mrs. Morse was especially pleased, since she received a message from her deceased husband, Dr. Morse, in his own handwriting!

Slate-writing mediums of this caliber no long exist; however, there were quite a few slate-writing mediums in Victorian times. Four come to mind—William Eglinton, P. L. O. A. Keeler, Laura Pruden, and Fred Evans. William Eglinton (1857–1933) was a famous British medium who convinced William Ewart Gladstone, prime minister of England from 1868 to 1894, of the reality of psychic phenomena. As a young man, William was highly skeptical of psychic phenomena. When his father formed a home circle, the son was "determined that if anything happened I would put a stop to it." However, he was surprised when the table moved vigorously. To Eglinton's surprise, "Something did happen, but I was powerless to prevent it. The table became animated and answered questions intelligently."[6]

He turned out to be a natural medium, demonstrating trance, slate writing, and levitation, all of which were reported by Archdeacon Thomas Colley in *The Spiritualist* on June 2, 1876: "The medium was next entranced and carried by invisible power over the table several times, the heels of his boots being made to touch the head of our medical friend [Dr. Malcolm]. Then he was taken to the further end of the dining room, and finally, after being tilted about as a thing of no weight whatsoever, was deposited quietly in his chair."[7]

Later, Eglinton concentrated on slate-writing mediumship. It took a good three years of daily sitting before any writing appeared, according to biographer John Stephen Farmer. When the spirits did come through on slates, the result was messages in English and other languages. On October 29, 1884, British prime minister W. E. Gladstone had a séance with Eglinton. He obtained answers to his questions, which were privately written on the hostess's own slates, both when the slates were held under the table and when they were laid upon the table in full view of all present, as well as when the slates were securely locked together with a clasp. Some of the questions were put in Spanish, French, and Greek and answered in the same language. Gladstone was so impressed that soon after he joined the Society for Psychical Research (SPR).[8]

Gladstone even gave Eglinton a special set of slates that "consisted of two slates of medium size, set in mahogany frames, with box hinges, and which, when shut, were fastened with a Bramah lock and key."[9] When Edgar Lee had a test séance with the medium, he used these slates. Time after time, Lee went into the next room and picked a word from a book at random. The exact word would appear on the slate. Then the medium asked the sitter, "Have you any friend in the spirit world from whom you would like to hear?" Lee answered that he did have a dear friend in spirit. The slates were cleaned and then locked. Within minutes he could hear scratching sounds as spirit wrote this message. When Lee opened the slates, he received an answer to his question:

My DEAR WILL, —I am quite satisfied with your decision respecting Bob. By all means, send him to the school you are thinking of. He will get on better there. His education requires more pushing than it gets at present. Thanks for all you have done for him. God bless you. —Your affectionate cousin, R. TASKER[10].

The message was from his cousin, who left the boy in Lee's charge. There was no way that the medium could have known that Edgar Lee was the sitter's nom de plume. His real name was William Tasker!

Just as William Eglinton was celebrated for his extraordinary work in England, Pierre Louie Ormand Augustus Keeler was praised for his physical mediumship in the United States. The Lily Dale medium started slate writing in the late 1870s and continued for over fifty years. Keeler is famous for producing the Abraham Lincoln slate on display in the Lily Dale Museum in New York. Written with chalk is the message "We come to you Sir because we see you are spreading the truth in the right way. I understood this phenomenon while in earth life, and had I lived, should have proclaimed it to the world. Press fo[r]ward My Brother. Never let thy step stray from the path of progress and truth. Your Friend, Abraham Lincoln."[11]

During his tour of the United States, researcher Sir Arthur Conan Doyle was impressed by Keeler's slate writing as well as that of Mrs. Laura Pruden. He attended several of her séances held at the Blackstone Hotel in Chicago. The séances were held in daylight. There were two slates with a bit of pencil in between, with individual questions being placed upon the slates. Since darkness was needed for the phenomena to fully transpire, Mrs. Pruden placed the slate under the table, draped with a dark cloth. She picked up one end of the cloth, and another sitter the other end, to form a "spirit cabinet." After about half an hour, the group could hear the sound of writing. Even though Mrs. Pruden did not see the question, Doyle received the answer to his question from his deceased son, Kingsley: "I had some business this morning of a partly spiritual, partly material nature with a Dr. Gelbert, a French inventor. I asked in my question if this were wise. The answer on the slate was "Trust Dr. Gelbert, Kingsley."[12]

While Laura Pruden's slate message from Doyle's deceased son was proof to his father, the most evidential slate writing came through the mediumship of Fred P. Evans during a public séance on June 21, 1885, in San Francisco. A skeptical gentleman was chosen from the audience to examine the slates with care. He was satisfied that they were "thoroughly washed, dried, and tied together, in a manner to make deception impossible."[13] He held the slate and did not let go. Fred Evans did not even touch the slates; yet, the bottom slate was "covered with about thirty messages, written in the usual patchwork manner peculiar to this psychic."[14] On June 21, 1885, Evans produced a slate that had thirty different languages. Later, many of the signatures were verified. The messages on the slates were most evidential. Germany's professor Johann Karl Friedrich Zöllner said,

"I have found an easy way for making known to science the proof of the return of the dead and shall soon give it to the world"

Two years later, on May 18, 1887, Evans produced a slate for Dr. Alfred Russell Wallace, who "was requested by the spirit control to tear off six sheets from a common writing pad of white paper at hand and place them between a pair of slates; which he did. In a few minutes we were assured by the medium that the forces were at work upon the paper, and soon it was found that upon each of five of the slips of papers was a finely executed crayon sketch of a prominent Spiritualist passed to spirit life, representing them as they appeared in earth-life, viz., D. D. Home, Dr. Benjamin Rush, Dr. Robert Hare, Jonathan Pierpont, Mrs. S. F. Breed, and upon one slip an unknown spirit picture not as well done as the others."[15]

In less than an hour, Fred Evans was able to produce six slates with crayon sketches and thirteen written messages. Professor Wallace pronounced the test séance a remarkable success: "The above appears to me to be a correct account of one of the most remarkable and convincing séances I have ever attended. I have never, on any occasion, witnessed phenomena of so wonderful a character appear with such rapidity and in a manner so entirely free from suspicion. ALFRED R. Wallace."[16]

It can take years to develop slate writing to the degree of Fred Evans; however, the process is fairly simple. According to researcher Nandor Fodor, "The medium and the sitter sit at opposite ends of a small table, each grasping a corner of an ordinary school slate, which they thus hold firmly pressed against the underside of the table."[17] If spirit is present, the sitters will hear the sound of scratching, followed by three raps. Mediums such as Laura Pruden and William Eglinton could produce writing that was "either a general message from the spirit world, or an answer to some question previously written down by the sitter."[18]

The Ascended Masters used another method. According to Madame Blavatsky, they precipitated their messages directly onto sheets of paper. Between 1880 and 1885, Blavatsky received scores of such letters in India and London. Many of the letters were written in response to queries from A. P. Sinnett. The author of *The Occult World* had a myriad of question for the Ascended Masters.

Master Morya and Koot Hoomi answered his questions directly through precipitation. As Edward Abdill, author of *Masters of Wisdom*, points out, "Many of the letters that were allegedly 'precipitated,' that is, delivered by phenomenal means rather than by post, have a curious look to them. It appears as though the ink is embedded in the paper, as though the writing and the paper were produced at the same time, and each individual word of every letter looks as though it had been produced by a dot matrix printer, except that instead of dots, each letter consists of tiny dashes."[19]

Even though they wished to oblige A. P. Sinnet's requests, the masters were hesitant to use supernatural precipitation. Morya was especially wary of psychic phenomena and warned against craving more and more phenomena. The Ascended Master stressed the need to develop a deeper philosophy of life, not reliance on occult phenomena: "It adds no force to our metaphysical truths that our letters are dropped from space on to your lap or come under your pillow. If our philosophy is wrong, a wonder will not set it right."[20]

INSTRUCTIONS FOR GROUP SLATE WRITING

First, assemble a group of like-minded people to sit on a regular basis for the phenomena. Once a week at the same time and place is ideal. Everyone should bring his or her own slates and a dark cloth or towel. Have each sitter put a bit of chalk in between the two slates—right in the middle of the bottom slate. Place the top slate over this and wrap them in a black cloth. The slates can be placed in front of each person or on a table in the middle of the room.

Keep a positive receptive attitude during the weekly séance. Start by singing upbeat songs such as "You Are My Sunshine" or "Row, Row, Row Your Boat." Then have the group sit in meditation for twenty minutes. Check your slates weekly to see if there are any marks. I did this with a group of students for six weeks, with just a few marks appearing. At first, tiny dots appeared. Later, milky patches. Alas, no faces of Indian chiefs or Victorian ladies manifested.

Disappointed, I put the slates away for a month. Then I took them out for class meditation and sat them on the living-room coffee table. When the meditation ended, I opened them—not expecting too much. I was happy to receive a stick drawing of an American Indian with arms up to a cloud. The slate is very evidential, since the guide that works with me on physical phenomena is named "White Cloud."

Two reasons for this modest success come to mind. One, the slate had been acclimated with six weeks of meditation. Second, I had given no thought to the matter for a month—which allowed spirit to intercede without my performance anxiety.

Author's slate. Note face of man in the center.

CHAPTER 6

Precipitated Writings, Paintings, and Cards

Beloved one,

I'll try to tell how it was done.

Rembrandt in spirit paints the picture here,

and it held aloft in psychic ray,

and on the canvas is repeated,

so the colors come to stay.

—Hypatia

As the Victorian era was coming to a close, a new form of spirit communication emerged—precipitated writing and painting. Few outside Catholicism had any idea what a precipitated painting was. The Virgin of Guadalupe is the most famous example of spirit-precipitated images; the image of the Virgin Mary was directly precipitated on the cloak of Juan Diego. The Vatican later authenticated this miracle.

There is a magical quality to the precipitated portraits that hang on the walls of Lily Dale Museum and Camp Chesterfield in Indiana. These portraits by the sisters Lizzie and May Bangs and the Campbell brothers were created in the late 1800s and early 1900s. The mediums involved created the precipitated spirit portrait during a séance in which a blank canvas and a pot of paints were placed at the spirit's deposal. After an interval of fifteen minutes to an hour, an image would gradually appear on the canvas.

Lizzie and May Bangs were the best known of the precipitation mediums. Elizabeth was born around 1860, and May was born in 1864. Their father, Edward, worked as a tinsmith and stove repairman, and their mother was also a medium. As they were growing up in Chicago, the two sisters exhibited natural psychic ability. Their gifts included independent writing in broad daylight and independent drawing and painting. Both girls also demonstrated the ability to do direct writing by typewriter (no human fingers touching the typewriter keys); however, it was the spirit paintings that made them legendary.

In 1921, May Wright Sewall had a session with May Bangs in which Mrs. Sewall wrote a letter to her deceased husband and sealed it in an envelope. She described her astonishment as spirit precipitated the answers to her questions, which she placed in a sealed letter between two slates tied together:

"Miss Bangs then dropped some ordinary black ink on a small bit of ordinary blotting paper and placed it on the upper surface of the top slate, I holding the slates firmly all the time, and I alone touching them. In a few minutes Miss Bangs said that my letter was answered. I thereupon untied the slates and on opening the envelope I found that the paper which I had put in blank was covered with clear script in black ink in a writing resembling but not duplicating that of my husband. There were six pages, which when read proved to be an orderly, coherent, categorical reply to my letter. The answers were numbered to correspond with [sic] numbered questions."[1]

Admiral William Usborne Moore also found the Bangs sisters to possess evidential mediumship. When he sat with Miss May Bangs in 1908, he placed an envelope with his letter to spirit between two slates, just as May Sewall had done. After a half hour, the two heard three raps, a signal to open the slates. When Moore did so, he found his envelope still sealed between the hinged slates. He was most pleased when he slit open the envelope:

I found, besides my questions, nine and a half pages of the blank paper covered with writing in ink, as if with a steel pen, duly numbered, and written at the instance of the spirit friend to whom I had addressed four out of five questions, and signed in full. The replies were categorical, giving or confirming information of great value to me personally; referring to facts and happenings of forty years ago, which the Spirit and I alone were aware of; and adding the names of individuals whom I had not named in my questions, but whom we both knew in the past, and who had participated in the events referred to by me. The reply to the fifth and last question was in the form of greetings from spirit friends who were known to me when they were in earth life, and now come to me as so-called "guides."[2]

Admiral Moore, a tireless researcher, even consulted Sir William Crookes (1832–1919), one of the most respected physicists of that century. He suggested that Moore add the chemical lithium citrate to his ink beforehand and then send to him the pages that had been precipitated by spirit. Moore took Dr. Crookes's suggestion. Later, spectrum analysis indicated that lithium citrate was discovered in the ink used by the spirits—proof that the spirits had precipitated the ink that Moore had placed on the séance table—even though it had in no way come in contact with the slates.[3] While few precipitated letters are still in existence, many of the Bangs sisters' precipitated portraits are on display at Camp Chesterfield in Indiana and Lily Dale Assembly in New York.

The Bangs sisters frequently demonstrated their art on stage, so everyone in the audience could witness the precipitation. Often a thin vapor swept across the blank canvas, followed by fine layers of color, then details of facial features, hair, and clothing. Usually in the development of a portrait, the outer edges of the canvas become shadowed, showing different delicately colored lines, until the full outline of the head and shoulders is seen. When the likeness is sufficiently distinct to be recognized, the hair, drapery, and other decorations appear. In many cases, after the entire portrait is finished, the eyes gradually open, giving a lifelike appearance to the whole face.[4]

One of the most spectacular portraits is that of Queen Victoria, a full-length portrait that was precipitated for Dr. Carson of Kansas City. He later donated it to Camp Chesterfield, which houses the largest collection of their paintings in the Hett Art Gallery. Dr. Carpenter of Olin, Iowa, took the precaution of bringing his own canvas nailed in a box to his session, which took three hours. He was just about to give up when spirit told him to open the box. "We accordingly opened the box and to my great surprise and joy beheld a complete life-sized picture of my wife and child in the spirit world. The picture is so natural and lifelike that many of my neighbors and friends fully recognize it although they have been in the spirit life for 33 years,"[5] Carpenter stated, adding that he had asked only for a portrait of his deceased wife. The addition of the daughter was totally unexpected. During the whole process, the box containing the canvas never left his sight.

Some of the portraits are so lifelike that they appeared to be photographs, yet no brushstrokes can be seen. When the colors were examined by experts, the pigment was found to be closest to that in butterfly wings. According to Irene Swann, author of *The Bangs Sisters and Their Precipitated Spirit Portraits*, the precipitated paintings were created with meticulous detail:

> *The hair in most of the portraits is in detail down to the most miniscule [sic] strands, waves, colors, top knots, and styles. Ringlets, braids, long luxurious flowing tresses, and curling tendrils can be seen. There are elaborate dresses, suits, silks, and Indian robes, delicate veils, lace, turbans, blouses, brilliant white dress shirts, and neckties, majestic long flowing beards, and stylish moustaches, necklaces, ruby red lips, turquoise, rings, cameos, and other forms of gorgeous jewelry and decorations; threaded seams, stitch work designs, intricate knots, exquisite pearls, bracelets, beads and buttons; vegetation such as red and white roses and other flowers, carved marble, and other flourishes of artistic beauty. The colors, most notably in the faces, are life-like and fresh and seem to have never faded; they look as if they were precipitated yesterday.[6]*

How did the Bangs sister accomplish precipitated portraits? According to researcher Dr. James Coates, "These precipitated paintings are the work of human intelligences operating on psychic planes, and through the agency of appropriate media. In the unique phenomenon of these remarkable spirit-produced paintings, the Bangs Sisters, in the history of the world's psychics, stand alone."[7]

Indeed, they were the work of several spirit guides. At least three are needed to produce such detailed portraits—one just for the colors alone and another for transmission. According to one spirit guide, Hypatia: "Beloved one, I'll try to tell how it was done. Rembrandt in spirit paints the picture here, and it held aloft in psychic ray, and on the canvas is repeated, so the colors come to stay."[8]

The Bangs sisters were not the only mediums to do precipitated painting; the Campbell brothers were famous for similar creations. Allan B. Campbell and Charles Shrouds were not related by blood, though they were called brothers. The two lived together in Lily Dale, New York, and made several trips to Europe. During their stay at Lily Dale Assembly, they produced several precipitated portraits, including one of Abraham Lincoln. The painting, which is on display at the Maplewood Hotel, was produced in a séance under the influence of their spirit guide Azur.

Their best-known precipitated portrait is a 40-by-60-inch portrait of "Azur, the Helper." When the portrait was produced, the room was dimly lit, with only a blank canvas and a pot of oil paint—no paintbrushes were permitted in the séance room. The process of creating a precipitated spirit portrait was considered a type of "séance." According the curator of the Lily Dale Museum, "During the process, the guests witnessed the gradual development of the painting on canvas. The painting was completed in one hour and thirty minutes."[9] When the picture was complete, six prominent witnesses signed an affidavit on June 15, 1898, verifying that they had indeed witnessed Azur appearing on the canvas. They also heard his spirit speak though trance medium Allen Campbell.[10] *Azur, the Helper* is on display in the lobby of the Maplewood Hotel at the Lily Dale Assembly.

Later, California medium Rev. Florence Becker (1892–1970) produced precipitated paintings, along with her gifts of dead trance, direct voice, and clairvoyance. Even as a child she communicated with the spirit of Lady Cologna, who would manifest to guide her. In due time, Mrs. Becker became a certified medium and was ordained a Spiritualist minister and a national Spiritualist teacher. She was first introduced by Doctor Allen, who told her she was a natural physical medium, and gave her a trumpet. Skeptical but curious, she took the trumpet home and sat with it in her closet. She challenged her guides: "Now, I'd like to see someone hit me with that trumpet." She said she never got such a beating in her life. Her American Indian guide Jonquil said, "See, Squaw, I told you that you had work to do."[11] Six month later, she gave her first séance. Later Florence Harwood Becker became a certified medium and Spiritualist minister.

Her church services attracted people from all walks of life, including Madame Nijinsky, widow of Vaslav Nijinsky. When she attended a blindfold billet service, she was ready to leave the church when Rev. Becker called out, "Romola, please don't go away. Vaslav is sitting next to you. He wants to talk to you about your daughter Kyra." In 1953, Rev. Becker gave Madame Nijinsky the message "I see a revolution in Hungary," correctly predicting the 1956 Hungarian Uprising, when Nijinsky's younger daughter took refuge in Canada.[12]

By 1950, she was famous for her precipitated paintings. The paintings began in 1913, when her guides told her to sit for spirit paintings. She was instructed to put a canvas, some pigment, and just a piece of wood in the darkened séance room. "The sitters sang the Marseilles, the French National Anthem. Rev. Becker would be taken into trance. The members of the circle would sing the song over and over, sometimes for up to 2 hours, I am told, until they would hear a loud 'clap.' After hearing the 'clap,' they knew the painting was on the canvas."[13] When the lights were turned on, everyone admired the paintings—many were of American Indian guides. The paintings were given to specified sitters with the provision that they be returned to the Golden Gate Spiritualist Church in San Francisco, California, when the owner died.

How did Rev. Becker create these works of art? Apparently her spirit guides drew energy from her solar plexus. "After a painting séance was held, she would find a large black-and-blue area about the size of a saucer somewhere on her body where substance had been drawn from her by Spirit to be used in creating the precipitated painting."[14] She was able to manifest twenty-seven precipitated paintings—many of which are on display at the Golden Gate Spiritualist Church.

Few mediums today possess the gifts of Rev. Becker, the Campbell brothers, or the Bangs sisters. In fact, only one comes to mind—Reverend Hoyt Z. Robinette. The Tennessee native first became aware of his gifts at thirteen, when he was contacted by a departed relative. Later, at twenty-one he met his mentor, Reverend Bill D. English, a Camp Chesterfield medium. Under Rev English's tutelage, Hoyt developed trumpet mediumship and the art of precipitated spirit cards. Spirit writing is similar to slate writing, by which Moses received the Ten Commandments.

Fortunately, this art of precipitation has not been lost. Rev. Hoyt Robinette, a Camp Chesterfield Spiritualist minister and medium, does precipitated spirit cards. Although Moses left no record of how long it took for him to develop his mediumship, Reverend Robinette explained that it took him seventeen years to fully develop. As the years have progressed, his spirit guides suggested that Hoyt use 3-by-5-inch index cards and crayons, markers, and colored pencils (with the tops on) so that they can dematerialize the ink and rematerialize it on the card. His initial cards were names of spirit loved ones and guides on one side—the back remained blank. Eventually the medium was able to create two-sided cards with writing on the front and a picture on the back. Now the cards have message writing on them, with signatures from loved ones—Grandma, Mom, Dad, and spirit guides—plus a detailed picture on the back. Portraits of guides are common.

I was introduced to a modern spirit precipitation of Rev. Hoyt Robinette in 2003, when Rev. Gail Hicks showed me her collection of spirit art cards—3-by-5-inch index cars with portraits and scenes drawn by spirit. I "knew" that I had to investigate. One year later, on October 22, 2004, she was to learn firsthand about precipitated art. My husband, Ron, a most practical man, and I, along with five students, including a doctor, nurse, and teacher, all piled into his green Suburban and headed for Fairhaven, Massachusetts, to attend a physical séance with Rev. Hoyt Robinette.

The séance was held at Arlene Pavia's Star of the Sea Chapel and Spiritual Center. When Ron and I arrived at the small church, which had once been a garage, we instantly felt the powerful vibrations. Rev. Hoyt, a gracious man who had driven from Camp Chesterfield to do the service, greeted us warmly. Then we seated ourselves in the front row—3 feet from the medium. We had purposefully arrived early so as to get front-row seats, to be sure of the medium's authenticity. However, we had little to worry about. Rev Hoyt Robinette turned out to be one of the most talented physical mediums—honest to a fault.

Before the séance, Rev. Robinette held up a snake basket and turned it upside down to show it was completely empty. Then he opened a brand-new, unopened package of blank, 3-by-5, white index cards in full view of everyone. He always has one of the sitters examine the cards to ensure they are completely blank. Before the séance, he had Michael, an accountant by profession, slowly go through the cards. He attested to the fact that all the cards were blank.

Then Hoyt placed the blank cards in the snake basket, along with a variety of colored pencils and markers with their caps on—layering them lasagna style. The basket was then placed in front of the room, where everyone could see it. Hoyt likes to use a snake basket since it is covered with an inside cloth that prevents light from entering. When the top is put on, the closed basket acts like a darkroom in which to precipitate the cards. It is interesting to note that the spirit guides work as a team to create the cards, with names of loved ones and guides written on the front and a picture on the back of the card.

For the next hour the basket remained in view and untouched as Rev. Robinette did a traditional billet séance in which he reads billets while blindfolded. I was impressed when Hoyt mentioned, "I have Katherine," but I kept still, since Katherine is a common name. Then Hoyt said, "Harry is here with Katherine," and I knew that my grandparents— Katherine and Harry Brickett—were in the room. Later their names, spelled correctly, appeared on the front of her spirit card with the name of a Native American guide, Bright Star, whose name had been given to her by a Long Island medium during a reading at Pine Grove Spiritualist Camp in Connecticut.

On the other side of the card was a green-and-gray picture of an older gentleman. I happened to be wearing gray pants and an emerald-green knit top that night. Apparently spirit knew that I wanted proof of their existence! At the conclusion of the billet séance, Hoyt turned and picked up the snake basket and began to hand the cards out. One with "Ronald Kuzmeskus" had a lovely scene of an American Indian campground against a background of purple mountains. Several names were impressed on the back; for example, "Ashtar," which was the same name that had been given to Ron during the billet séance.

The students were equally impressed. Dr. Gina received a precipitated picture of Mother Cabrini, whom she greatly admired, and Nora, a nurse and alternative healer, received a picture of Edgar Cayce.

Apparently, spirit tunes in to the thoughts of each sitter before each séance. For instance, when Sylvia invited her Catholic mother to a spirit card séance, the seventy-five-year-old Italian lady worried that it might not be the right thing to do. She prayed to the Virgin Mary to guide her. When she received her card, there was a picture of Mother Mary, a duplicate to her prayer card on her table at home. It seems that Mother Mary was also present during the séance in March 2009. Later, Mother Mary had appeared on Ronald's spirit card, after he had been told by spirit that he would receive a picture of Mary and Joseph in their middle years.

Every spirit card séance is unique. During my second séance with Robinette, I decided to test the medium. Shortly before the séance, I sent the thought out to Arthur Ford, asking the deceased medium to place his name on my spirit card that night. Arthur Ford's name appeared on my card in the faintest ink—as if it were last to be precipitated. Other cards have been evidential as well. The names of Carl Hewitt, Yogananda, Gladys Custance, and Kenneth Custance, and those of my grandparents—Katherine Brickett and Harry Brickett—have appeared on subsequent cards. In March 2015, I received a picture of Dr.

Oswaldo Cruz and the following names: Gladys Strohme, Clifford Bias, Gladys Custance, Kenneth Custance, Dr. Peebles, Dr. Oswaldo Cruz, Eleanor Hoffman, Ethel Post Parrish, Crazy Horse, and Mom.

Spirit cards can also predict future events. In 2008, a year before my granddaughter, Zinnia, was born, I received a lovely card of a little girl with zinnias on it. Another card that I cherish was precipitated at a Maryland séance. It was a picture of medium Margery Crandon. At the time, I was doing a biography on the 1920s medium. Many times as I was doing the research for *The Medium Who Baffled Houdini*, I could sense Margery Crandon's presence.

The day after my birthday, March 26, 2011, I received a very special precipitated spirit card. During the billet séance, I was most pleased to hear from Connecticut medium Rev. Carl Hewitt. I tend to be serious, but Carl always made me laugh at his gentle humor. He said to me that evening, "I am putting my image on the card. I am having a little trouble with the hair—it is darker." When I saw my card, I understood his message. Carl had sandy blond hair and a square build. The image on the card was that of a brunette with a slender build. I turned the card over, and there in the middle, spirit had written "Rod Serling" in red letters!

When I attended a séance with Reverend Robinette on Monday, May 13, 2019, in New London, Connecticut, I received another special precipitated spirit card. That evening I asked the spirits to "please list the guides who will work with me on the next book." While in trance, the medium gave this reply: "Rod Sterling, Bias, Dorothy Lynde, Baba. We are here together. Don't know who. Margery is here with you. Gladys Strom is here. You have lots of people that are beckoning to me. D. D. Home is here. D. D. Home wants you to know that some of the best things come in small packages. Going to show you a likeness of myself. I was not a large person." Naturally, I was most pleased to find the slender image of New London physical medium Daniel Dunglas Home.

INSTRUCTIONS FOR PRECIPITATED CARDS

It takes a great deal of dedication to become a physical medium—even more so to do precipitation. Remember, Rev. Hoyt Robinette sat for seventeen years for development to unfold his gift of precipitated cards. At first he received dots or scribbles, and then a bit of writing. Eventually the spirits produced two-sided cards. The front was filled with names of guides and loved ones, and the back with an evidential picture. The truth is, it takes patience and dedication to develop this gift.

To work with developing the skills with precipitated cards, it is best to sit with a group dedicated to physical mediumship—at least once a week at the same time and place. When the group is ready, prepare a box for blank 3-by-5 index cards. The container can be a lined basket or even a shoebox. Put in a layer of cards, followed by a layer of colored pens with their caps on, then add a second and third layer lasagna style. Sit every day with the basket or box with the lid on for at least ten minutes. Meditate more if the group feels inspired.

This is the important part of the instructions: the group must meditate each day. When the person entrusted with the basket or box goes on vacation, he or she must bring the box along. The guides need daily meditation to acclimate to your energy and produce spirit marks. Be patient! It could take a year or so to see any results. By all means, arrange to bring the card basket to other physical development groups the owner may attend, or to séances with physical mediums such as Reverend Hoyt Robinette. This procedure can greatly speed personal development.

Precipitated portrait of Bernal Tobias. Creators: Mary E. Bangs and Elizabeth Snow. *Courtesy of Hett Art Gallery and Museum at Camp Chesterfield, Chesterfield, Indiana*

Precipitated portrait of Rose Carson. Creators: Mary E. Bangs and Elizabeth Snow. *Courtesy of Hett Art Gallery and Museum at Camp Chesterfield, Chesterfield, Indiana*

Precipitated spirit portrait of Abraham Lincoln, produced at a Campbell brothers séance. *Courtesy of Lily Dale Assembly, Lily Dale, New York*

Precipitated spirit portrait of Azur, helper, produced at a Campbell brothers séance.
Courtesy of Lily Dale Assembly, Lily Dale, New York

Precipitated card with image resembling Margery Crandon. Medium: Rev. Hoyt Robinette, dated April 25, 2012.

Margery Crandon, 1923

Precipitated card with image of Rev. Arthur Ford, March 26, 2011

Rev. Arthur Ford

Names on the back of precipitated card included Rod Serling. Medium: Rev. Hoyt Robinette, dated March 29, 2017.

CHAPTER 7:
Voices of Spirit

Believe me, my friends, I know; there is only one way, and it is a way of love. When man forgets himself in love and in service, then he begins to live, then he begins to perceive God and his purpose for him. Then you are shown your path, and how you can live it, and what you can do with it, and how you can enable others to find it also.

—Mahatma Gandhi through direct-voice
medium Leslie Flint

Not only can images of spirits be captured on film, but spirit voices can also be heard and even recorded. The most-common methods are trance mediumship, direct voice, and electronic voice phenomena. In trance mediumship, spirit overshadows or, in rare cases, takes over the body of the medium. Eileen Garett and Edgar Cayce were considered the best of the trance mediums in their day. Both contributed much to the field of trance mediumship. Eileen Garrett was one of the most respected trance mediums of her generation—also the most tested. Uvani, a fourteenth-century Arab soldier, was her control, but Abdul Latif, a seventeenth-century Persian physician, dealt with healing. Tahotah and Ramah, who claimed no prior earthly incarnations, discussed philosophy. Each spoke in his own voice and gave information that would not available to the medium. After many tests, veteran researcher Hereward Carrington pronounced Mrs. Garrett "a medium's medium."

On the other hand, Edgar Cayce did not submit to rigorous testing, preferring to concentrate on medical mediumship. In order to do so, he positioned himself on a couch with his head to the north. As he drifted out of his body, his eyelids began to flutter. Once his control, known as "the Source," took over his body, he was able to contact the universal consciousness. The Source was really a group of spirits that came to help humanity. Once the Source located the person needing advice, the session would begin with "Yes, we have the body here." As long as the correct procedure was followed, the guide did not hesitate to answer the question posed while Cayce was in trance. However, if the designated questioner was not present, the guide would pause for a moment and say, "We are through for the present."[1]

Even though Edgar Cayce was a trance medium, some physical phenomena did take place in Cayce's home. According to Harmon Bro, Cayce's deceased father, Leslie Cayce, could be heard walking around the upstairs bedroom. He even went through papers in Cayce's office until he was told he was dead. Bro also related how a family helper—a superstitious African American woman—tried to get into the Cayce home. For several nights, "Bunchie" kept tapping on their bedroom window to get their attention. Finally, wishing to get some sleep, Edgar informed the old woman that she was now in the spirit world.

In reality, it is not unusual for spirits to make rapping sounds—even footsteps are common. Direct-voice mediumship, however, is most unusual. It takes a strong physical medium to bring through the voices of spirit through a trumpet or directly in the room. Spirit operators need to create an ectoplasmic voice box, through which they can speak physically and audibly to all present. This voice box may be over the throat, on the side of the face, or elsewhere in the room. Trumpets are often utilized to amplify the signal, and directed-voice mediums are sometimes known as "trumpet mediums." The ectoplasm has to be drawn both from the medium and the sitters. In order to do this, the room must be completely dark, since even a speck of light can destroy ectoplasm—a fine etheric substance.

Also it is important to maintain a high degree of harmony and focused attention to levitate the trumpet. At first, voices that come through may be a soft whisper; however, as the power builds, the volume and quality of the spirit voices improve.

Only a few mediums have been successful in producing direct voice—the most famous being Elizabeth Blake, Emily French, Etta Wriedt, John Sloan, George Valliant, and Margery Crandon. Perhaps the most thoroughly researched was Emily French of Buffalo, New York. The elderly medium came from a well-known family and never accepted money for her séances. Over and over again the medium demonstrated that the voices did not originate from her own vocal cords. She was investigated by Edward C. Randall, who attended a weekly séance in her Buffalo, New York, home for fourteen years. Eventually Randall wrote a book about French's séances, *The Dead Have Never Died*, extolling both Emily French's high moral character and genuine direct-voice mediumship.

In 1905, Edward C. Randall contacted the owner of Funk & Wagnalls Publishers, Isaac K. Funk, to arrange for Mrs. French to be scientifically investigated. He agreed to do so, and Mrs. French came to New York City for a two-week stay. In Dr. Funk's book *The Psychic Riddle*, he described his first séance with Mrs. French. To ensure that there was no trickery, the medium placed her mouth on the back of Funk's hand while the spirits were talking. Even so, everyone in the room could hear her guide Red Jacket:

> *While Red Jacket delivered an address his voice suddenly seemed to die out like the notes of an organ when the wind fails, and he exclaimed "Sing!" When his voice came again he explained that the cause of his voice failing was lack of vibrations, and he entered upon a discourse regarding the wonderful atmospheres, electrical conditions, ethers, and vibratory forces of which mortals were quite ignorant, that formed the conditions that enabled spirits to throw their voices into our atmosphere.*[2]

Even at seventy-two, with a heart condition and nearly deaf, Mrs. French gave amazing direct-voice séances: "Her Indian control 'Red Jacket' had an exceedingly loud, masculine voice that would have easily filled a hall with a seating capacity of 2000 people. The medium at that time was a frail old woman with a weak heart and was deaf, yet the sitters could hear every remark of the communicators."[3]

Elizabeth Blake of Ohio was a contemporary of Emily French. While not as affluent as the Buffalo medium, the poor illiterate medium from Bradrick, Ohio, was just as gifted. Even Sir Arthur Conan Doyle was intrigued by her gift. When Mrs. Blake was present, spirit voices were heard—sometimes when the medium herself was speaking. Over the years, the same spirit voices were heard with the same personality and intonation.

Mrs. Blake willingly submitted to tests by scientists and physicians—yet no fraud was ever detected. According to Professor James H. Hyslop's report, spirit voices could be heard from 20 to 40 feet away. The voice gave names and facts about their lives. Here is an example of a typical trumpet séance:

When Mr. Clawson next took the trumpet the voice of a girl spoke and said, "Daddie, I am here."

He said, "Who are you?"

The voice replied, "Georgia," which was correct.

Mr. Clawson then said, "Georgia, is this you?"

"Yes, Daddie," she replied, "Don't you think I know my own name?"

He then said, "I thought you did, Georgia, and could not understand why you would not tell me. Where do we live, Georgia?"

The voice replied, "In Kansas City," which was correct.[4]

As a result of witnessing such remarkable séances, Dr. Hyslop believed that the voices were from spirit, but he was at a loss to explain how this was done. According to N. Riley Heagerty, author of *The Direct Voice*, spirit uses the trumpet as a tiny spirit cabinet. "With her slim trumpet, Mrs. Blake was even able to produce voices in the light: 'The reason Mrs. Blake sat in the light, with the exception of her dark séances that she would do upon request, was because the trumpet was so slim and small at the ends, enabled the middle of it, the distended part to be completely dark, which allowed the spirits to manifest their voices while séances were held in the dark.'"[5]

Another direct-voice medium, Mrs. Maud Lord-Drake (1852–1924), was a star of the séance circuit for sixty-five years. Queen Victoria even invited the medium to Buckingham Palace. The noted medium's main control was the spirit of an American Indian girl by the name of "Snowdrop." Early on, the spirits had encouraged her mediumship: "Maud was christened 'Daughter of the Orient' by the spirits who compared her favorably to the medium at the Temple of Delphi 4,000 years ago."[6]

Mrs. Lord-Drake did not work in the light, but she would position herself in the center of the circle and clap her hands when spirit voices were heard—just to prove she had not changed her place during the séance. During the direct-voice séances, spirit spoke in their own voices and played a music box, to everyone's delight: "A small music box was played and passed from one hand to another, the spirit hand playing on it and passing it around. Voices—notably among them, the voice of the son of our host—were heard in many parts of the circle at once, the medium all the time clapping her hands and talking in another part of the circle; small hands and large hands passed continually and touched us, accompanied by voices: 'Mother!' 'My child, God bless you!' 'George is here!' and at the same time Mrs. Lord would be describing accurately some spirit friend or group of friends to those in another part of the circle."[7]

The medium made it a point to clap her hands at regular intervals so sitters knew that she was not passing the music box around. The ethical medium had many talents. In addition to direct-voice mediumship, Maud Lord-Drake "was reported to produce full-form materializations in daylight, independent music from a levitated guitar, independent voices and singing, and clairvoyance."[8]

Etta Wriedt (1859–1942) was another evidential direct-voice medium. The Detroit medium became well known for her trumpet séances. One of the most frequent spirit voices to emanate from the trumpet was that of her guide, John Sharp, who said he was born in Glasgow, Scotland, in the eighteenth century. When she visited England, she held séances for William Stead and Vice-Admiral William Usborne Moore, author of the book *The Voices* (1913). While Moore believed that spirits were speaking, he was not quite sure how they did it.

Etta Wriedt never entered trance; instead she conversed freely with the spirits—sometime even disagreeing with them. Two weeks after William Stead perished with 1,500 *Titanic* passengers, his daughter, Estelle, attended a séance with the direct-voice medium and quickly recognized her father's voice speaking through Etta and talked with him for about forty minutes.[9]

According to Miss Edith K. Harper, who attended two hundred private sittings with Etta Wriedt, several spirit voices would be talking at the same time, giving messages to different sitters. The private secretary to Mr. W. T. Stead explained, "Messages given in foreign languages—French, German, Italian, Spanish, Norwegian, Dutch, Arabic, and others—with which the Medium was quite unacquainted. A Norwegian lady, well known in the world of literature and politics, was addressed in Norwegian by a man's voice, claiming to be her brother, and giving the name P——. She conversed with him, and seemed overcome with joy at the correct proofs he gave her of his identity."[10]

While Etta Wriedt charged a modest fee only if the séance was satisfactory, John Sloan did not charge at all. He would even get upset if anyone offered to pay for his séances, since he considered his mediumship a sacred gift. He liked to begin his séances with hymns. Soon after the preliminaries, his spirit control White Feather, an American Indian from the Rockies, took over and spoke to the group through a trumpet.

John Campbell Sloan (1879–1951), a contemporary of Etta Wriedt, became known for his demonstrations of direct voice. When Findlay, a Scottish stockbroker, first visited the medium on September 20, 1918, he was initially suspicious of the slight, middle-aged medium slumped in a chair. His opinion quickly changed when Sloan went into trance. According to Findlay, "Voices from all degrees of strength and all spoke from what appeared to be different parts of the room, but it was difficult to say where they originated as center of the circle where two megaphone or trumpets each about two feet long and from the metallic ring of the voice occasionally they were used to speak through."[11] Incidentally, Sloan's control was an American Indian, White Feather ("Whitie"), who took over the "old box" of his medium. Whitie, who spoke in broken English, apologized for his poor vocabulary.

During the next five years, Findlay attended several séances at Sloan's home and became certain that spirit voices were speaking through the medium. The spirits gave their names, earthly addresses, and personal details of their life. For example, when Findlay came as a stranger in the circle, the medium said, "Your father, Robert Downie Findlay, is here." Sloan then went on to talk about an event his father, Arthur, and one other knew about. After twelve years, the researcher concluded, "I can say with conviction he is the best trance, direct voice, clairvoyant, clairaudience medium with whom I have ever sat."[12] Findlay chronicled Sloan's direct-voice mediumship in his 1931 book, *On the Edge of the Etheric* (1931).

Psychic researcher J. Malcolm Bird also investigated Sloan. According to Bird, "Spirits flock to the room to communicate with the people, just as people flock to the room to communicate with spirits. Sometimes the control actually relays the messages, sometimes they appear to come directly from the communicating spirit."[13]

One of the spirit voices was that of Cornelius Morgan. In an exchange of remarks, the spirit of Cornelius Morgan provided Bird with verification of his knowledge of Bird's life. "Cornelius stated categorically and without hesitation or prompting, and addressing me unmistakably, that about three weeks previously on a Friday afternoon about 7:30, I had been walking across the Brooklyn Bridge with a lady and gentleman." When Bird's memory was sketchy, the spirit rebuked him for "speech without thought"—a "vicious" habit that was sure to get Bird in "a peck of trouble."[14]

Excited by the positive evidence of spirit communication, Malcolm Bird crossed the Atlantic to interview Boston medium Margery Crandon. The editor for *Scientific American* magazine had his first sitting with the attractive blonde medium on November 15, 1923. Unfortunately, the séance was disturbed by the presence of a less-than-desirable spirit. After demonstrating table tipping, Margery passed into trance, and the spirit of her brother Walter loudly told the evil spirits, "Get the hell out of here," articulated in the tones of "mud-gutter" rather than Back Bay.[16] Walter was in a better mood for phenomena at the next séance, November 26, when to everyone's amazement a live pigeon appeared with a registration tag on one leg marked 1921 R I.[15] After the second séance, Malcolm Bird was favorably impressed by his sessions with Margery Crandon. He continued to attended séances in the Crandons' Beacon Hill's home, which he described in his book *Margery*.

Margery Crandon continued to impress researchers here and abroad. By all accounts, her English séances were a success. During her final European session on December 17, 1923, at the invitation of Sir Arthur Conan Doyle, Margery sat in the makeshift cabinet: "With no light save that which filtered in accidentally from without, Walter came quickly, tilting the table in greeting. Then he did some very high levitation—at times the table rose as high as eight inches. Walter's spirit gave his characteristic whistle."[16] Then he whistled in Sir Arthur's ear in recognition of his deafness; after which he whistled behind Lady Doyle. Next he shook the cabinet and brought the rug down over the psychic's head.[17] When Sir Arthur Conan Doyle left the séance, he became Margery Crandon's lifelong champion.

Even no-nonsense Harvard professor William McDougall could not dispute the physical phenomena that he witnessed when he attended one of Margery's séances. The professor heard raps coming from every corner of the room, witnessed a profusion of lights, and saw the trumpet levitate. He was so impressed that he recommended that Harvard University test the medium in a laboratory. In order to rule out ventriloquism, Dr. Richardson devised a voice-out machine. Even with stringent test conditions, Walter's voice continued to be heard—to Richardson's satisfaction.

However, when a committee from *Scientific American* magazine investigated the medium, they were not as convinced as Dr. Richardson. The committee consisted of Harvard University professor Dr. William McDougall; Massachusetts Institute of Technology professor Dr. Daniel F. Comstock; president of the Society for Psychical Research, Dr. Walter Franklin Prince; distinguished British investigator Hereward Carrington; *Scientific American* editor Malcolm Bird; and magician Harry Houdini. Malcolm Bird offered to act as secretary for the committee, and Dr. Austin C. Lescaboura, another editor on *Scientific American*, agreed to assist in arranging the tests. In the end, they could not rule out fraud. However, Hereward Carrington, the most experienced psychic investigator on the *Scientific American* committee, believed in Margery Crandon's physical mediumship. According to Carrington, "As a result of more than forty sittings with Margery, I have arrived at the definite conclusion that genuine supernormal phenomena frequently occur. Many of the observed manifestations might well have been produced fraudulently; however, there remains a number of instances when phenomena were produced and observed under practically perfect control."[18]

Another direct-voice medium, George Valiantine from Williamsport, New York, also fascinated researchers. As in the case of Margery Crandon, who became aware of her mediumship as an adult, Valiantine did not discover his talent until age forty-three, when he began to hear voices, including that of his deceased brother-in-law. Eventually he developed direct-voice physical mediumship. He worked primarily in the United States, but he did travel to Britain and other countries in Europe to give sittings in 1924, 1925, 1927, 1929, and 1931.[19]

When H. Dennis Bradley attended a George Valiantine séance in New York City, he was impressed with the fact that phenomena happened even though luminous bands were placed around Valiantine's wrists. His sister who had passed away ten years earlier spoke to him in "clear, audible tones," which were heard by everyone present. Bradley asserted that the other sitters could not have known of his sister, or the family matters that were discussed with her for some fifteen minutes. He also observed that "she said sayings in her own characteristic manner. Every syllable perfectly enunciated and every little peculiarity of intonation was reproduced."[20]

Even more evidential was the séance given by Valiantine on February 27, 1924, for the novelist Caradoc Evans, who heard his deceased father's voice, which he "described as struggling through the floor and coming up between his feet." He tested the spirit by asking his father to speak in his native Welsh language. Hannen Swaffer was equally impressed when he attended a séance with Valiantine on February 25, 1925. One of the sitters, a Chinese countess, heard from her father, followed by the voice of Lord Northcliffe advising Swaffer on the title of a forthcoming book. Swaffer confirmed the spirit communication: "I have heard Northcliffe's voice speak to me on, at least, eight occasions at Valiantine sittings. Once he spoke to me in daylight, in a way which precluded any chance of fraud or trickery."[21]

Valiantine gave his most sensational séance in New York City in the 1920s. Dr. Neville Whymant, an expert on Chinese ancient literature and philosophy, was invited to attend. The group heard the words "K'ung-fu T'Zu." Whymant missed the first séance due to illness. However, he was well enough to attend the second séance, in which "K'ung-fu T'Zu" (Confucius) spoke. Confucius spoke directly to the scholar: "The trumpet floated in front of Whymant and he heard a 'voice' come through in an ancient Chinese dialect: 'Greeting, O son of learning and reader of strange books! This unworthy servant bows humbly before such excellence.' Whymant recognized the language as that of the Chinese Classics, edited by Confucius 2,500 years earlier."

While Valiantine utilized a trumpet to amplify spirit voices, direct-voice medium Leslie Flint (1911–1994) needed no such apparatus. When the medium gave séances, everyone in the room could hear the voices of spirits. There were no levitating trumpets or, for that matter, an altered state. According to Flint, "All my séances are held under normal, natural conditions. There are no flying trumpets . . . no tilting tables."[22]

How was this possible? Flint was a natural-born medium who saw spirits of deceased loved ones as a child. When he grew up, he continued his mediumship and attracted a team of spirit operators. Eventually his guides had to build a voice box of ectoplasm. Sometimes he would use a spirit cabinet or a cupboard—since complete darkness was also required. In any event, his mouth was taped and his hands were held down or bound to his chair. Within minutes, everyone in the room could hear voices "located in a space a little above my head and slightly to one side [of the medium]. The sitters are allowed to record these messages from spirit."[23]

It wasn't long before Flint became well known in England for his direct-voice séances. In the August 3, 1940, edition of *Psychic News*, the newspaper reported, "Flight Lieutenant Peter Kite who was killed in the Norwegian offensive in April has succeeded in transmitting perfect proof of his survival."[24] When the spirit of the young airman spoke at a séance given by medium Flint, he asked to give a message to his mum and dad. When one of the sitters, W. J. West, agreed to do so, the spirit of the twenty-year-old replied in his own voice, "I have three Christian names: Peter William Handford Kite."[25] After spelling out his last name—K-I-T-E—the deceased airman gave his parents' address as 85 Upland Way, Grange Park. All the information turned out to be true. His mother in fact did live at the address provided, and she confirmed that Christian William Handford Kite, an airman, had perished a few months before. Even though Mrs. Kite was not a Spiritualist, she was grateful that her only son had materialized to tell her, "I am not dead."[26]

Flint, who had worked as a theater usher in his youth, was a great fan of Rudolf Valentino (1895–1926). Naturally, he was thrilled to receive a personal message from the movie icon in a séance that took place on December 15, 1962. The spirit explained the tie between the medium and the actor: "Valentino described the fact that his eyes had been opened when he crossed into spirit, and he understood that his meeting Leslie Flint after his passing was not due to chance; it had been planned centuries before."[27] According to the legendary Italian actor, "There is no such thing as death."[28]

Flint was boxed up in a spirit cabinet, tied up, sealed up, and gagged, yet he still produced direct voices with messages of life eternal. Flint became well known for contacting other famous spirits such as Helena Blavatsky, Frédéric Chopin, Winston Churchill, Arthur Conan Doyle, and Mahatma Gandhi. On June 21, 1961, Mahatma Gandhi spoke directly to tell the world about death. According to the noted Hindu philosopher, love is the way: "Believe me, my friends, I know, there is only one way, and it is a way of love. When man forgets himself in love and in service, then he begins to live, then he begins to perceive God and his purpose for him. Then you are shown your path, and how you can live it, and what you can do with it, and how you can enable others to find it also."[29] This recording and others are stored at the University of Manitoba.

Celebrities and royalty alike have attended Leslie Flint's séances. Shortly after the Earl of Spencer died on March 29, 1992, John Bolton spied his daughter, Princess Diana, slumped in the back seat of an official black car, looking "the picture of misery." The psychic investigator decided to write to the princess because he thought she might find comfort in a session with Leslie Flint, who lived a short drive from the palace. Apparently Bolton's hunch was correct. Diana later wrote a note of thanks for the introduction to the direct-voice medium. Leslie Flint later confirmed that the séance had been "successful and helpful."[30]

INTO THE FUTURE EXERCISE

Hypnosis can be used to meet your guide, as explained in chapter 2. Hypnosis can also be utilized to view the probable future. Try this exercise to remote-view the future. You can have a friend read it to you or record it yourself and play it back.

Find a comfortable position with your legs straight. You may choose to sit, lie down flat, or recline, with two pillows supporting your head and upper back. The ancient Egyptians favored reclining at a 135-degree angle.

Now take three deep breaths in through the nose, out though the mouth.

Relax.

Now take a second deep breath through the nose and out through the mouth.

And a third deep breath through the nose and out through the mouth.

Visualize white lotus blossoms serenely floating in a pool of aqua water. See your eyes as beautiful lotus blossoms, completely tranquil. Just peacefully floating in water.

Let this feeling of relaxation go into your forehead, erasing all cares.

Then gently into cheeks, chin, and throat. All tension is released in the throat.

Next this relaxation flows into the shoulders, releasing all pressure in the muscles.

Now visualize this relaxation going down your right shoulder to your right elbow to your right wrist to your right hand.

Completely relax.

Allow this relaxation to flow into your left shoulder, down your left arm to your left elbow to your left wrist, so your whole left arm is completely relaxed.

Your shoulders, spine, and back are completely relaxed.

Your chest is relaxed. All tension is released from your shoulders, chest, lungs, heart, and stomach. All organs are operating smoothly.

This relaxation goes into your hips, down the right hip to the right knee to the right ankle, so your whole right leg is relaxed. Then down your left leg to your left knee to your left ankle, so your whole left leg is relaxed. Your whole body is now relaxed from the top of your head to the soles of your feet.

You have the ability absolutely to project into the future.

You have a strong desire to see the future.

You are protected with white light and wisdom.

Imagine yourself at the table having your morning beverage. Visualize the kitchen or dining area clearly. You feel rested, well, and peaceful. As you look around the table, you spy a folded newspaper, the *New York Times* (or the name of the daily news in your community). Bring the paper up so it is in front of you. On the count of three, but not before, you will open the newspaper and be able to read the headlines for one year from today.

One, you have the paper in your hands.

Two, you are ready to open it.

Three, open it and read the headlines.

What does it say? Take your time. Now look at the front page. Are there any pictures? If so, describe them. Look around the front and carefully read the articles there. Take your time. You will remember all details when you return. Is there any other interesting news? If so, turn to that page and read about it. Take a few minutes to read the paper.

When you are ready, close the paper and relax. See yourself walking onto a long white corridor back to present time.

Now you are ready to return to the present. On the count of seven, you will wake up, feeling wonderful in every way.

One: You are ready to return.

Two: You feel rested.

Three: You feel wonderful in every way.

Four: You have peace of mind.

Five: You are becoming more aware of your surroundings.

Six: You are back to your normal state.

Seven: Eyes wide open.

Write down your experience in a journal. Remember that the future is not fixed. Prayer and meditation can bring about a more positive future.

Music List

Marcy Hamm, "Inward Harmony"

Music for Deep Meditation, "Tibetan Singing Bowls"

Steven Halpern, "Deep Theta"

Paul Horn, "Music in the Great Pyramid"

Monroe Products, "Between Worlds with Hemi-sync"

Carlos Nakai, "Mystic Dreamer"

Valley of the Sun, "Eternal Om"

Reading List

Stewart Alexander, *An Extraordinary Life*

Arthur Hasting, *On the Tongues of Angels*

Eileen Garrett, *Many Voices*

Charles Hapgood, *Voices in Spirit*

Brian Inglis, *Trance*

Sidney Kirkpatrick, *Edgar Cayce: An American Prophet*

Jon Klimo, *Channeling*

Janet Nohavec, *Where Two Worlds Meet*

Kevin Ryerson, *Spirit Communication*

Jess Stearn, *The Sleeping Prophet*

Michael Tymn, *Resurrecting Lenora Piper*

Leslie Flint. *Courtesy of Wikipedia Commons*

CHAPTER 8

Electronic Voice Phenomena

Our senses only allow us to perceive a minute

portion of the outside universe.

—Nikola Tesla

Direct voices are rarely heard in the modern séance room. Nowadays, spirit voices are more likely to be captured on digital tape recorder—a technique known as electronic voice phenomena (EVP). EVP was discovered in 1959 by Friedrich Jürgenson, a Swedish film producer who was recording birdsongs in his backyard. When he turned on his reel-to-reel tape recorder, he was surprised to hear his mother's voice in German: "Friedrich. You are being watched. Friedel, my little Friedel, can you hear me?"[1] He continued to record voices from spirit and wrote two books: *Voices from the Universe* and *Radio Contact with the Dead*.

When Latvian psychologist Dr. Konstantin Raudive read one of Jürgenson's books, he was skeptical. However, he was sufficiently intrigued to contact the author. Convinced that the voices were real, Jürgenson taught Raudive how to record EVPs. "Their efforts were rewarded with voices in a mixture of languages. The sound was unusual as sometimes the speech was nearly double the usual speed and the voices had a pulsed quality such as one would find in chants or poetry."[2] The voices on tape often gave messages that indicated the spirit was aware of current circumstances. When Peter Bander, the editor of *Breakthrough: An Amazing Experiment in Electronic Communication with the Dead*, listened to an experimental tape, he heard a familiar voice say in German, "Why don't you open the door?" In addition, the voice was unmistakably that of his mother. Also, the message made sense to Bender, since he insisted on keeping the door of his office shut—even though his colleagues teased him about his isolation.[3]

Not only are the deceased interested in giving personal messages, but they also give professional advice. George and Jeanette Meek worked with psychic William O'Neil to recorded EVPs using radio oscillators. Their efforts were rewarded by conversations with the spirit of a dead NASA scientist: "The spirit collaborator soon identified himself as Dr. George Jeffries Mueller, a college physics teacher who died in 1967 and had now come close to the vibration of the Earth to assist Meek and O'Neil in opening a communication bridge between the two worlds. O'Neil and Mueller went on to record more than 20 hours of dialog between 1979 and 1982."[4] The spirit of Dr. Mueller gave very precise instructions. "In one dialogue, Doc Mueller was giving O'Neil technical advice on how to improve the Spiricom equipment: 'William, I think the problem is an impedance mismatch into that third transistor.'"[5] With a bit more communication, O'Neil was able to rectify the problem.

EVP continues to be popular with many research groups—chief among them the American Association for Electronic Voice Phenomena (AA-EVP), which was founded by Sarah Estep in 1982. When she stepped down in 2000, Tom and Lisa Butler took over as codirectors. At the time, both had demanding corporate jobs, but they were willing to give up their careers. The AA-EVP, which became the Association TransCommunication in 2010, encourages people to collect EVPs of their own. Tom and Lisa Butler wrote the book

There Is No Death and There Are No Dead to explain how to experiment with EVP. More information is available on their website: https://atransc.org.

EVP researchers cite two important functions of the phenomena. The first is to gain knowledge such as demonstrated in the seminar given by Tom and Lisa Butler at Omega Holistic Institute in October 2005. When I attended the Butlers' four-day class on EVPs, I received two very evidential EVPs from two gentlemen who had died within the year. The first was from Connecticut medium Rev. Carl Hewitt, who died on January 26, 2005. He was born in rural North Carolina with the gift of clairvoyance and had tested at the Rhine's Institute in Durham, North Carolina. The successful medium attracted clients as far away as Hong Kong, the Philippines, Ghana, and Saudi Arabia. Everyone in the group of twelve students heard Carl on the cassette recorder clearly state his name, "Carl," in his characteristic southern accent. The second EVP was from her father-in-law, Anthony Kuzmeskus. He also stated his name, "Anthony," and added the word "protect."

The second reason to investigate EVPs is to give comfort to the bereaved—particularly parents such as Martha Copeland, whose twenty-year-old daughter Cathy died in a car accident—two days before Christmas on December 23, 2001. Copeland was devastated. A few months later, she flew to Long Island for a reading with medium George Anderson, which provided some relief; Cathy gave comfort to her mother. As Anderson explained, "She insists, too, that you recognize that she had an accomplished life. 'A short one and an accomplished one,' she says, especially to her mom, who feels she was cheated out of her life."[6]

Still, her grief knew no bounds. "I tried everything I could think of, such as grief therapy and antidepressants, to get through the darkness. But the first time I heard Cathy's voice after her death, saying these words, 'I'm still here,' I told them, 'I felt hope.'"[7] That first EVP communication from Cathy was received by her cousin Rachel five months after Cathy died. The two girls had walked away from a car accident a few months earlier. They then made a pack that if one died, the survivor would try to communicate with the other. After many attempts to record an EVP on her computer, Rachel was about to give up when she decided to give it one last try. That is when she received the message in Cathy's voice: "I am still here."

After hearing the EVP, Cathy's mother wanted to receive her own message, so she opened her computer and turned on the audio to record. At first, all she got was silence. Frustrated, Copeland thought, "Why can Rachel reach you, but I cannot?" This time when she played the audio back, she heard Cathy's voice at last, "Mama," she said, "I'm right here."[8] Other messages from Cathy soon followed. In early June, which would have been Cathy's grand-mother's ninety-first birthday, their beloved Nanny became very ill. I received an EVP from Cathy saying, "Mom, Nanny's coming."[9] Eventually Copeland wrote a book about EVP communications with her daughter, *I'm Still Here*, that attracted the attention of Universal

Studios. In 2000, Martha Copeland, along with members of the national group AA-EVP, were a part of a movie trailer for *White Noise*, starring Michael Keaton.

Some of the most evidential EVP studies have been conducted in Brazil. Since 2001, Dr. Sonia Rinaldi has investigated EVP with good results. Guided by the spirit of none other than Konstantin Raudive, the Brazilian researcher has been able to make contact with spirits of deceased children and even an unborn child. In 2017, Dr. Rinaldi began receiving messages from Nikola Tesla, the inventor of AD/DC current. In July 2017, she started receiving the messages in English—before that, the communications were in Portuguese. "Apparently, he worked out a way to link her South Portuguese–speaking station to the North American English-speaking station. Since then she has been getting very clear messages in English."[10]

Many spirit scientists—including Nikola Tesla; Dennis Gabor, the inventor of holography; and Michael Faraday, known for his contribution in the field of electromagnetic induction—are working to bring electronic spirit communication to the public. According to Tesla, there is much more to discover in the universe: "Our senses only allow us to perceive a minute portion of the outside universe."[11]

INSTRUCTIONS FOR EVP RECORDING

Recording Equipment

If you wish to record EVPs, you will need a recording device—preferably a digital one. Less expensive digital recorders are preferable since they produce more internal noise, which is useful for voice creation. In addition to a digital tape recorder, you may wish to use an EMF meter to locate an electromagnetic energy field, which often indicates spirit activity. You will also need to create some form of white noise, which assists spirit to help produce sound. A hairdryer or even running water is sufficient. Also, it is also a good idea to bring extra batteries for your recorder.

Location

Take time to find a location with paranormal activity or a place where spirit has been spotted. Check out local history books or look on the computer for ghost stories. If there is a paranormal society in your community or historical society, they can you give additional tips.

Scheduling

If you are visiting a private home or historical site, you will need to get permission. Try to visit during a quiet time of day or ideally when the building is closed to the public.

Preparation

Be sure to be well rested. When you arrive, meditate to gain rapport. Then say a prayer of protection.

Session

Turn on you recorder. It may be necessary to add white noise. If there are no background sounds, be prepared to add some with a fan, a hairdryer, or running water. Often, entities will come through as soon as the recorder is on; however, some may need coaxing. Remember your recorder will pick up all sounds—so when you are recording, be aware of noises that could be mistaken for EVPs. For instance, a dog barking or a door slamming shut may be mistaken for spirit sounds. If there are any extraneous sounds during the session, simply explain the source. If the dog barks, explain, "That was my dog barking," or if a door shuts, say, "A crew member just shut the door."

Most entities respond well to questions. Talk to the spirits in a normal tone of voice. Leave adequate space between your questions to pick up any possible responses. It is best to keep the session short. Start with a few preliminary questions such as "Who is here?" Then wait thirty seconds. Next, you could ask permission to record them. Wait thirty seconds. Next, you might ask if spirit has a message. Wait a minute, then announce you are closing the session and ask spirit if they have any last-minute information. Wait another thirty seconds before you turn off the recorder.

Playback

Usually, spirit voices will not be heard until you play back the recording. Be sure to use headphones and amplification for best results. If you wish to obtain a voice graph, hook the recording to computer software such as Audition or Audacity sound editor, which can amplify, filter, and even reverse sound files. Watch the graph on the computer. Tune into the valleys between the sound peaks, since EVPs will often come in between the human voices.

At first, EVPs may be mere whispers, but the voices become stronger as spirit gains experience. Voices that are clear and understood by those present are class A. With class B the voices are heard but are not as audible, and people may disagree on the words. Reviewing EVPs can be time consuming. It may take thirty minutes to carefully analyze a five-minute EVP.

Keep a Log

Keep a record of your EVPs. Be sure to include the date, time, and seconds into the recording; the message itself; and the question asked. Label and save the audio file.

Publish Results

If you've captured what you consider good-quality EVP, share your success with other researchers. Many paranormal organizations welcome EVPs. If you have a website or Facebook page, take time to write a blog. With practice, paranormal researchers can record EVPs. Sometimes a group effort will speed things along. For example, Robin and Sandy Foy and Diane and Alan Bennett tried their hand at EVP in Scole, England. Since the four were experienced in mediumship, they were able to communicate with spirit guide Manu, who gave wholehearted assistance from the other side. Their collaborative efforts resulted in extraordinary EVPs. The group even received a class A performance of Rachmaninoff's Second Concerto.

Tom and Lisa Butler. Photographer: Elaine Kuzmeskus.

CHAPTER 9

Spirit Photography

One picture is worth ten thousand words.

—Chinese proverb

Physical mediumship entered a new era with the invention of the camera. Now spirit images could be captured by the camera. Spirit photography was discovered quite by accident when Boston engraver William H. Mumler (1832–1884) noticed the ghostly image of a deceased female assistant on a photograph he had taken of Moses A. Dow in 1862. He shared his discovery with his wife, a well-known "healing medium," who maintained her own practice.[1] News of his amazing photographs quickly spread, and soon people were coming to the photographer for pictures of "spirit extras," for which wealthy clients paid ten dollars a photograph.

Many Boston Spiritualists had their portraits taken, including Fannie Conant (1831–1876). She served as message medium for the Spiritualist newspaper *Banner of Light*. These messages were later preserved in a book, *Flashes of Light from the Spirit World*. In 1868 Fannie visited Mumler's studio for a photo of "a spirit extra." She was pleased to see the shadowy figure of her brother Charles H. Crowell, who died earlier in the year. The image of Charles leaning over his sister's right shoulder was recognized by everyone who knew him.

The following year, 1869, William Mumler's most famous patron, Mary Todd Lincoln, requested a photograph. When Lincoln's widow arrived for a spirit photo, she gave the name of Mrs. Tydall. After the photographer asked her to be seated, he went into his dark-room to prepare a plate. According to Mumler: "When I came out I found her seated with a veil still over her face. The crepe veil was so thick that it was impossible to distinguish a single feature of her face. I asked if she intended having her picture taken with her veil. She replied, 'When you are ready, I will remove it.' I said I was ready, upon which she removed the veil and the picture was taken."[2] It was only when he developed that plate that Mumler realized his sitter was Mary Todd Lincoln—since the familiar figure of President Abraham Lincoln is seen behind his wife. The original photograph also had the outline of their deceased son—however, the faint image faded.[3]

William Mumler also took pictures of trance medium Fanny Conant with the "ghost" of her brother Charles, and of Moses A. Dow, the editor of the *Waverly Magazine*, with the spirit of his assistant Mabel Warren. Robert Bonner had the spirit image of his wife, Ella Bonner, in his photograph. Noted Spiritualist and opera singer Emma Harding Britten received the image of Beethoven in hers.[4] During his lifetime, Mumler attracted his share of critics as well as supporters. One very vocal critic, P. T. Barnum, took him to court in 1869. Mumler's most prestigious supporter was Charles Livermore. The Wall Street financier was part of a team sent by the *New York Sun* to investigate Mumler. Livermore was delighted with the image of his deceased wife, Estelle, that appeared in his spirit photograph. The photograph appeared in the May 8 edition of *Harper's Weekly*.[5]

While Mumler was taking spirit photographs in Boston, another photographer, Edward Wyllie (1848–1911), was photographing spirit extras in California. He was born in Calcutta, where his father, Colonel Robert Wyllie, was secretary to the government of India. Wyllie also served as a captain in the Maori War in New Zealand before he moved to Southern California in 1866. Later, he made his living as a photographer; however, extraneous lights and orbs threatened his livelihood—until he realized the images were spirits.

As demand for Wyllie's psychic photography increased, his work came under the scrutiny of self-appointed investigators, as well as photography experts and some psychic societies. After visiting the photographer in Pasadena in 1901, Dr. H. A. Reid insisted that the spirit photography was genuine: "As to the work of Edward Wyllie, the medium photographer, the proofs and testimonies that the phenomena were genuine, and no trickery were so open, untrammeled, fair, and conclusive that to reject them is to reject the validity of all human testimony."[6]

What set Wyllie apart from others in the field was the fact that he was never accused of fraud. While not every photograph produced a spirit image, the vast majority did. Dr. James Coates, who conducted experiments with the photographer, summarized his findings as follows: "About 60 percent of the photographs taken exhibited psychic extras, and 25 percent of these were identified as those of departed persons. To all the subjects Mr. Wyllie was a complete stranger, and of the origins of the psychic extras or portraits he could have no knowledge; and except in the cases where flowers—roses and lilies—were produced there was a marked absence of symbolism in the photographs taken."[7]

Since Wyllie was also a gifted psychometrist, he could obtain photographic spirit photos by holding an object. For example, when Coates sent him locks of his and his wife's hair, two faces appeared in the photograph—one was recognized as Mrs. Coates's grandmother.[8] In 1910, James Coates's deceased daughter, Agnes, appeared in a photo next to Mrs. Shaw. How could this be possible? Mrs. James Coates, a trance medium, gave this explanation during a séance. "When we think of what we were like upon the earth, the ether condenses around us and encloses us like an envelope; our thoughts of what we were like, and what we would be better known by produce the forms and features. It is here that the spirit chemists step in using their own magnetic power over the ethereal matter they mold it so, and give to it the appearance such as we were in earth life."[9]

William Hope (1863–1933) was the next noted spirit photographer. He was not a photographer by trade, but a carpenter. He became interested in spirit photography quite by chance, when he and his friend took pictures of each other with their new cameras. Both were just as surprised as William Mumler to find spirit extras. Soon Hope was taking spirit photos at the local Spiritualist church. Unlike Mumler, he did not charge exorbitant fees—just his hourly wage as a carpenter. According to British medium Lionel Owen, whose uncle attended many sessions of Crewe Circle Spiritualist group, William Hope's spirit photograph were authentic.

One of Hope's most evidential sittings took place on May 6, 1912. The sitter was William Walker, who had two plates exposed. He received a message from his old friend William

T. Stead, who drowned on the *Titanic* in the early hours of April 15, 1912. The message, "I will try to keep you posted. W. T. Stead," was a poignant one: "Mr. Stead was interested in all psychic experiments and before leaving England on his last voyage to America, he had discussed the mediumship of Hope and the Crewe circle with Walker and requested him 'to keep him posted' of any further developments."[10] Later, in October 1915, Stead's daughter Estelle Stead sat for another spirit photographer, Ada Deane. She was most pleased to see the image of her father in a cloud of ectoplasm over her left shoulder.[11]

William Stead continued to make his presence known through psychic Pardoe Woodman and his daughter Estelle: "By 1917, Pardoe Woodman had learned automatic writing, and Estelle communicated with her father that way. She said she could sometimes see light surround them in the room, and sometimes see the figure of her father during their weekly session."[12] In 1922, these sessions were published in a book, *The Blue Island: Experiences of a New Arrival beyond the Veil.*

Mrs. Deane was a working woman and medium and discovered her talent for spirit photography later in life. When her spirit guides asked her to photograph the upcoming November 11, 1922, event at the Cenotaph War Memorial in Whitehall, England, she refused because she did not have access to the event. However, the day before, one of her clients gave her a ticket to a front-row seat—and the rest is occult history. "Just before the two[-]minute silence she removed the cap from her camera and made an exposure of four minutes. It showed no less [*sic*] than sixteen faces of soldiers and sailors with the face of an Indian and the late father of Estella Stead, whose face on the photograph is almost covered in ectoplasm."[13] Wide publicity was given in the daily press to the remarkable photograph taken. She was assisted by Miss Estelle Stead.

Mrs. Deane became "one of Britain's busiest photographic mediums, holding over 2,000 sittings, many of which were for ordinary people."[14] She was also a sought-after speaker at Spiritualist societies. When John Myers attended a séance by the spirit photographer, he prayed to be able to capture extras on photographic plates. He had been aware of the spirit world since he almost died due to a rabid-dog bite. "It was after this event that John began to be aware of another world and its inhabitants, that could not be seen by others, e.g., he saw children, and a woman whom he described as his 'guardian angel.'"[15]

The Victoria Psychic Research Society was willing to help Myers form a circle dedicated to spirit photography.[16] However, success did not come immediately. Each member of the circle did his or her best to receive psychic impressions on the photographic plates. Only when Myers took a turn did an image appear. The spirit image was later identified as that of a woman who had died some weeks earlier.[17] The picture made the front page of the very first issue of *Psychic News*, much to the delight of its founder, Maurice Barbanell. During this period, Barbanell would give Myers the name and information of a deceased person who could be identified if their image appeared. When the photographic plates were developed, one had the image of the "very person to whom John had referred."[18] Barbanell was so impressed by Myers that he wrote a book on the spirit photographer, *He Walks in Two Worlds*.

Later, members of the Press Portrait Bureau conducted a test. "They were to purchase the plates and be present when loaded, together with signing them and monitoring the development. Before the test, John advised Barbanell that he believed the playwright, Edgar Wallace, would make himself known and asked for Hannen Swaffer, who had known Wallace, to be present at the test."[19] When the plates were developed, there was a perfect image of Wallace.

John Myers's spirit photography was even verified by other mediums. Such was the case for Mr. and Mrs. Farebrother, whose son, Jackie, appeared in a photograph taken by Myers. They had been told by Estelle Roberts to expect a picture. The noted English medium explained that "Jackie, their youngest son, communicated and mentioned that he had attempted to show himself on the photograph but had been unsuccessful; he further added that on the next occasion he would succeed. When Mr. and Mrs. Farebrother had another sitting with John, 'to their great delight Jackie kept his promise'"[20]

There were also spirit photographers in the United States. In the heyday of Camp Chesterfield, there were many spirit photographers such as Mable Whitfield. Here is one example of her sitting in front of her cottage. Notice the materialized faces in the windows and the ectoplasm over the roof of the house.

Medium Mabel Whitfield. *Author's collection*

Rev. Charles Swann of Camp Chesterfield in Indiana became well known for his spirit photography in the 1950s until his death. His wife, Pauline, would cut 6-inch silk squares to be used in spirit photography. During the séances, which were held in complete darkness, sitters would place the silk square over their solar plexus. The result was pictures of loved ones and guides impressed on the fabric. When Jeanette Strack-Zanghi attended one of Swann's séances, she received a picture of a biblical guide: "Cards were given to us. We were told to hold the blank cards against our lower stomachs or solar plexus. The Rev. Swann went into prayer, as we went into meditation. I then looked at my former blank card and it now had a skotograph or picture of Master Amos from biblical times."[21]

According to Reverend Hoyt Robinette, who attended several of Swann's séances, "Charlie Swann was genuine." Both he and Reverend Bill English amassed a large collection of spirit photos, which sadly were destroyed in a house fire. Fortunately, the art is not lost, since Hoyt Robinette conducts his own spirit on silk séances. I attended one of his spirit-on-silk séances in Maryland with twenty-three other people. As the guests entered the basement turned séance room, I noticed a table with a stack of "silks" that Hoyt had prepared earlier, some containers of ink, and a stack of normal construction paper of various colors. The lights were on, everything was clearly visible, and the participants were invited to inspect everything.

After he explained the process, he gave each of us a 6-inch white silk square. The lights were then turned off so that the basement/séance room was pitch black. Rev. Hoyt led the group in "The Lord's Prayer" before he went into trance and his guide, Dr. Kenner, took over. The guide gave messages, while spirits imprinted the images on the silk squares. At the close of the séance we were instructed to roll up the silks and the construction paper beneath it and to keep it away from the light for twenty-four hours—to give the images time to develop completely. When I opened my silk the next day, I was most pleased to see a picture of my godmother, Aunt Ruth, who had passed to spirit in 1953!

Since the séance with Hoyt Robinette, I've learned to do spirit photography. When I teach the art to students, the first thing that I ask is "What is the difference between real and fake psychic photography?" The correct answer is intention. A Spiritualist would explain, "It is important to begin with sincere intention to capture spirit on film to prove the continuity." An amateur ghost hunter may simply wish to satisfy his or her curiosity. Obviously, each will attract different spirits. If you are simply curious, mischievous spirits will accommodate you. However, if you have honorable intention, you will attract the attention of the spirits of loved ones and spirit guides. To get the best result, be clear in your intention.

After the right intention, meditation is essential to spirit photography. Take time to relax your mind and body with meditation. Send the thought out that you wish to connect with spirit. While amateurs can be successful, the best spirit photographers need to have some degree of intuition. Then contact spirit guides through meditation. As you send the thought out that you wish to communicate with the other side, spirit will come through your thought field as well as guide you telepathically.

Faith also plays a huge role in spirit photography. Agnes, a devout Catholic, is a good example. When the young mother and artist attended a weekend meditation retreat, she received communication from Mother Mary, who told her she would appear in person. She was then told to go to a grotto not too far from her house and to bring a camera. When Agnes snapped a picture, she did not know what to expect. However, her faith was rewarded. When the film was developed, there was Mother Mary's serene image.

A similar incident happened to Mary, a recently retired second-grade teacher, on a trip to see John of God. When she visited Brazil, she was charmed by the South American Indian children. Often she stopped to talk with the youngsters as she would purchase the small items they had to sell. When the natives who owned a local gift shop invited her to attend one of their ceremonies, she agreed to come back that evening. She found the energy exhilarating, but she saw nothing unusual as she took pictures. That is, until she returned to the States. As she reviewed her pictures, they were full of orbs. The first had only a few; the second, more orbs; and finally, in the last frame, a multitude of orbs with an image of Our Lady of Guadalupe in the background.

It seems that when you least expect it, spirit images will appear. I've had my share of spontaneous spirit orbs, faces, and even figures show up in photos. One of the most unusual occurred at the Danbury Music Center. I was trying to capture electrical voice phenomena in the elevator area; however, there were no sounds that night. Disappointed, I felt impressed to snap the last picture in my throwaway camera and was rewarded with several spirit images—even though I did not see them with my naked eye.

Spirit photography is not an exact science; it takes time to develop. Most psychic photographers would agree that spirit will allow them to take their picture at the right time. Sometimes the spirits are shy, but other times they will come in great numbers.

Take your time when you arrive at a location. Allow a half hour to gain rapport with the spirits present. Walk around the location and try to tune in to the energy. I did this when I researched the old copper mines in East Granby, Connecticut. As I sat quietly in the side yard, I tuned in to layers of energy. First I heard music similar to that of the 1920s, and then I saw small spirit animals. When I asked the guide if the property had always been used as a prison, he answered, "No, it was a tavern in the 1920s and later, in the 1940s, a children's zoo."

Also note signs from nature. When visiting the Harriet Beecher Stowe House, I was amused at the sight of two blue butterflies that flew side by side. Later, I learned that both Harriet and her husband were interested in the spiritual. Was this their sign they were present?

When ghost hunting, bring a notebook, a thermometer, an electromagnetic field (EMF) meter, and a camera. Write down any impressions that come into mind. What energy are you picking up as you walk around? Note any changes in temperature, sparkly lights, cool breezes, or even fragrances. Use a thermometer to document hotspots or cold spots. Sometimes the temperature can go down 10 to 20 degrees in one area if a ghost is present. Finally, an EMF meter can detect electromagnetic energy that is present.

As for the choice of camera, experts prefer a digital camera, since it eliminates any criticism of flaws in the film. Even more important then a camera is patience. Do not expect instant results. If the conditions are right, orbs, lights, and ectoplasm can crop up in photo; however, it may take several shots. Often it is good to take three shots in one location to capture movement. For example, when Ron, my husband, took several pictures of a séance room at Camp Casadaga in Florida, he was able to capture a funnel of energy traveling across the room.

Once you have taken your photos, take your time examining them. The first sign you have made contact with spirit is orbs—round spheres that are often transparent and sometimes colored. Occasionally, a face may appear in the middle of the orb. Another common occurrence is ghost lights—lights with no external source—sometimes they will have a distinct color.

Next, a foggy substance may appear. This is ectoplasm. This is the first step in materialization. Sometimes faces or figures will form out of the substance. When I tried to take a picture of Theodate Pope outside my second-floor bedroom, a mist formed over the picture. Since Theodate was a believer, I felt that this was her spirit coming through.

Even amateur spirit photographers can capture images on camera if they choose the location carefully. Are there historic homes or cemeteries known to be haunted in your area? Look online for a list of places with paranormal activity. Another choice would be a historic site such as Gettysburg. When you feel ready, point your camera in the direction of spirit energy. Do not be overly concerned if you cannot spot any orbs or spirits, since most spirit photographers do not see orbs or ectoplasm with the naked eye. With practice, most spirit photographers can capture these images:

orbs: transparent or colored round spheres

ghost lights: streaks of white light with no external source

lightning rods: sticks of light that sometimes will swirl or bend in shape

vortex: funnel shape that can sometime be seen moving on video camera

ectoplasm: light-gray mist

It takes skill and a bit of luck to capture a full figure such as the photograph taken by Robert Chaney, a resident medium at Camp Chesterfield. The author of *Mediums and the Development of Mediumship* was also a gifted medium and spirit photographer. One day in 1944, he stopped to take a picture of the statue of an American Indian while he was strolling the grounds of the camp. When the photograph was developed, he was surprised to find the image of a spirit Native American next to the stone statue.

Perhaps the best example of spirit photography is the photos of Silver Belle, the spirit guide of Ethel Post Parrish. While the medium was in trance, Silver Belle materialized and allowed Jack Edwards to take several pictures of her materializing in front of eighty-one people during a 1953 séance. The photographer took pictures every fifty seconds, using infrared film, and obtained amazing results, as you can see from the picture below:

Séances such as that of Ethel Post Parrish require special attention. Never use a flash during a séance while the medium is in trance, since the flash can upset both spirit and the medium. The white light of flash may even burn the medium and produce internal

The fully formed Silver Belle is now able to speak with the people attending the séance.

injuries! Occasionally, a picture can be obtained if you ask permission beforehand. If possible, use an infrared camera.

Scotography or photographing in the dark is another type of spirit photography. Two very important factors are needed: One, there must be communication from a spirit team—usually three or more spirits are needed, including a spirit chemist. Second, the medium must possess the right chemistry. When the spirit team arrives, they can then use the medium's body to create ectoplasm, needed for spirit to be photographed in the dark.

Rev. Charles Swann was able to produce scotographs as well as photographs on silk. When Rev. Gladys Swann, on July 13, 1976, received a scotograph of Master Amos, she said, "Cards were given to us. We were told to hold the blank cards against our lower stomachs or solar plexus. Then Rev. Swann went into prayer, as we went into meditation. I then looked at my former blank card and it now had a skotograph or picture of Master Amos from biblical times."[22]

Scotography can even be done with unopened rolls of film, which was the method used by the Scole group. Their circle began in 1993, when Robin and Sandy Foy and Diane and Alan Bennett sat for physical mediumship in the basement of a home in Scole, England. When the group attempted scotography with Polaroid film, the spirit team kept a careful watch on the film: "The spirit team did not so much acquiesce in the investigators' bringing and controlling their own film as to positively commend this course. Since the initial expectation was that films could be produced only after a gestation period extending over a week or two, it was necessary to agree on the sort of security container in which to house unopened rolls of virgin film."[23] For security purposes the rolls of 35 mm Polaroid color film were kept in a locked box.

With the help of spirit, images were imprinted on unopened rolls of film. These images included actual photos of people and places, sometimes from the past, and various obscure verses and drawings that took some effort to identify. There were also pictures of other dimensions as well as newspapers. "This *Daily Mirror*, dated 1936, was one of two newspapers which were apported. It (like the *Daily Mail*), was in mint condition when it arrived but within a week the paper had yellowed—despite being kept in air-tight conditions."[24]

INSTRUCTIONS FOR SPIRIT PHOTOGRAPHY

1. Research your location carefully for paranormal activity.
2. Always ask for permission before taking spirit photographs. Avoid areas that are marked "Prohibited." If possible, visit the area before the actual shoot to be familiar with the terrain, traffic, or both.
3. Be respectful of the site. Clean up after being at an investigation site, and leave the area just as you found it.
4. For best results, go with a partner to witness any paranormal activity. Be sure to let everyone know that they may not cross in front of the camera.
5. Do not smoke or use perfume or aftershave, since you want all light and fragrance to come from spirit.
6. Document any activity that could interfere with photos, such as a cat jumping in the picture or a lightning storm.

Mary Todd Lincoln with the spirit of Abraham Lincoln. Spirit photographer: William Mumler. *Courtesy of Wikipedia Commons*

Reverend Charles Lakeman Tweedale, his wife, and the spirit of her deceased father (September 5, 1919). Spirit photographer: William Hope.

Elderly couple with the spirit of their daughter. Spirit photographer: William Hope.

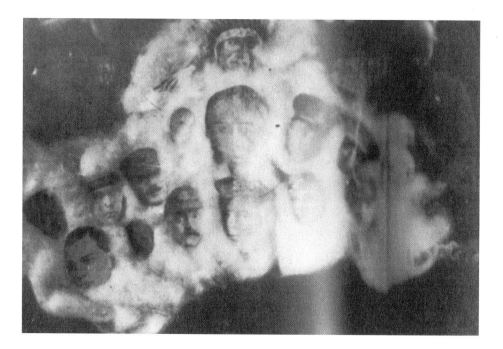

Armistice picture also in 1922 on Armistice Day, taken just before the eleventh hour of the eleventh day. Spirit photographer: Ada Deane. *Courtesy of Wikipedia Commons*

Edward Whyllie, spirit photograph with writing, *Courtesy of Wikimedia Commons*

CHAPTER 10

Trance and Transfiguration

After six days, Jesus took with him Peter, James, and John, the brother of James, and led them up a high mountain by themselves. There he was transfigured before them. His face shone like the sun, and his clothes became as white as the light. Just then there appeared before them Moses and Elijah, talking with Jesus.

—Holy Bible, Matthew 17:1–3

As exciting as it is to hear the voices of loved ones and guides, it is even more amazing to see their faces. Not only can the departed speak, but they can also materialize. Spirit manifestation has three stages—transfiguration, ethealization, and materialization. The first phase requires the least amount of energy, since spirit transfigures only over the face of the medium who is in a trance state. During ethealization, more ectoplasm is drawn from the medium, so a full spirit form can appear in a light ethereal state. When the trance medium is fully developed, he or she will be able to produce enough ectoplasm for the final phase—a full materialization.

In all three phases of materialization, some amount of ectoplasm is extruded from the medium's body while he or she is in an altered state of consciousness. However, not every medium can do physical mediumship, since a certain chemistry is needed to produce ectoplasm, as well as the help of a spirit chemist. The job of the spirit chemist is to extrude the ectoplasm needed for spirit to make an appearance. In order to do so, knowledge of both human and etheric anatomy is necessary.

Ectoplasm is produced within the body; the pancreas plays a major role. Once formed within, it is extracted from all of the orifices—mouth, ears, and, for female mediums, the vagina. Ectoplasm, once extracted, is a cloudy substance with a musky smell. It is usually misty; however, at times it can become as hard as plastic. The hardened ectoplasm in necessary for levitation and table tipping. Yet, for transfiguration, which is less dense, a small amount of ectoplasm will suffice.

Trance can vary from light to deep states of awareness. Transfiguration can be done in a light to medium trance state, while materialization requires deep trance—with ethealization falling in the middle. Methods of testing the depth of trance vary as well. For instance, old-time Spiritualists were known to stick a pin into a medium's arm to be sure the medium was indeed in deep trance. Today, science uses an electroencephalograph to measure brain waves. The lower the frequency of cycles per second (cps), known as Hertz (Hz), the more awareness is turned inward, and the lower the cycles per second.

beta (14–40 cps): awake and alert
alpha (8–13 cps): relaxed, light trance state
theta (4–7 cps): deeply relaxed state, ideal for hypnosis
delta (0.5–3.5 cps): unconscious state, full trance

While a clairvoyant or clairaudient medium would be fine in an alpha state, transfiguration mediums need a deeper state of trance. Most trance mediums usually operate in the theta trance, with some conscious awareness; only a few are full-trance mediums in the delta state of consciousness. In mental mediumship, spirit uses the medium's mind to communicate mind to mind. Whereas in trance mediumship, spirit overshadows the medium as in light trance and may actually take over the medium's body in full trance.

The key to any trance state is focused attention. This can be obtained with meditation or through hypnosis. Once a medium can relax, he or she is in a natural alpha state. With practice and deeper relaxation, the medium enters theta, in which there is still awareness of surroundings. In deep trance—known as "dead" trance—the medium loses all consciousness of what is said during the session. Most trance mediums usually operate in the theta trance, with some conscious awareness; only a few are full-trance mediums in the delta state of consciousness.

In addition to the level of consciousness, there is a shift in spirit communication with each phase of mediumship. In mental mediumship, spirit uses the medium's mind to communicate mind to mind. However, in trance mediumship, there is a closer connection as spirit overshadows the medium as in light trance. In full trance, known as "dead" trance, spirit may take over the medium's body. This, of course, is done only with the medium's permission.

Cora L. V. Richmond, Edgar Cayce, and Elwood Babbitt all had the gift of full-trance mediumship. Richmond was noted for doing lectures in trance. Her topics varied from astral travel to materialization. She advised, "Never believe or disbelieve anything. If something cannot be proved, then it must be shelved, until one day when it can be proved."[1]

Edgar Cayce, on the other hand, became well known for dispensing medical advice while in trance. According to Cayce, "Mind is the builder." He often pointed out that mind is the bridge between the physical world and the spiritual world. Cayce used hypnosis techniques to induce trance. As he took slow, deep breaths, his assistant (usually Gladys Davis) would watch the psychic's eyes flutter. She could then pose questions to the Source, Cayce's guide. However, if she started too soon or waited too long to ask questions, then Cayce would be out of trance and not able to answer the queries.

Once the medium is in a state of light trance, ectoplasm can be extracted. When enough ectoplasm is present, spirit can overshadow the medium's face so that the spirit's face is present. Sometimes a spirit cabinet is used to collect the ectoplasm. The medium is seated inside a cabinet made of wood or draped in black cloth. Then spirit guides and loved ones can press their faces into the ectoplasm and make their features visible. Since ectoplasm is destroyed by light, this type of séance usually takes place in conditions of low red light.

Queenie Nixon (1918–1989), one of the most evidential of transfiguration mediums, used red light to demonstrate transfiguration. A natural medium, she was known both for her transfiguration and direct-voice demonstrations. During trance, she often took on the features of her main spirit guide, Paul, as well as loved ones from the spirit world. Those present could also see the faces of spirit loved ones as these loved ones transfigured over the medium's face:

Whilst in deep trance, one could watch her face altering in shape, age, and sex. In every case the new face appearing upon Queenie Nixon was recognized by someone in the audience, at which stage the spirit person would then commence talking to that relative[,] and some of these two[-]way conversations went on for 10–12 minutes. One of the most amazing of the above described was the appearance of the "dead" mother of a French[-]born woman who lived in Perth[;] not only did the dead mother speak to Monique in French, she used a dialect peculiar to a district 30 miles south of Paris.[2]

Sometimes faces would even appear to the side of Queenie Nixon. Her séances could last as long as three hours, and they often included independent voices of spirit. All her séances were done in the dark, with only a dim red light shining on the medium's face. At times, forms appeared above and to the side of Nixon.[3]

Later, Jean Skinner became notable for her demonstrations of transfiguration. Jean had a spirit guide by the name of Chan, who was known to appear in ectoplasmic form over her face. During one séance at Stansted Hall in England, a photographer captured the spirit world placing a mask of her spirit guide Chan over Jean's face. The photograph is posted on the Jean Skinner website (psychictruth.info/Medium_Jean_Skinner.htm).

Rev. Richard Schoeller, a noted transfiguration medium from Long Island, New York, discovered his mediumship with a visit from two sets of deceased grandparents one evening in 1997. At first he thought he was dying. "They reassured him that it wasn't his time to join them in the afterlife and that their visit was to help him understand that he could now see them."[4] Transformed by the experience, Schoeller began taking mediumship lessons.

By the time I saw him, he had advanced to cabinet mediumship. The cabinet was set up in the basement of the First Spiritualist Church in Springfield, Massachusetts. Schoeller was dressed all in black. He sat in the cabinet to build up ectoplasm while the group of about forty sang songs to raise the vibration. When the curtains to the cabinet were opened, a red light shined on the medium's face so everyone could see the spirit faces as they transfigured. The faces appeared rapidly—about ten or so a minute. People began to call out the names of loved ones as they appeared. For instance, one man shouted, "That was my uncle—I can tell by the scar on his face." I too saw faces; I was especially pleased to see the spirit of trance medium Elwood Babbitt appear over Richard Schoeller's face.

A few years later, in 2013, Babbitt appeared over the face of another medium—Rev. John Lilek from Toledo, Ohio. Rev. Lilek was ordained in 1992 through the Universal Spiritualist Association. Rev. Lilek conducted two séances at my office in Suffield, Connecticut. He did not use spirit cabinet but simply sat on the couch at the far end of the room in pitch darkness. Once he was in trance, Ronald Kuzmeskus shone a dim red light over Lilek's face. During both sessions, the faces of spirits rapidly transfigured over John's. Elwood Babbitt came in, and later we all saw the face of Abraham Lincoln. Many sitters saw the faces of their deceased loved ones along with colored lights and spirit images in the room.

Diana Palm had a similar experience: "People who sat for John's demonstrations claimed to see spirits manifest and walk around the room, experiences of physical touch, see colored lights, spirit hands, and multiple full-bodied spirit apparitions appear on or near him."[5]

Many people were surprised by the sight of loved ones and historical figures. At one point, Rev. James Tingley, John's mentor, made an appearance. Several sitters were able to confirm that it was Rev. Tingley from photos in the séance room shown after the séance. Mabel Riffle came through to say she was looking forward to being with John and working with him.[6] Sadly, Rev. John Lilek passed to spirit six days later.

INSTRUCTIONS FOR A TRANSFIGURATION SÉANCE

The first step in transfiguration requires trance. Once a medium can go into trance, he or she is ready to try transfiguration. The basic requirements for transfiguration are a pitch-dark room, a red light, and spirit control. Before you begin, have these materials ready:

   black drop cloth for the wall behind the medium

   red lightbulb, 7.5–10 watts

   lamp with a dimmer (a lamp with a narrow shade works best)

   extension cord if needed

   set of black pants and a black top

Then prepare the room. A basement or room without windows is ideal. However, windows can be covered with black curtains—black garbage bags will do. Then have a chair—preferably with arms—for the medium, and chairs for the sitters. The medium should dress in black or dark clothing and remove all jewelry.

Explain the rules to the sitters, since they are part of the séance. It is important they keep a positive expectant attitude. They should also sing or hum (if they don't know the words). Choose easy songs such as "Row, Row, Row Your Boat" or "I've Been Working on the Railroad."

Start the séance with a prayer such as "The Lord's Prayer" and an invocation:

Father-Mother God, we ask for the highest and best. We call upon loved ones, guides, and ascended masters to be present this evening. May everyone here experience the miracle of transfiguration.

When they see a loved one or guide, it is important for them to call out their name. For example, "I see my mother Dorothy's face" or "That's Elwood Babbitt."

Explain that the first portion of the séance is in complete darkness. Then, once the medium is in trance and the energy is high enough, a red light will be turned on by the medium's assistant. Before you begin the séance, ask if there are any questions.

Once all questions are answered, turn off the light. Have the sitters sing to bring up the energy. You may wish to end with a signature song. In my transfiguration group, we sang four or five tunes and ended with a lively rendition of "Jingle Bells." During the singing, the medium who was seated in front of the group does deep breathing and prepares for trance. The medium's attendant can tell when the medium is ready, and will ask for a dim red light to be shone on the medium's face.

At this point, the sitters should be able to see an ectoplasmic face quickly transfigure over the medium's face. People will begin to call out names of deceased relatives and friends. Sometimes famous people such as Abraham Lincoln may appear. If this happens, everyone in the room will recognize the face.

Rev. John Lilek. Photographer: Elaine Kuzmeskus.

CHAPTER 11

Materialization

The most difficult phenomenon to produce, and the hardest to accept, even by Spiritualists themselves, is materialization. First come hands and faces, and then the full forms.

—Maud Lord-Drake

Spirit contact can take many forms—spirit voices, psychic photography, even materialization. While materialization is the most convincing proof of survival, even some Spiritualists find his rare form of mediumship hard to accept. This was not always the case. In the 1870s, materialization first became common in séance rooms. The entranced medium would bring through spirit, who could touch the cheek or hands of the sitters, ring bells, move objects, and even leave their fingerprints in wax. Sometimes luminous forms would appear, such as Katie, the spirit control of Florence Cook; Silver Belle, the spirit control of Ethel Post Parrish; and Peggy, the spirit control of Helen Duncan. Everyone in the room could see the guides and converse with them.

Learned scientists such as Professor William J. Crawford, Dr. Gustave Geley, Sir William Crookes, and Cesar Lombroso all have examined materializations. In 1914, Dr. William J. Crawford, a lecturer in mechanical engineering at Queen's University of Belfast, Ireland, meticulously examined the mediumship of sixteen-year-old Kathleen Goligher. He estimated that on average, only one in one hundred thousand human bodies contain the chemicals necessary for a full-form materialization. In a full materialization, spirit seemingly appears from a cloud of ectoplasm—gradually becoming more distinct in features. There is a science behind materialization, even though it appears to have no visible source.

However, materialization is accomplished by invisible spirit chemists who draw ectoplasm, a cloudy, white, semifluid substance, from within the medium. According to Dr. Gustave Geley, head of the Institute Metaphysique International in Paris, "Ectoplasm is an externalization of decentralized energy in solid, liquid, or vaporized states. This decentralized expended great vital energy, which could manifest through rapping, phosphorescence, telekinesis, or the production of Ectoplasm."[1] Under test conditions, Frankel Klushi was even able to produce spirit fingerprints in wax in several séances—a feat Margery Crandon later duplicated in Boston.

Occasionally, physical mediums such as Warren Caylor will allow sitters to hold ectoplasm. This is done only in red light or candlelight, since ectoplasm will dissipate under pure white light. When Warren's guide Yellow Feather gave me permission to hold a mound of ectoplasm, the substance was light and sticky—a bit like wet cotton candy. It had a weblike texture and a distinctive musky odor. During a 2017 séance held in Suffield, Connecticut, spirit went even further and materialized a man's arm and hand. One of the sitters, Steve, was allowed to touch the ectoplasmic hand, and he said, "It feels solid—like a regular hand."

In the heyday of physical mediumship, there were several excellent materialization mediums. Mrs. Maud Lord-Drake was one the most popular. When she did a materialization séance, she insisted on being tied to a chair when she sat in the spirit cabinet. She also made sure that the doors and windows were kept locked, to avoid any allegation of trickery. Under these strict conditions, very credible materializations took place, such as a woman in a bridal dress: "The lady in bridal costume was recognized by Mrs. Hutton, Mrs. Knapp, and members of my father's family as an acquaintance who had been buried in her wedding dress similar to the one in which she presented herself."[2]

At the same séance, several other spirits materialized, including that of the medium's tiny guide, Snowdrop. "Among the number was a beautiful little Indian girl who parted the curtain and threw a bouquet of flowers which struck me on the shoulder, and who said: 'Here's the medium's flowers for you, Brave.'"[3]

Maude Lord-Drake's materializations provided conclusive evidence. "On December, 1886, J. S. Drake explained, 'What was the most convincing of all was the appearance of two forms at the same time, both addressing us in different voices while the medium was talking.'"[4] At another séance the medium gave in Oakfield, Wisconsin, the spirit of a man materialized and gave his name. The spirit stated that he had lived in western New York, near Jamestown, and that he was a relative of Mrs. Hooker in Fondulac and that he would like to have the medium tell Mrs. Hooker that he was dead and he had come to inform her before the funeral. In a few days Mrs. Hooker did indeed receive a letter to inform her of the death of the gentleman who materialized in the séance room.[5]

Helen Berry was not as well known as her contemporary Maud Lord-Drake. However, many Bostonians, such as Dr. William James, attended her materialization séances. The Harvard professor investigated Helen Berry and pronounced her "the best of her class."[6]

Florence Marryat, author of *There Is No Death*, concurred with Professor James. When she saw an advertisement in the papers for one of Helen Berry's séances, she decided to attend incognito. The writer was glad she did. During the materialization séance, she was surprised to see the spirit of her daughter Florence with a small spirit child: "I went up to the cabinet, the curtains divided, [and] there stood my daughter Florence as usual, but holding in front of her a little child of about seven years old. I knelt down before this spirit of my own creation. She was a fragile[-]llooking little creature, very fair and pale, with large grey eyes and brown hair lying over her forehead. She looked like a lily with her little white hands folded meekly in front of her. 'Are you my little Gertie, darling?' I said. 'I am the Princess Gertie,' she replied, 'and Florence says you are my mother.'"[7]

Gertie was the stillborn child Florence Marryat had lost years before. Apparently the baby had grown up in the spirit world, much to her earthly mother's surprise: "At that time I had hardly believed it could be true that the infants who had been born prematurely and never breathed in this world should be living, sentient spirits to meet me in the next, and half thought some grown spirit must be tricking me for its own pleasure. But here, in this strange land, where my blighted babies had never been mentioned or thought of, to meet the Princess Gertie here, calling herself by her own name, and brought by her sister Florence, set the matter beyond a doubt."[8]

Mr. Brackett also witnessed the spectacular phenomena. During one of Miss Berry's séances, the spirit of his deceased cousin emerged from a cloud of ectoplasm and walked toward Mr. Brackett. As he studied the spirit girl's face, he noticed that "her hair had all the warmth and glossiness of a girl of eighteen. She said to me, 'Don't you think that I am very strong today?' and putting both hands in mine allowed me to caress and converse with her freely."[9]

Even more astounding were the séances of Florence Cook (1856–1904). She was thoroughly investigated by Sir William Crookes, who pronounced her materialization genuine. The teenaged medium could not have had a more distinguished champion. Crookes was noted for his discovery of the element thallium and pioneering research into vacuum tubes. His research paved the way for atomic physics. The British physicist became interested in Spiritualism after the unexpected death of his brother Philip in 1867. In July 1869, he visited medium Mary Marshall, who was known to produce spirit raps, table levitation, writing on glass, and direct voice of the guide John King.

Between 1871 and 1874, Crookes investigated Kate Fox, Daniel Dunglas Home, and Florence Cook. He became so fascinated by Florence Cook that he held a series of sittings with "Florrie" between December 1873 and May 1874. During these séances, the spirit of Katie King materialized. The spirit claimed to be the daughter of Henry Morgan, the buccaneer.[10] She was Florence Cook's control from the 1850s to the 1870s. At first, Katie King was more ethereal; however, with practice the spirit was able to materialize more fully a long dress and headscarf. She reached the point where she could walk out of the spirit cabinet and allow herself to be photographed with a flash. "On March 12, 1874, Katie King, after materializing, came to the opening of the cabinet, pushed aside the curtain, and summoned Sir William to the assistance of the medium. Katie was in white. Sir William immediately went into the cabinet and found Florence Cook, clad in her customary black velvet dress, lying across the sofa."[11]

Naturally, Florence Cook had her critics. Some claimed that the medium impersonated Katie King. Sir Arthur Conan Doyle explained that "as is apparently typical of materialized spirits, Katie's exact height and weight varied, though Katie was always taller than Florence Cook, with a larger face, and different hair and skin. According to those present, the two were both visible at the same moments, so that Florence could not have assumed the role of the spirit."[12]

In a letter published in *The Spiritualist* (June 5, 1874), Crookes describes the photographing of Katie King: "I frequently drew the curtain on one side when Katie was standing near[,] and it was a common thing for the seven or eight of us in the laboratory to see Miss Cook and Katie at the same time under the full blaze of the electric light. We did not on these occasions actually see the face of the medium, because of the shawl, but we saw her hands and feet; we saw her move uneasily under the influence of the intense light and we heard her moan occasionally. I have one photograph of the two together, but Katie is seated in front of Miss Cook's head."[13]

Later, Trevor H. Hall in his book *The Spiritualists* (1962) claimed that Florence Cook had an affair with William Crooks. The author, a skeptic of mediums, based his allegations on Frances G. H. Anderson's statement to the Society of Psychical Research in 1922 and 1941.[14] Sir William Crooks's biographer William Hodson Brock seriously doubts that an affair between Florence and Crookes ever took place.[15] Even if the suspicious allegations were true, though an alleged affair with a married man might sully Florence Cook's character, it would not invalidate her materializations, which were witnessed by researchers other than Crookes.

Physical mediumship always seems to be clouded by controversy. Even the brilliant Brazilian medium Carmine Mirabelli had detractors—though few in number. According to author Brian Inglis, he was "the most remarkable physical medium in recent history, outshining even D. D. Home in his ability to produce phenomena."[16] Mirabelli was born in Botucatu, São Paulo, Brazil, on January 2, 1889. He suffered greatly when his father died on February 22, 1914. His sensitivity to the spirit world grew when his father died. His deceased father became his "guiding star."

For whatever reason, the spirit activity increased. His physical mediumship became a source of concern when he went to work at the Villica Footwear Company. It wasn't long before strange noises were heard and shoeboxes literally flew off the shelves. People believed the young man to be possessed. He was persecuted at work and beaten up on the streets. Eventually it was all too much for Mirabelli, and he was hospitalized with what the doctors termed "nervous energy." Eventually, psychic researchers convinced Mirabelli of his rare psychic ability.

In 1919 the committee of Academia de Estudos Psychicos "Cesar Lombroso" tested the medium for trance speaking, automatic writing, and physical phenomena. He sat for 392 sessions. When in trance, the medium spoke in twenty-six languages and wrote in twenty-eight languages. The script was nothing short of amazing.[17] "Mirabelli to write a treatise of 9 pages on the independence of Czechoslovakia in 20 minutes, Camille Flammarion inspired him to write about the inhabited planets, 14 pages in 19 minutes in French, Mirabelli delivered five pages in 12 minutes on the Russo-Japanese war in Japanese, Moses wrote in Hebrew on slandering, Harun el Raschid made him write 15 pages in Syrian and an untranslatable writing of three pages came in hieroglyphics in 32 minutes."[18] The young medium was also observed levitating and on one occasion was seen to be levitating 6 feet into the air while sitting in an automobile. He even made a violin play with spirit hands. There were also reports of Carlos Mirabelli dematerializating from one sealed séance room to another room. "He was soon discovered in a side room lying in an easy chair and singing to himself."[19]

The scientists were amazed by Mirabelli's astounding materializations of Dr. Jose de Carmago Barros, who died in a shipwreck. They carefully examined the materialized form: "The mist, glowing as if of gold, parted and the bishop materialized, with all the robes and insignia of office. He called his own name. Dr. de Souza stepped to him. He palpated the body, touched his teeth, tested the saliva, listened to the heart-beat, investigated the working of the intestines, nails and eyes, without finding anything amiss."[20] Once everyone had ample time to examine his form, bishop slowly dematerialized.

In another séance the deceased daughter of Dr. de Souza materialized for thirty-six minutes. Her father recognized his daughter dressed in the same outfit in which she had been buried. Her father was even allowed to embrace his daughter and take numerous photographs.[21] Carmine Mirabelli continued his remarkable mediumship until his death in 1950.

Perhaps the most astounding feat was the materialization of Giuseppe Parini, the Italian Enlightenment satirist and poet of the neoclassical period. Dr. Carlos de Castro was surprised by the event. Apparently, the deceased poet materialized between him and the entranced Carmine Mirabelli during a séance at the Cesare Lombroso Academy of Psychic Studies. Fortunately, the image of Giuseppe Parini seated between Dr. Castro and the entranced was caught on film.

Brazil was not the only country to produce materializations. In America, the Eddy brothers produced apparitions—solid enough to be measured and weighed. The brothers hailed from a long line of sensitives dating back to Salem witches. At first glance, William and Horatio seemed more suited to the farm than the séance room. Both had a clumsy demeanor and were ill at ease with strangers. Yet, the two farmers turned mediums had the gift of levitation, spirit writing, and clairvoyance and produced excellent materializations at the family inn.

In a typical séance, William Eddy would enter a spirit cabinet at the front of the room. He would be tied to his chair. Then he would prepare for trance. While William sat in a spirit cabinet in trance, his brother Horatio sat outside as a cabinet attendant. Most of the séances were held with some light from a shaded lamp. However, those held in complete darkness produced stronger manifestations. Musical instruments would start playing music on their own, and there were psychic lights and materialized hands and figures observed by the attendees. At times, "Mad Indian dances shook the floor and the room resounded with yells and whoops."[22.]

In 1874, a reporter from the *New York Sun*, Colonel Henry Steele Olcott (1832–1907), investigated the Eddy brothers for several weeks. Initially skeptical, the colonel brought a platform scale to weight the spirits and measure them as well. However, after witnessing more than four hundred materializations in ten weeks, he became convinced that the brothers' materializations were genuine. According to Colonel Olcott, "He saw in the course of ten weeks no fewer than four hundred apparitions appear out of the cabinet, of all sizes, sexes, and races, clad in the most marvelous garments, babies in arms, Indian warrior, gentlemen in evening dress, a Kurd with a nine-foot lance, squaws who smoked tobacco, ladies in fine costumes."[23]

When Helena Blavatsky read Olcott's account of the materializations in the New York newspapers, she made a trip to Chittenden, Vermont, to see the apparitions. There was a change of forces. The materialized spirits were not Native American, but spirits from many nationalities: "There was a Georgian servant boy from the Caucasus; a Muslim merchant from Tiflis; a Russian peasant girl; and others. Another evening there appeared a Kourdish cavalier armed with scimitar, pistols, and lance; a hideously ugly and devil-ish-looking Negro sorcerer from Africa, wearing a coronet composed of four horns of the onyx with bells at their tips, attached to an embroidered, highly-colored fillet which was tied around his head; and a European gentleman wearing the cross and collar of St. Anne, who was recognized by Madame Blavatsky as her uncle."[24] At the sight of her uncle, who materialized with the cross and collar of St. Anne, Madame Helena Blavatsky was also convinced that Will Eddy was a genuine medium.

Olcott was only too happy to tell the world of the remarkable mediumship. In 1875, the reporter wrote a book about the Eddy brothers, *People from the Other World*, which was published by the American Publishing Company of Hartford, Connecticut. His book received praise from noted British scientists Sir Alfred Russel Wallace and Sir William Crookes.

After World War I, the public's interest in mediums surged. During the 1920s, there were several physical mediums that emerged: Franek Kluski, Willi Schneider, Helen Duncan, and Ethel Post Parrish, to name a few. Franek Kluski (1874–1949) did not attract the level of attention that was given to the Eddy brothers, but he produced some spectacular materializations during his seven-year stint. At times, he materialized the hand and face of a hairy *homo sapiens*: "The Spirit World produced through Franek a spiritual bird something like an European Nightjar, also a lion like creature which would walk around the table; a dog on occasions appeared and placed itself on the lap of a sitter and licked the other sitters as would the hairy humanoid. The humanoid creature would sometimes, when asked, lift the heavy library sofa above the heads of the sitters, a very heavy bronze statue was lifted above the heads of the sitters and taken around the séance at height."[25]

Kluski was born February 13, 1874, to an upper-middle-class family in Poland. His father and uncle also had psychic powers, but they did not demonstrate their gifts publicly. As a child of six, Franek began to see spirits. The sensitive child grew up to become a journalist and a banker. It wasn't until he was forty-five that Kluski actively pursued his mediumship. His séance phenomena are described in *Reminiscences of Séances with the Medium Franek Kluski*, published in Poland in 1926. At first he demonstrated table tipping and the movement of objects, then automatic writing, lights, and finally apparitions. In one session, on August 30, 1919, a large hawklike bird appeared out of nowhere. "Prior to the exposure, there was a whirring sound, like that of large unfurling wings, and slight blasts of wind. The sitting was held in the light of a red lamp, about 3 metres away from the medium, and in this light the participants could see the outlines of a grey moving mass, which was identified as a bird only after the plate had been developed."[26]

Kluski conducted his séances in difference locations. Sometimes he was subjected to doing a séance in the nude or a brightly lit room, which was not the best venue. However the spirit entities more often provided their own light or used a luminous plate that spirit hands held to illuminate a face: researcher F. W. Pawlowski claimed that "the light from the plaque is so good that I could see the pores and the down on the skin of their faces and hands. One frequent [spirit] visitor not only provided enough light to ensure that he could be seen, but this also illuminated the sitters and much of the séance room."[27]

The figures were nothing short of miraculous. "The participants exchange observations, they see ginger facial hair, a wrinkled face, wide[-]open eyes looking ahead under the brim of a cap, an irregular nose, and pale, sunken cheeks. . . . The Colonel remarks that this is a Russian general. The author has no doubt that it is the uniform of a Russian officer, with details such as the cap with the officer's oval bow in the middle, and gold officer's stripes on the shoulders."[28] The spirit is later recognized as Komarov, who speaks to the phantom is Russian. Another spirit "Assyrian priest" "looked like a beautiful old man, reminiscent of the inspired Rabindranath Tagore in a flowing white robe."[29]

One of the most impressive materializations was that a phantom who bowed in the Eastern manner, touching its forehead and chest, and stood speechless. "It claimed to be a Turk captured during a battle between the Polish army and Turks 250 years previously. It also claimed not to be able to speak because its tongue had been cut out by an ancestor of one of those present. It was noted that while at times the phantom seemed to be just like a living person, every so often it would become transparent and misty, with its contours blurring, and that its eyes and eye sockets seem to burn with a strange light."[30] The spirit even accepted a cigarette before he dematerialized.

Ethel Post Parrish was America's most prominent physical medium. She had several spirit guides, including Silver Belle, a beautiful Indian girl and granddaughter of the famous Chief Baconrind. She also had Sir Joseph Banks as a master teacher. While on the earth, Banks (1743–1820) was an English naturalist who explored the Pacific with the famous navigator James Cook. As might be expected, Silver Belle was lighthearted, with a musical lilt to her voice. Sir Joseph Banks, on the other hand, patiently answered questions with his seasoned philosophy.

Parrish's gifts of materialization attracted attention worldwide. A devout Spiritualist, she established a school for Spiritualist ministers and mediums in 1927 in Miami, Florida. Later, in 1932, she opened a summer camp in Ephrata, Pennsylvania, which she named after her spirit guide, Silver Belle. Many Spiritualists traveled to her camp, situated at the Mountain Springs Hotel in Ephrata, to learn more about mediumship and attend her séances. Ethel Post Parrish demonstrated physical mediumship at the hotel until her death in 1960.

Ethel Post Parrish's séances were astounding! Mrs. Parrish would sit in a spirit cabinet, often with her cousin Mabel Riffle as attendant, and go into trance. While she was in a state of dead trance, her American Indian guide would materialize and speak so everyone could hear her. Often other guides and departed relatives would appear as well: "On August 8, 1943, at Camp Silver Belle in Pennsylvania, she materialized several figures before an audience of twenty-five. The first to materialize was the medium's guide, Silver Belle, who promised, 'I am going to work hard tonight and try to get as many of your loved ones through as possible.'"[31] It wasn't long before the 6-foot spirit of Silver Belle's grandfather, Chief Baconrind, emerged from the cabinet, accompanied by other spirits: "In rapid succession, the following phenomena occurred: Ella Carter and a Dr. Baker, both in spirit, materialized for Joseph Graham, Bryn Mawr, Pennsylvania. These two held the floor simultaneously and for several minutes talked to Mr. Graham. Ella Carter moved from the center of the room to her right and stopped a few feet away from me. I [Graham] could see that she was a very beautiful spirit."[32]

Another amazing séance took place on August 25, 1945, at Camp Silver Belle in Ephrata, Pennsylvania, where a group of thirty-two men and women gathered to witness a materialization. Before Ethel Post Parrish went into trance that Saturday evening, three members of the audience inspected her spirit cabinet. Then the group was instructed on séance protocol: "We were told how to hold the co-worker's hands to form a battery, and warned against touching the forms, unless Silver Belle, the little Indian girl who is the Medium's cabinet guide, gave her permission. We were also warned not to step between the Medium and the materialized form as an invisible cord connects the two and an injury to it could cause great harm to the medium."[33]

Then the lights were turned off, with only a "very low spirit light" in the room. To raise the vibrations, the group said "The Lord's Prayer" and sang a hymn. "Before the group finished the song, Silver Belle materialized with long dark hair, and radiant white robes. She asked, 'Can everyone see me?' She told the group their loved ones were ready to greet them. When the singing ceased, one materialized spirit after another emerged from the cabinet."[34] While there were materialized individuals on the floor, talking with their loved ones on Earth, at the same time during the entire séance there were voices singing in the cabinet.

Silver Belle's images were captured in photographs taken by Jack Edwards in 1953. Parrish materialized her spirit guide Silver Belle while sitting in her curtained cabinet. The pictures, taken at fifty-second intervals in infrared light by Edwards, show Silver Belle growing from a cloud of "ectoplasm." The series of photographs show the process of materialization of a full spirit form so detailed that even Silver Belle's eyelashes were visible!

Camp Silver Belle continued after the passing of Ethel Post Parrish in 1960. When Jeanette Strack-Zanghi attended séances at the camp in the 1970s, several physical mediums were still doing materializations. She and her husband, Eddy, attended a séance with medium Warren Smith and Penny Umbach in 1974. The two mediums sat in spirit cabinets to build sufficient ectoplasm for materialization. Smith's guide, Miss Firefly, materialized first. The spirit, elegantly dressed in a white gown, sang several songs in her characteristic operatic voice. When the spirits were ready, "Miss Firefly announced CLAYTON NELSON. A spirit came up to Eddy and said hello. Eddy answered, 'Hi, Nelson, how are you doing?' Nelson had been an employee in the Dania post office where Eddy worked. Nelson—'I am studying here and getting along fine.'"[35]

"Later Miss Firefly announced Oma, Jeanette's deceased mother[,] who was incapacitated in later years. Oma was now able to walk. According to her daughter, Gerda Slater, 'She then came in front of me and raised her glittering gown, showed me her legs[,] and said, 'Sehe meine Beine. Ech kann wieder Gehen.' She continued in English, 'I can even dance.' And she danced and I wept with joy.'"[36]

When the Slaters returned to Camp Silver Belle the following year, they attended a séance with medium Bill Donnelly on June 19, 1975. Oma appeared again at Camp Chesterfield. The medium's guide, Crystal, said, "Gerda, your mother is here." Oma appeared to her daughter: "She appeared beautifully in white gauze and spoke a few words of German to everyone in the room."[37] The Slaters and their daughter, Ann, received several visitations: Jeanette had four spirits materialize; Eddy and Ann each had two spirits appear. Edgar Cayce and Ethel Post Parrish made appearances as well.

Author Joyce Keller attended Camp Silver Belle as a young woman. At the time, she had been enjoying Paramahansa Yogananda's book *Autobiography of a Yogi*. She shared her enthusiasm with her husband, Jack, and friends. When they attended a materialization séance at the camp, Yogananda appeared in the séance room. "His white translucent figure floated directly toward me. My heart beat so loudly I could hear it in my ears as Yogananda stopped in front of me and said clearly, 'Joyce, thank you for your appreciation of my book and for speaking so kindly of it to so many people.'"[38] She had not mentioned anything to people at Silver Belle regarding her interest in Yogananda.

Few people outside of Spiritualists have heard of Camp Silver Belle. Spiritualists both here and abroad are wary of prejudice and police intervention. Up until recent times, mediumship and fortune-telling were against the law. For example, Helen Duncan (1897–1956), one of the most talented physical mediums, spent nine months in Holloway Prison when she was convicted of witchcraft. She had caused quite a stir when she materialized the spirit of a sailor with HMS *Barham* on his cap. He came to tell his mother that he had recently died when the ship was sunk by Germans.[39]

Sir Winston Churchill was beside himself when he heard that security had been breached, and ordered an immediate investigation. The British Admiralty then found an archaic law—the Witchcraft Act of 1735—and charged Helen Duncan with the crime of witchcraft. However, forty-one witnesses testified on her behalf, including Air Force officer and wing commander George Mackie, who stated that he had seen his deceased father and mother materialize at one of Helen Duncan's séances.[40] Mary Blackwell, the president of the Pathfinder Spiritualist Society, also testified that she had attended a hundred or more of Duncan's séances and "witnessed the spirit forms conversing with their relatives in French, German, Dutch, Welsh, Scottish, and Arabic."[41]

When Helen Duncan was released from prison in September 1944, she vowed to never do another séance. Eventually the gifted medium consented to do séances for those seeking proof of the continuity of life. Duncan was arrested one more time in Nottingham, England, during a séance in a private home. This time the police were even rougher. They rudely interrupted the séances, turning the lights on and grabbing the medium, still in trance. They even took flash photographs. As a result, Helen Duncan suffered severe burns to her abdomen, which undoubtedly contributed to her death five weeks later.[42]

When Alec Harris and his wife, Louie, visited Helen Duncan's circle, they were pleased to hear the voice of her control, Albert Stewart. He spoke in a cultured voice with a strong Cambridge accent, in contrast to the medium's strong Scottish accent. Louie was "utterly fascinated" when "a tall figure of a man in a flowing white robe stood beside her, his hand on her shoulder."[43]

Alec was also transfixed when his sister Connie, who died from TB, materialized: "After a while, a beautiful young girl stepped right out of the cabinet. It was Connie. Every feature was as it had been when we last saw her."[44] During a second séance at the church with Duncan, "With that the curtains parted and my beloved father stepped out of the cabinet! He came forward, his arms outstretched to mother. 'Poll,' he said gently, 'I am with you.'"[45] According to Louie, he was as solid as she was.[46]

Alec and Louie decided to form their own circle. They meditated at night as part of their development. One night, the trumpet that had been sitting on the mantel moved, to their amazement, "It rose up, glided silently across the mantelpiece, and came to rest on the opposite side, carefully avoiding two vases which stood in its pathway."[47]

The couple was encouraged to try materialization by medium Helen Hughes at the Park Grove Spiritualist Church in Cardiff. The medium's Red Indian guide noted, "You will also have full-form materialization before very long." This seemed hard to believe. He explained, "This will be so because Alec is a very powerful physical medium."[48]

They formed a Sunday night development circle with six members after they were advised to sit for materialization. It took only a few sessions before they had success: "To our amazement a luminous ball began forming in the centre of the cabinet curtain. A face could be seen within this luminous mass, not very clearly, but still a face. While we pondered who this was, the head began to turn. The feathered headdress of a Red Indian could be discerned. I knew then who it was. White Wing!"[49]

As Alec Harris's mediumship progressed, not only did faces appear, but full forms would also appear when the séance cabinet curtains parted. One spirit, Rohan, took over the duties of master of ceremonies: "At the beginning of our circles Rohan always came first and quietly addressed the sitters. He explained that it was not easy for loved ones to build their materialized forms. The Guides had much experience of building, therefore found it comparatively easy."[50] Rohan also emphasized the importance of a harmonious and relaxed atmosphere and suggested that the sitters not concentrate too much on one particular person to come through.

The editor of *Two Worlds* Spiritualist magazine, Ernest Thompson, witnessed this extraordinary and lifelike materialization of a perfect female form through a male medium. "A charming Spanish girl gracefully glided through the curtains and enthralled us with a dancing display. It was fascinating to watch her elegant movements. As she turned quickly on her toes the hem of her billowing white dress flicked my cheek."[51] When the dancer then opened her robes to reveal her nude body, there was no doubt in Thompson's mind that she was indeed a female.

The guides did their best to prepare the group for the coming world changes. "In the early hours of the morning of January 1, 1941, we had come downstairs to celebrate, when White Wing unexpectedly took control of Alec. He spoke to us, with a serious note in his voice, 'There have been many dangers in the past year,' he said, 'and I have come to warn you of a greater danger at hand, to prepare you for this. But have no fear. Know that we, on this side, will do all in our power to protect you. Only trust in the Great White Spirit.'"[52]

INSTRUCTIONS FOR A SPIRIT CABINET

Obtain the necessary materials: gray electrical pipe (8¾ inch by 10 foot) and fittings (8¾-inch tees, 8¾-inch-long elbows), and a small can of plastic cement. When complete, the cabinet is approximately 6 feet, 2 inches in height, 5 feet in length, and 4 feet wide.

Begin by assembling the pipes to make a base 5 by 4 feet. After that is sturdy, make a top 5 by 4 feet out of pipes and connect the base to the top with 6-foot, 2-inch pipes. To do this, use four cups, each placed in a corner. Do not cement the four posts, so you can take it apart. Once the base is assembled, you will need to drape black curtains. If you cannot purchase them, buy blackout material and have them made, plus a piece to place over the top. Finally, place a chair with arms in the cabinet, so the medium can relax completely and meditate.

Have the medium sit in the cabinet, with the curtains drawn. Assign two advanced students on either side of the cabinet to act as attendants. Turn off all lights. Begin with a prayer, then start singing lively songs such as "Jingle Bells" or "I've Been Working on the Railroad" to lift the vibrations. Once spirit has entered the medium, the spirit will often allow a red lamp to be turned on, so when spirit is ready, open the curtains and turn on the red light. If no permission is given, the séance can be conducted in total darkness. However, red light is needed to observe.

CHAPTER 12

Apports

They are said to come from sunken ships, old ruins, large factories with such vast quantities of small, inexpensive objects that a few would never be missed, or somewhere of like nature. The alleged spirits seem to be very careful to do nothing really dishonest in securing the apports.

—Susy Smith

Apports are gifts that manifest from the nonphysical to the physical world. The word *apport* means "to bring" in French. Spiritualists believe that spirits bring small items of jewelry, coins, and gemstones as presents from spirit loved ones. For example, Captain Bronson received a ring from his deceased sister when she materialized at one of Mrs. Maud Lord-Drake's séances. The captain could hardly believe the sight of his deceased sister, who materialized in a form solid enough to hand her brother a ring that had been on her finger when she was buried in Keokuk, Iowa. In her book *Psychic Light*, Maud Lord-Drake details the séance and the aftermath: "Disturbed by the event, the captain couldn't rest until his sister's coffin was opened to see if it was really the same ring. When they opened the coffin, they found that the ring was no longer on her hand."[1]

The majority of apports are not handed to sitters during a séance; rather, they come through a spirit trumpet or just mysteriously materialize in the séance room. Indeed, apports are the most baffling aspect of physical mediumship. For the most part, rapports are small items—coins, jewelry, or even flowers. However, spirit has been known to apport larger items, such as an Egyptian bust on display at the Hett Museum in Camp Chesterfield.

Apports are not a new phenomenon. Miraculous appearances are even recorded in the Holy Bible. Numbers 11:31, Kings 17:14–16, Psalms 78:24, and Ezekiel 2:9–10 mention materialization. For example, God sent an apport in the form of a scroll to warn Ezekiel of the consequences of the rebellious nation. "Then I looked, and I saw a hand stretched out to me. In it was a scroll, which he unrolled before me. On both sides of it were written words of lament and mourning and woe."[2]

Jesus also knew the laws of physical mediumship. The Master used them to produce miracles such as the materialization of the loaves and the fishes to feed the group of four thousand followers. "Taking the five loaves and the two fish and looking up to heaven, he gave thanks and broke the loaves. Then he gave them to his disciples to distribute to the people. He also divided the two fish among them all. They all ate and were satisfied."[3]

The first apport recorded in modern times was witnessed by a Dr. G. P. Billot during a séance on March 5, 1819, in Paris. In attendance were somnambules and a blind woman. He received an apport that reportedly came from Saint Maxime and Saint Sabine: One of the seeresses said she saw a dove flying around the room. It was carrying something in its beak that it finally deposited before a person. When Billot examined the contents of the packet, he found three pieces of paper with a small bone glued to each, and beneath was written, "St. Maxime, St. Sabine, and Many Martyrs."[4]

Everyone needs reassurance, and spirit has been known to go to great lengths to contact loved ones as well as the faithful. When Sir Arthur Conan Doyle died, he was anxious to contact his wife from the other side. Within weeks, Doyle came through to medium Mrs. Caird Miller to give a message plus his wife's phone number. When Mrs. Doyle required more proof, the medium found a key on her pillow. "Conan Doyle informed her that it was the key to his study. Mrs. Miller called his son Denis this time. When she told him what had happened, he drove 40 miles to pick up the key. When he returned, he found that the key did fit the study door."[5]

Researcher Malcolm Bird was just as impressed when he received his first apport during a séance with Frau Vollhard. To avoid trickery, the medium had a sitter on either side, holding her hand in complete darkness: "We had been so (sitted) but a moment or two when the medium began to make her weird noises. These worked up to a climax quite rapidly, there was a faint rustling[,] and the medium groaned wildly and repeated and insisted that something happened. Dr. Schwab flashed his light and there on the table was a branch of box-tree perfectly fresh."[6]

Later, Bird observed apports of Boston medium Margery Crandon. In November 1923, Bird traveled to Boston to observe the medium. For weeks her group had been discussing apports. The ABC group (named for participants with the last names of Adler, Brown, and Crandon) was especially interested in bringing through a living apport. Margery's spirit guide was also keen on the idea. The spirit began issuing orders: "There must be a man in every room. We must do this scientifically."[7]

Dr. and Mrs. Crandon, Dr. Brown, Aleck Cross, Mr. Adler, Dr. and Mrs. Mark Richardson, and Charles Caldwell attended the séance. The servants were dismissed for the evening of November 26, and Margery's son, John, was tucked in for the night. At Margery's spirit guide Walter's insistence, all the rooms of the four-story home had to be searched to verify that no live animal was present. The doors and windows were closed at 11:05 p.m. At 11:06, Dr. Brown led the way into the dining room; he saw something white on the floor, which he picked up. It was to everyone's amazement a live pigeon with a registration tag marked 1921 R I on one leg. When they attempted to trace the registration, the group discovered that the bird to which it had been originally issued was dead, so it must have been transferred from this dead bird—not an uncommon practice.[8]

At a later séance held on Valentine's Day 1924, the ladies received fresh flowers: "On Valentine's Day 1924, Walter (Margery's spirit guide) had some fun with the ladies. Mrs. Litzelman said to Walter, 'I have three red, red, red, roses for you.' To which the playful spirit replied, 'I have you a yaller, yaller, yaller rose, and Kitty (Mrs. Brown) I have brought you a yaller, yaller, yaller rose, and Ma I have brought you a yaller, yaller, yaller.'"[9] Then, according Malcolm Bird, who was present in the séance room, he witnessed single roses land in the laps of the three ladies addressed. When the lights were turned on, each had in her lap "a small rosebud, yellow and crumpled with stems obviously fresh cut."[10] Apparently spirit had just picked the flowers!

How do spirit operators manage to bring flowers into the séance room? Strange as it may seem, the flowers had to be picked, dematerialized, and rematerialized into the séance room. According to spirit helpers, they "by an act of will power, disintegrate the object that is to be transported into its molecular elements without altering its form, in this state the matter may pass through any other matter and become re-integrated be a second act of will power, de-materialization, and re-materialization."[11]

After Margery Crandon, there were few physical medium in the United States until the 1950s, when Keith Milton Rhinehart (1936–1999) began his work. He founded the Aquarian Foundation in Seattle, Washington, in 1955. His physical mediumship progressed rapidly from reading billets to direct voice, materializations, and apports.

Susy Smith, the noted parapsychology author and a medium herself, believed that Rhinehart exhibited genuine physical mediumship, as exhibited in an amateur movie she was shown. "In it the medium is seen spewing from his mouth quantities of small objects as he did in the Japanese séance. The most curious thing about this film, however, is that apports are seen in his ears."[12]

According to Smith, Rhinehart's apports came from a variety of sources: "They are said to come from sunken ships, old ruins, large factories with such vast quantities of small, inexpensive objects that a few would never be missed, or somewhere of like nature. The alleged spirits seem to be very careful to do nothing really dishonest in securing the apports."[13] During her first apport séance, which was held in complete darkness, Susy Smith received two dozen white carnations, which dropped into her arms as she was seated in the third row. Though impressed, the researcher could not vouch for the séance since she did not have the opportunity to search the medium and hall beforehand.

Keith Rhinehart gave an even more evidential apport séance in Japan in 1958, under very stringent test conditions. The medium had been stripped, thoroughly examined, and given a simple dark kimono to wear. He was then securely locked in a specially constructed chair, designed to record even an inch of movement. After a gag was securely placed in his mouth, Rhinehart began the séance. At the end, he motioned for the gag to be removed. When it was removed, Rhinehart literally spat agates from his mouth in rapid succession. "After this more agates came from the trumpet that was poked through the cabinet curtain. There were a total of 720 pieces of agate which were later examined by Kenichi Ikeda, a jeweler who valued them at more than five hundred yen apiece."[14]

More recently, Indian guru Sathya Sai Baba (1926–2011) materialized articles in broad daylight. Several members of the Sai Baba group from Windsor, Connecticut, received rings. For example, a devoted middle-aged Hindu couple was pleased to receive matching rings with nine stones. Baba also materialized a silver ring with "Sai" on it for a retired gentleman. On close examination, Jim saw that there was a notch carved in the top. A carpenter by trade, he had never worn a ring—fearing he might catch it on machinery. Apparently Baba had picked up Jim's fear and made the ring with a notch so it would crack open if necessary!

In 1992, I visited Sai Baba's ashram in Puttaparthy, India, where I was able to observe the guru firsthand. Before leaving, I viewed a video of the guru producing sacred ash known as *vibuthi*. There seemed no rational explanation for the phenomenon. As luck would have it, I was seated in the first row during morning devotions. When Sai Baba came to bless the devotees, he stopped in front of me, outstretched his hand, and produced vibuthi. The sacred ash literally bubbled up in the center of his upturned palm. Usually Swami makes vibuthi with his palm down—unless a spiritual aspirant needs to see how vibuthi manifests.

In 1993, Robin and Sandra Foy and Alan and Diana Bennet decided to sit for physical phenomena in Scole, England. For the next six years, they met twice a week in the basement room, 15 by 30 feet, which was painted midnight blue. The two couples sat around a circular wooden table in complete darkness—all wore luminous armbands so all could observe their movements.

Even though the four were experienced mediums, it took almost a year before any results were observed. By October 1995, their efforts were rewarded when a coin literally appeared out of the air and landed on the séance table. In the ensuing years, they received over 150. These apports included "a silver necklace; a Churchill coin; a small rose quartz crystal ball; a 1940 British penny; a 1928 one franc piece token; a Silver charm of the 'Grim Reaper'; an original copy of the *Daily Mail* dated 1st April 1944; an original copy of the *Daily Express* dated 28th May 1944; and many others."[15]

Their most impressive apports were copies of the *Daily Mail*. The first newspaper that was apported was a pristine copy of the *Daily Mail* dated April 1, 1944. The newspaper headlined the story of how Helen Duncan had been sent to prison under the "Witchcraft Act" for holding materialization séances and that included an article about medium Duncan's eighteen-month prison sentence.[16]

The second apport arrived as unexpectedly as the first: "On Monday 11 July 1994, after Manu's initial greeting, the 'plop' as an object dropped on to the table sounded different from normal. Manu explained to Robin that the apport was 'from one of your spirit helpers and you will understand why this particular item has been chosen when you see it.'"[17] The newspaper reported the defeat of Winston Churchill's party by Labour in the 1945 election. It is interesting to note that "the apported *Daily Express* was printed on paper of the type used in the early- and mid-1940s, but it was in almost mint condition. . . . There was no sign of the usual yellowing which would have occurred if it was an original from the end of wartime Britain."[18]

The apports were varied in nature. While some were quite serious in content, others were more whimsical. For instance, after the group had been watching a TV program on monkeys in the wild, they received an evidential apport. "During the séance, a massive 'thump' was heard on the table. We all jumped, as it was so loud, we thought that it might be a house brick that had been apported! In fact, the apported object turned out to be a wooden carved monkey—about 8 inches long—with one hand extended in a hook, as though designed to hang on a rail."[19] Apparently the spirit team wanted to lighten the mood of the group.

How did the Scole group achieve their remarkable results? First they gave credit to their guides—especially Manu: "In a typical session, Manu—a powerful guide who was the 'gatekeeper' from the spirit world—would come through first, welcome everybody, and then 'go behind the scenes' and blend the energies so the work could begin."[20] They also received guidance from the spirit of Thomas Edison, who drew a schematic for a device to directly speak with spirit:

> We basically had a technically-minded friend build the device for us (just a little larger than the average matchbox), using two coils and a germanium chip, as per the schematic on the film which had been drawn for us by Edison. It took many months of sitting with the device (which was connected into the microphone socket of a cheap cassette tape recorder to utilize its amplifiers; and therefore clearly hear the results) during Scole Group sessions to achieve even a "white noise" background effect, and many more months before we started to receive excellent and positive results.[21]

The Scole group also experimented with a glass dome. "The team scientists explained that it would take a number of sessions to gradually build up the charge of energy within the dome and that no-one should touch—or even come within one foot of—the dome between experiments." The dome was to be used like a Leyden jar—an early form of capacitor. Eventually the group observed light in the dome, which lasted as long as fifty-two minutes. The group continued to experiment with the design. Eventually, "They placed the flat wooden base on a clear Perspex platform. This was then set on Perspex supporting legs, each about one inch in diameter."[22] With this design, with a space between the dome platform and surface of the table, light could enter the plastic legs and illuminate them.

While I've never seen the work of the Scole group firsthand, I've observed two mediums who produced apports—Warren Caylor and Mychael Shane. Warren is an English medium who grew up in New Zealand. His spirit team includes Yellow Feather, Luther Tommy, and Winston Churchill.

Over the years, I've attended many of Warren's séances. One event in particular stands out. On July 25, 2017, Warren sat in the cabinet at our home, ready to do the séance. I was on his right and another woman was on his left. He was bound and gagged in the séance cabinet, ready to begin the séance, when he started mumbling. Warren's guides go to great lengths to produce apports—sometimes even dislocating his jaw, so I was concerned about his safety. Just as he went into trance, he started mumbling for us to take off his mouth gag. One of the woman on the right removed the gag. Then the group saw a 5-inch crystal apport in Warren's mouth. With some effort, he was able to dislodge the apport into a towel. It was pristine in nature! He then handed it to Amanda, one of the students from the New England School of Metaphysics.

Since then, I've observed Warren produce a variety of apports, from small crystals to large colored ones. He has also produced beautiful rings for several students. One, Sylvia, received a ring at a Warren Caylor séance on February 18, 2017. I was two seats away when the apport formed quickly in his mouth. Again, Warren literally seemed to cough it up as it came out of his mouth!

Mychael Shane is another amazing apport medium. He has been producing apports since childhood. At only seven years old, he found a 16-carat sapphire while playing with his toy soldiers in the backyard. After a hiatus from physical phenomena, he returned to mediumship. According to Mychael, he works with Ascended Masters: Jesus, Saint Germain, Master Kuthumi, Lord Buddha, and Lady Nada. When I attended his Ascended Masters séance at Lily Dale Assembly on July 28, 2017, I was astounded by his apportation at the end of the event. He literally "coughed up" about fifty or more small crystals. He gave one to each person in the audience, with a few to spare. The crystals are charged with sacred energy, which strengthens our connection to the Masters. I received a green stone for healing from Lord Buddha.

The following year, my husband and I attended two of Mychael's séances. On July 29, 2018, Mychael produced about forty faceted crystal stones of various sizes. His method was the same. After a brief meditation in the spirit cabinet, he sat in front of the group in light and began coughing up the stones. Within a minute or two, a large number of small crystal apports came out of his mouth. Obviously, it took a great deal of effort, and at times he seemed to be in pain. The group, which included several mediums, was relieved when the apports were safely delivered.

Everyone in the group felt blessed as Mychael channeled a message from the Masters as he handed each of us a crystal. My husband and I each received a crystal from Lord Maitreya. I was especially pleased to receive a triangular crystal stone with the message "You have worked hard for others. Now more leisure time." Others were given stones from archangel Michael and other Ascended Masters. The energy in the room was phenomenal—just being in the room with the presence of Ascended Masters was a transformational experience!

INSTRUCTIONS FOR TRUMPET MEDIUMSHIP

Apports are a rare phenomenon; however, they are real. It is possible to develop physical phenomena under the right conditions and with the use of a trumpet. Spirit trumpets are used for direct voice as well as the production of apports. In the case of independent voice, spirit makes an ectoplasmic voice box to move. For apport séances, the trumpet serves as the cabinet to contain the apport as it forms and becomes solid.

Trumpets come in two sizes—student with three segments and professional with four segments. Start with a student trumpet. Then cleanse the instrument by smudging it with sage or incense or misting with a solution of sea salt (not table salt) and water. Mix a half cup of sea salt into a quart of water. Put the solution into a spray bottle. Shake it up, then gently mist the trumpet. As you wipe off the saline solution, say an affirmation such as "This trumpet is dedicated to the highest and best."

Once the trumpet is cleansed, it can be placed on a table in the center of the room. Often it is wise to begin by placing the short end of the trumpet on top of the two larger segments. Place six to twelve chairs around the table for the sitters. If there is more than one medium in the group, the two strongest should sit opposite each other to generate power.

For best results, it is essential to meet with a medium at the same time and place each week, and to be clear in the group's attention. For example, in the Scole group a group of four mental mediums made a conscious decision to sit for physical phenomena each week. While most mediums need several years to produce physical phenomena, the Scole group was able to do so early on. This is because the group had several trance mediums.

Usually the trance medium begins by saying a prayer of protection, then leads the group in meditation before he or she goes into trance. Once the medium is in "dead" trance, then the spirit guides take over. It is the job of the spirit control to locate items of significance, change the vibration of an article to dematerialize it, then transport it into the séance room, where it is rematerialized.

According to noted physical medium Ethel Post Parrish, "The Spirit Operators know how to change the vibration of matter so that it may be passed through other matter. In other words they dematerialize the article they wish to apport and in its new state they are able to pass it through solid matter—they then materialize it again after they have accomplished their purpose. They say that sometimes it is necessary to dematerialize a part of the wall or door so that the apport can pass through it in its original state."[23]

Students who wish to sit for apports need to make a long-term commitment to a physical-mediumship group. It is very important to be clear in your intention. For instance, if you wish to produce phenomena as evidence of spirit survival, send the thought out to your guides. By your intention, you will attract the spirit chemists who will assist in the production of apports.

Even so, it may be hard to comprehend the work of spirit. When Ethel Post Parrish's guide, Silver Belle, apported a vase of gladiolus from the lobby to the séance room, the Native American spirit told her medium that the feat was very hard work. "You see, the vase and the flowers were of different vibrations. I had to dematerialize the flowers first and then when I got them out in the lobby I materialized them again. I then came back and on a different rate of vibration did the same with the vase—then I put them together and set them on the table."[24] While Silver Belle's explanation of apports made perfect sense to her, such miracles exist beyond the scope of modern physics.

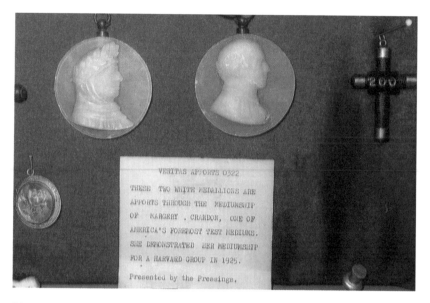

Blue medallions apported by Boston medium Margery Crandon. *Courtesy of the Hett Art Gallery and Museum, Camp Chesterfield, Chesterfield, Indiana*

Ring materialized for Sylvia at a Warren Caylor séance.
Photographer: Elaine Kuzmeskus.

Apports from Mychael séance, July 29, 2018. Photographer: Elaine Kuzmeskus.

Blue pyramid stone apported at a Warren Caylor séance. Photographer: Elaine Kuzmeskus.

CHAPTER 13

Today's Physical Mediums

There are more things in heaven and earth, Horatio, than are dreamt of in your philosophy.

—Hamlet (1.5:167–68)

By the 1980s, physical mediumship had just about become extinct in the United States. Camp Chesterfield went into decline—largely because of Tom O'Neill's article published in *Psychic Observer* on July 10, 1960. O'Neill and psychic investigator Dr. Andrija Puharich were at first enthusiastic about Camp Chesterfield.

They even arranged to film two séances at Camp Chesterfield, using infrared film to capture spirit materializations. However, the film revealed obvious fraud, such as familiar figures dressed as ghosts. Later, in 1976, one of Chesterfield's premier mediums, Lamarr Keene, confessed to faking séances in his book *The Psychic Mafia*, "as told to" Allen Spragett. With brutal honesty, Keene explained how he created ghostly apparitions and floated trumpets in darkened séance rooms. Even his church message services were aided by a hidden microphone used to pick up material for his message service. Lamarr's confession showed that there were more than a few mediums willing to stoop to fraud to further their careers. Such revelations brought skepticism regarding mediumship—particularly physical phenomena.

In England, there was still a smattering of interest in physical mediumship that in the 1990s was fanned by the Noah's Ark Society. The group began in 1990 as a Spiritualist home circle in Ilkeston, England. "The people sitting in attempt to communicate heard an independent voice message (heard apart from any of their member's speaking), that urged those present to form an organization specifically devoted to the promotion of physical mediumship and the development of mediums in whose present physical mediumship occurs."[1] The spirit identified himself as Noah Zerdin, who had been a mentor to direct-voice medium Leslie Flint, one of the last psychics to use direct-voice mediumship. According to Robin Foy, Zerdin asked the group to "start a Society which would educate the public about physical mediumship—ensuring its safe development, demonstration and practice—as well as generally promoting physical mediumship and its phenomena to the public."[2] Later, Florence Marryat, the noted Victorian novelist and author of *There Is No Death*, became a regular communicator in the Ilkeston group.

Stewart Alexander joined the Noah's Ark Society early on. He had been introduced to physical mediumship in 1968, when he read *On the Edge of the Etheric* by Arthur Findlay. It detailed Findlay's investigation of the independent voice medium John C. Sloan (1869–1951). The 1931 book inspired Alexander to form a physical-phenomena circle, which met weekly at his home. While the ten or so sitters were loyal, it took many years before they were able to levitate a trumpet. When they did, they were rewarded by the voice of Alexander's guide, White Feather. The guide was able to speak through a small megaphone known as a spirit trumpet.[3]

Eventually his trumpet mediumship developed to the point of intelligent movement. When Tom and Lisa Butler visited Alexander's circle in Hull, England, they saw the trumpet respond to questions. For instance, the instrument made a "yes" gesture and other times moved as if laughing. "The trumpet tapped on the table and danced on the floor. Another trumpet joined in, and while one tapped on the table, the other moved about on the floor."[4] Stewart Alexander also materialized two spirits that evening: "One of the women near Stewart announced that she felt hands touch her head[,] and Carol on the other side of Stewart also said that she was being touched on her head. Dr. Barnett spoke, saying that he and another person had partially materialized in the room."[5]

Several guides came through, including the motherly spirit of Freda Johnson, a young Christopher, and Dr. Barnett, who did psychic healing, as well as the late Alan Crossley. One of the most remarkable materializations was the one that took place on May 15, 2003, when the spirit of Alan Crossley, who wrote a biography of Helen Duncan, appeared. "The cabinet curtains flew open and a person's footsteps could be heard walking from the cabinet, saying excitedly, 'It's Alan. It's Alan,' in the unmistakable tone of Alan Crossley. He went around the circle and enthusiastically approached and greeted only those persons whom he knew."[6] The spirit materialized sufficiently to shake the hand of the former president of the Noah's Ark Society.[7]

The hand demonstration was the idea of Stewart's guide Walter Stinson—the same Walter who acted as spirit control for his sister, medium Margery Crandon. In order to facilitate materialization, Stewart's guide Walter Stinson requested a specially constructed table—one with a glass top that was lit with a red light underneath. Often the spirit would form a hand from a lump of ectoplasm, one finger at a time. Walter often allowed sitters to place their hand on the table and to touch the materialized hand to confirm that the spirit hand was a perfectly normal human hand. When Dr. Neal Rzepkowski visited Stewart Alexander's group in England, he was allowed to clasp the hand of spirit. According to the physician, the spirit hand was solid and warm to the touch. He could even feel the bones just as one would in a normal hand.

Leslie Kean had a similar experience when she attended one of Alexander's séances in England. Walter asked her, "Would you like to feel the hand of a man dead to your world for over a hundred years?" With her permission, Walter materialized his hand. According to the author of *Surviving Death: A Journalist Investigates Evidence for an Afterlife*, "the ectoplasm crept over the edge of the table and I watched it form again into a living hand, which moved close to my hand and touched it. I held that materialized hand in mine. It felt completely normal and human, with joints, bones, and fingernails, but much warmer than my hand and larger, with sort of stubby fingers and very soft skin. Once again, it withdrew."[8]

While I have never had the opportunity to attend any of Stewart Alexander's séances in England, I have witnessed many physical mediums in the United States, five to be exact: Reverend Hoyt Robinette from Camp Chesterfield in Indiana; Kai Mugee from Frankfurt, Germany; Warren Caylor from England; Reverend Mychael Shane from

Seattle, Washington; and David Thompson from Australia. They were all amazing and generous in sharing their gifts of physical phenomena.

The most evidential of the physical mediums is Rev. Hoyt Robinette. His gifts include trumpet mediumship, clairvoyance, blindfold billets, spirit cards, spirit pictures on silk, and direct voice. The medium from Tennessee became aware of his psychic abilities at thirteen. When he was twenty-one, he met Rev. Bill D. English, a noted trumpet medium at Camp Chesterfield. Under English's guidance, Hoyt developed his spirit gift. He sat for development for fifteen years, before his physical mediumship manifested. In the beginning his spirit cards were symbols and simple designs. Later, more-complex pictures appeared. Eventually, portraits of spirit were on the front of the card, with the names of spirit guides and loved ones on the back. In 1980, he was ordained as a Spiritualist minister by the Universal Spiritualist Association. He also continued his formal education while studying mediumship and received a master's degree in clinical psychology.

Over the past fifteen years, my husband and I have attended about twenty or more spirit card séances with Rev. Robinette. Some were held in Suffield, Connecticut, with others in nearby Agawam, Massachusetts; at Camp Chesterfield in Indiana; and metaphysical centers in Maryland. Wherever the location, Reverend Robinette is amazing. He places a pack of plain white cards in a basket—layering the cards with colored pens with their caps secured. Then the medium puts the cover on the basket and places it where the sitters can view it throughout the message service. After the clairvoyant messages are given, Hoyt opens the basket to view the cards. When he opens the basket, spirit has written the name of each person, with the names of their guides on one side and a picture on the other.

At the first spirit card séance, I was naturally hesitant. However, when Rev. Robinette gave the names of my grandparents—Kathryn and Harry—during the message service, I was intrigued—but still not convinced. Only when I received my card—it was the only picture in gray and green, matching my gray pants and emerald-green T-shirt—did I know, at that moment, that spirit was present. At the next séance, she sent the thought "Arthur Ford, if you are my guide, please put your name on the card." I did not tell a soul about her intention, yet there was Arthur Ford's name in faint green letters as if it had the last one to be put on the card!

After I finished my book *Connecticut Ghosts*, I took a trip to Camp Chesterfield. When I asked Hoyt about doing a séance for a small group of her students, he graciously agreed to meet the next evening. I received a spirit card in rust and an eerie green. When I received a copy of *Connecticut Ghosts*, I was surprised to see the cover in rust and green—the exact shades on my card. In no way could the publisher, Schiffer Publishing, have known about the spirit card, nor did I have any input on the cover design.

Spirit has also offered input on other books as well. In 2013, I asked Hoyt this question:

"Please give specific names of guides who are helping me with my next book." I was working on a biography of physical medium Margery Crandon but had told no one about this project. Rev. Robinette answered my query with "One, Walter Prince." The response made sense, since Walter Prince had been on the Scientific America Committee that investigated the medium. At the time, he was highly skeptical of Margery the medium. Apparently, Dr. Prince has had a change of heart!

Over the years, my husband and I have received many other beautiful spirit cards. When Ronald Kuzmeskus requested a picture of his guide Ashtar at a summer séance in Camp Chesterfield, he was told he would receive one next time. It seemed that spirit had already impressed a picture on the card in the basket. At the next séance, he received a beautiful likeness of his guide. He also had the names of many of his relatives, including his father, whose nickname was Tony the Tiger. One of Ron's favorite cards is a picture of a city on the other side that includes many spirit faces and the names of loved ones and guides on the back.

Hoyt Robinette also does incredible trumpet séances. One of his most evidential séances was held April 13, 2013, at a student's home in Agawam, Massachusetts. The hostess made sure that her finished basement room was completely blacked out, since even a speck of light can affect the séance. Hoyt brought along his professional-grade trumpet, which comes in four parts. In the past, the medium has been known to get two trumpets in the air at the same time. However, on this occasion he placed the smaller segment on top of the three other parts, since he said it is not necessary to place all four segments of the trumpet upright. After singing to raise the energy, spirit voices were heard clearly emanating from the trumpet.

Our messages from spirit guides were personal and inspirational. For instance, Saint Francis came through to speak to Ron. He said that Ron was "a diamond in the rough"; good with animal communication, and also nonjudgmental. Furthermore, his joy guide, a spirit child by the name of Wild Flower, was present. Since I had been sitting for trumpet mediumship, I was thrilled to hear the voice of the great trumpet medium Clifford Bias. He said in direct voice, "Writing the thing that lasts. You have been dragging feet on Margery book. It's going to be a good publisher." Her American Indian guide, White Cloud, came in with Wild Rose. Then the spirit of Daniel Dunglas Home confirmed that he had been involved in the slate drawing of White Cloud earlier in February. He said that he had drawn the picture of the American Indian with his arms raised up to a cloud.

We all received apports as well as messages from our guides. My husband and I were given almost identical light-blue stones. Another sitter, Dr. Laura, received a stone that "came from a long distance." She had prayed for a stone from beyond this world! Mary, a shaman, received a green stone from John of God and a message from Jesus. Sal, a devotee of Sai Baba, was thrilled to receive an onyx stone that came from Sai Baba.

More American mediums are beginning to take note of physical mediumship. For example, Reverend Neal Rzepkowski has visited England and Spain to investigate physical phenomena. When he has invited German medium Kai Muegge to visit his home center in Lily Dale, New York, I have made it a point to attend several of Muegge's events. The Frankfurt medium began holding séances in the basement of his parents' home. It wasn't long before the spirit of his deceased grandfather, Felix, an eye doctor, made contact. The group dubbed itself the Felix Circle in his honor, and they experimented with many aspects of physical mediumship, including table tipping. Often Kai's guide would lift his mother's wooden tables so high they crashed, to her dismay. Eventually, he switched to plastic tables.

When people encounter Kai for the first time, they are surprised to see a man who sports a short spiked haircut and dressed casually in loose, white drawstring pants and a black T-shirt, which exposes the colorful tattoos in his arm. At forty-four, Kai is completely sincere in his work, which includes past experience as a social worker and a filmmaker. Now the demand for his mediumship has increased to the point where he works full-time as a physical medium.

The medium is aided in his work by his wife, Julia, who keeps order in the séance room. Julia, a slim, attractive woman with long brunette hair streaked in red, is also very dedicated. She is attuned to spirit and sees that the séances go smoothly. Security is very important to the Felix Experimental Circle, whose main control is the spirit of Hans Bender. The séance room was inspected by members of the séance circle before we entered, and everyone was told to remove all jewelry; the men were also told to remove their belts. Next, the medium explained the rules: No going beyond the tape, which marked about 2 feet in front of the cabinet—a tent improvised with black cloth and a hula hoop. Kai went on to explain how phenomena could occur within the circle and a 2-by-4-foot force field directly in front of the cabinet. No one was allowed in this area, which was marked by duct tape on the floor. The séance began in complete darkness. Only after Kai induced trance would the red light would be switched on, so the sitters would have the opportunity to see ectoplasm.

Another important rule involved his "gatekeeper," Julia. When she gave the command, we were to link hands. When she said, "Silence," we were to cease talking. Kai then showed us how to hold hands in the chain position. We were also encouraged to sing or hum a tune during the séances in order to raise the vibrations in the room. To bring up the energy, our host, Neal Rzepkowski, selected songs for the circle. His CDs included classic Beatles' tunes such as "Let It Be," "Imagine," and "My Sweet Lord," along with standards such as "Row, Row, Row Your Boat," "You Are My Sunshine," and "I've Been Working on the Railroad."

Before the séance, as part of the protocol a gentleman was asked to examine the medium. The author's husband volunteered to watch Kai undress for the séance, to be sure he was completely naked under the séance garb. Two other people were asked to examine Neal's séance room—a large room approximately 20 by 15 feet—for hidden wires or other contraband. Julia even examined each sitter with a flashlight, checking for contact lens cameras and other recording devices. To be sure all activity was from spirit, Kai's arms and legs were tied to the cabinet and he was gagged. Volunteers checked to be sure the cable ties and gag were all in place. To produce the optimal amount of ectoplasm, the séance was held in red light.

In the course of the evening, August 17, 2014, Kai Muegge produced rapping sounds, shook rattles, levitated trumpets, and floated handkerchiefs, as well as producing ectoplasm. The first phase of the two-hour séance began with three loud spirit raps emanating from the ceiling. Then we all heard the voice of a kindly old man come through the entranced medium. This was the spirit of Professor Hans Bender, the noted German parapsychologist. For some reason, the Germans were more interested parapsychology in the 1920s and 1930s, while Americans were more fascinated by Spiritualism.

Dr. Bender explained how Kai worked in the tradition of Rudi Schneider (1908–1957), the young Austrian medium known for manifesting breezes, levitating of objects, and materializing various forms—all while tied to a chair. As the séance continued, the parapsychologist from the other side talked about spirit hands around D. D. Home and Margery Crandon. At this point, I felt a chill as I sensed the spirit of Margery Crandon in the room. Dr. Bender ended his talk on a note of humor: "Don't worry about your dead relatives; they have just taken an early exit off the highway. You will catch up with them later."

During the second phase, ping-pong balls, a trumpet, and a handkerchief were levitated. To begin the demonstration, Julia sprayed a phosphorus substance on three ping-pong balls to illuminate them. We witnessed the three ping-pong balls levitate from a bucket on the floor. They moved deliberately, as if lifted by unseen hands.

Hans Bender, Kai's spirit guide, then asked for the illuminated plaque, an 8-inch tile square that was prepared with phosphorous paint. After a short burst of singing by the sitters, a dark fingerlike mass was clearly visible on the illuminated plaque. Then, to their amazement, everyone saw a crude hand manifest on the 8-inch tile in the middle of the floor. The hand had three and then four fingers. It seemed alive with energy.

Next, the trumpet quickly rose and began darting around the room. It purposely hit Ron in the chest several times with a staccato beat, and on the bridge of his glasses. Next, I felt the metal trumpet on my left side, then on my right side, and finally on the bridge of my glasses. The movements were rapid and forceful. We both saw white lights spontaneously appear and crisscross the room, as well as a small green light chased by a red light.

During the third phase, Hans Bender came in and talked about human consciousness. The professor explained the role of aliens in human consciousness. He said that alien consciousness was mixed with human consciousness about six thousand years ago. The first group was quite humanistic, while the second mingling produced a more materialistic group. The whole talk was well organized, with many details—previously unknown to historians.

Ever protective of Kai, Dr. Bender was upset with dust on the floor left over from a shaman ceremony. He said it could be detrimental to the medium. After the reprimand, two attendants opened the cabinet carefully, since ectoplasm can stick to the curtain. There was Kai, covered with ectoplasmic cobwebs over his face and chest and some at his feet. In the center was a 10-inch oval photograph of a brunette middle-aged woman. It took a bit of prodding from the spirit of Professor Hans Bender to identify the spirit. When he urged the sitters not to be shy, one man said it looked like the face of his friend Barbara, who had died recently. Apparently pleased by the group effort, a spirit hand appeared at the base of the cabinet and waved playfully to us.

When the séance ended around 1 a.m., everyone was charged with energy. There was no way we could go to sleep, so we went to Denny's Restaurant for breakfast. As we sipped our coffee, we were not surprised to see sitters from the séance in the booth in front of us!

The following year, on Wednesday, July 29, 2015, I attended a table-tipping séance with Kai Muegge at Neal Rzepkowski's Lily Dale home. It was an incredible demonstration of table tipping. Kai did not go into trance as he did for the cabinet séances, and he remained conscious throughout the evening. The protocol remained the same. We were divided into two groups of six or seven each. We were seated around a square plastic table and instructed to place our hands lightly on the table—the full hand palms down. When the music played we were to sing or hum along with the song.

Within minutes, I felt a force emanating from under the table suddenly lift the table 3 feet. We all had to stand up to keep our hands on. To test the force, the author pressed lightly on the table—but there was no give. Whatever spirit hands were holding the table aloft were quite strong! The table remained suspended in midair for about two minutes. Then, just as suddenly as it had risen, the table crashed to the ground.

The spirit team had an even-bigger surprise for the second group. At the end of their session, we heard a loud thump as if something or someone had fallen in the middle of the table. We urged Julia to turn on the red light. In the center there was a chair, which had been a good 10 feet away before the séance. No one heard or felt the chair pass over their heads, yet there it was!

Unfortunately, I was able to attend only four of Kai Muegge's séances, but I've been at a dozen or more of Warren Caylor's—including four at my home. When I first met him, I was surprised to see an ordinary man in his forties, casually attired with tattoos down both his arms. He can be quite candid in his speech. The father of three is willing to travel, even though he misses his two young sons and daughter. Since Warren has stayed with us in Suffield, I've had the opportunity to get to know him better and can assure sitters that he is absolutely genuine in his gift. Even while we were having coffee in the dining room, the spirit would rap on the ceiling and the heavy mahogany dining-room table would vibrate.

Warren Caylor began to see spirits at the age of nine. He was born in England on October 30, 1969, and he moved to New Zealand with his family. Sadly, his father died in a race car rally when Warren was nine. About the same time, he discovered his first invisible friend—only later did he realize that he was seeing spirits. However, Warren did not become aware of spirit communication until he was an adult. He was quite surprised to hear the voice of his deceased mother.

He first became aware of materialization when he attended a séance with David Thompson. His grandfather materialized and spoke to Warren. "My grandfather did have a very strong tobacco smell about him, and that's what I had smelt when he approached me in the séance. He also had a very strong Cockney accent and trembling hands, both of which were evident again tonight, but more important than ever was that he knew not only where I lived in New Zealand but the name of my brother, father, mother, and even the family dog's name."[8] However, he was still not convinced, so he asked his grandfather how his brother was doing on the other side (Warren's brother was actually still alive). Grandfather immediately replied, "You know very well he is in New Zealand."[9]

His grandfather is now one of Warren Caylor's guides, along with Yellow Feather, a Native American guide who acts as a master of ceremonies. Warren's other guides include Luther, a Nubian Egyptian who had lived over nine hundred years ago. According to Luther, the guides had been working on Warren for about twelve years to develop his physical mediumship, which includes spirit lights, direct voice, trumpet levitation, materialization, and apports.

For anyone witnessing a Caylor séance, his materializations are nothing short of phenomenal. At one séance, a woman's husband materialized and gave evidence of attending his own funeral. "There had been in the crowd a woman who had not long buried her husband, on which she laid a single yellow rose on his coffin. He also walked across the séance room floor and thanked her for the rose; she had buried him two days prior to the séance."[10]

Warren's other guides include Sir Winston Churchill; Tommy, an eight-year-old boy; and Jessica, a three-year-old girl. Each speaks directly to the group in their own voice. For instance, Luther has a deep voice with an aristocratic tone; Yellow Feather, on the other hand, is more genial and likes to lighten the mood with a joke. Tommy and Jessica have the high-pitched voices of children their age. Tommy likes to pick up the drumsticks with the fluorescent tips and play a beat on the floor with such verve that attendees would imagine him to be a professional drummer! For example, on September 27, 2018, Tommy materialized sufficiently to take the drumsticks lying on the floor into his spirit hands to beat out a lively tune—all while the trumpet flew about the room and bells placed on the floor jingled merrily along.

In the past five years, I have attended over fifteen of Warren's séances. I witnessed countless demonstrations of direct voice, teleportation, production of streams of ectoplasm, materialization, and apports. Sometimes the spirit children like to have a bit of fun with Warren. During a séance in May 2017, one young spirit unwrapped duct tape placed on the floor and wound it about twenty times around Warren—front and back! All these events took place while the medium was in trance—tied and gagged in the cabinet.

One of the most evidential demonstrations of materialization occurred when Warren's guide Luther spoke in direct voice and asked me if I would like to come up to the chair. I said, "Yes," to the disembodied deep voice. As I sat there, Luther said he would put his hands on my head. When he did, I physically felt a very large hand gently press on the top of my head. It was a wonderful demonstration of direct voice and partial materialization.

At a later séance, in September 2018, Warren's guide Yellow Feather even brought some ectoplasm over and put it on my head. It weighed about 2 ounces. Knowing that the ectoplasm was attached to Warren, I remained very still and was rewarded by a gentle healing—and a sense of peace. At another séance, I had a second chance to touch ectoplasm. While in full-trance control of Caylor, Yellow Feather led the medium about 6 feet and placed him in front of me. He said, "Go ahead and touch the ectoplasm gently." I made note of the fact that ectoplasm felt like wet cotton candy, but with a rougher or netlike texture. By the way, Yellow Feather spoke in direct voice since Warren was gagged in the cabinet.

It is always thrilling to hear spirit speaking in his or her own voice in the room—even more so if the voice is that of Winston Churchill. When Churchill spoke to the séance group assembled in my office on July 25, 2017, everyone in the room could hear his distinct British accent. He allowed questions. When I asked how we can increase our spirituality, Churchill emphasized understanding others and where they are in the world.

At the September 27, 2018, séance, one young man brought at copy of Churchill's *A History of the English Speaking Peoples*. When Churchill came through, the young man asked him if he would sign the book. The spirit agreed and picked up a nearby pen. When the lights came up, we gathered around to see Churchill's signature boldly written on the book.

The most amazing aspect of Warren's séances are materializations and apports. On July 25, 2017, Warren and his spirit team materialized a hand for all to see. At first there was a great mass of ectoplasm—about a 9-inch circle. Then the mass changed into man's arm and hand. When one of the sitters was allowed to touch it, Steve said it was solid and felt just like a human hand.

Warren Caylor is perhaps best known for his apports. During a February 2017 séance in Glastonbury, Connecticut, Warren appeared to be in distress. Since I was sitting about 3 feet away, I could see why. An object had formed in Warren's mouth. He literally coughed up a ring. Since this part of the séance was held in candlelight, everyone was able to see the beautiful ring with three diamonds, which he gave to Sylvia, a parapsychology student.

One of Warren's most incredible apport séances took place a few months later in Suffield, Connecticut. On May 13, 2017, I witnessed Warren producing an apport at close range. We had the séance room prepared in total blackout, with a red light on. The medium was gagged and tied to the chair. Within minutes, he appeared to be in distress, motioning at the gag. His assistant removed it, as I stood by. When Warren opened his mouth, I had a good view of a crystal literally forming in the medium's wide-open mouth. We quickly placed a towel under his chin, and he spit it out. Warren then took a few deep breaths to relax before he handed the 4-inch crystal to Amanda, one of the attendees.

Sitters were also treated to apports during the September 27, 2018, séance in Glastonbury, Connecticut. Several "diamond" rings and loose diamonds were produced. The stones were round, about 2 carats and faceted. Two mediumship students received apports with messages from the masters. The stones varied in size from small ones about a half an inch to 5-inch crystals.

One of the most delightful—and evidential—séances took place on November 19, 2018. This was an early Christmas séance—complete with a pine tree and presents for the spirit children. All twelve of the sitters brought presents for the spirit children to unwrap and play with. I chose a brown-and-white toy dog that barked when someone pushed the button on his left ear. During the session, the medium remained in a spirit cabinet with his arms and legs taped to the chair and his mouth gagged, while the spirit children entered the room. We could hear them even chatting with Tommy as he encouraged them to come in. Just like their earthly counterparts, the spirit children tore off wrapping paper and began to play with their new toys. As soon as I heard the bark of a toy dog, I knew one of the spirit children had unwrapped my gift.

In 2017 and 2018, I was able to sit with another medium, Mychael Shane, famous for apports. He grew up in a family who attended séances with Seattle materialization medium Keith Rhinehart (1936–1999). Mychael was born on July 2, 1963, a Tuesday. The following Sunday, his mother brought him to a séance at the Aquarian Center in Seattle. She was told that her baby would grow up to be a powerful medium with gifts similar to medium Rhinehart's. As a youngster, Mychael showed tremendous psychic abilities, so much so that he began training at four years old in the Spiritualist church of his grandmother.[11.]

When he was seven, Mychael produced his first apport while playing in the backyard. At first, his mother was skeptical of the 40-carat sapphire her son produced, but later realized it was a genuine apport. From age seven to twenty-eight, he did not practice mediumship; instead he did a stint in the military and later tried his hand as a rock musician.

By the time he was twenty-eight, Mychael was ready to sit for mediumship unfoldment. However, an earthly teacher could impart only so much knowledge, so the Ascended Masters stepped in to guide his development. He progressed rapidly under their tutelage. Within a year, he was sitting in a cabinet for trumpet mediumship. After eight months, the trumpet levitated and communicated with taps—one tap for "yes," two for "no," and three for "I don't know." At this point, Mychael proceeded to go into a deep trance, and Lady Nada came through.[12]

Within a short time, Mychael began producing apports. Some simply appeared or fell to the floor, while others came out of his body. According to the medium, "I feel if a cloud appears above everybody and objects fall on the floor, that it is great, but when objects come out of the body, it has a greater impact on people."[13] Mychael became so well known for his apports that Dr. Wayne Dyer invited him to conduct a séance in Hawaii. During the televised event, Mychael Shane apported more than forty gemstones before Dyer's amazed eyes.[14]

I was fortunate to attend several séances with Mychael in Lily Dale, New York. Since he is a physical medium, he uses a spirit cabinet much like Warren Caylor's. During his séance, Ascended Masters—Lady Nada, Germaine, Master Kuthumi, and Lord Buddha, to name a few—come through. While there is never a guarantee of apports, Reverend Shane often produces them at the end of the event. The first time I witnessed his apportation was in July 2017 at Lily Dale. It was amazing. During the séances, the trumpet levitated, and we heard the high-pitched voice of Lady Nada, and masculine voices of Ascended Master Kuthumi and Ascended Master Saint Germain speak through it. At the close of the séance, everyone received apports. Ron and I received gemstones of jade, amethyst, and smoky quartz!

When we went back on July 29, 2018, we received more apports. This time Mychael apported about forty faceted crystal stones of various sizes and gave each one of us with a crystal with a personal message. Ours was from Lord Maitreya. Others received stones from archangel Michael and other Ascended Masters. We both received crystal triangles with the messages "You have worked hard for others—now more leisure time." At the end there were about twenty crystals left. Mychael allowed people to choose crystals as gifts for those in need. Ron picked up one for his brother, who was recovering from cancer. I felt guided to choose one for our daughter for abundance in her life.

In addition to séances in Lily Dale, my husband and I have attended séances with David Thompson, a New Zealand physical medium known for his spirit materializations and direct voice. The medium has been holding meetings with a group in Australia called the Silver Cord Circle. In order to maintain strict security, both the medium and room are inspected before each séance. David is then gagged and tied to the chair by the wrists and ankles before the séance begins. His cardigan sweater, buttoned up the front, is also secured with plastic ties. Then two people are asked to check the medium to make sure he is securely bound. They are also allowed to inspect the room, the furniture, and the equipment before the séance. They can also check the sheet of plywood placed on the floor in the center of the room for the spirits to walk on.

In September 2019, David Thompson gave a series of séances at the Unity Church in Santa Fe, New Mexico. I attended the September 19 and September 21 séances. During the first, I was seated midcircle about 12 feet from the cabinet, which gave an excellent view of the séance activity. Several spirits spoke, including William, his control. The majority of the two-hour séance was conducted in complete darkness, since ectoplasm is highly sensitive to light. However, William allowed some activity to be viewed in red light for a short time. If red light is turned on for too long, it can drain the energy, so that there is little left for reunions.

As instructed, everyone held hands once the séance began. Then our host, Reverend Tom Newman, played songs. We remained silent for the first and sang with the next three to bring up the energy level. After a few minutes, the sound of footsteps was heard as the spirit walked across the sheet of plywood. Then a deep male voice announced himself in quaint English: "My name is William Cadwell, I am a very close friend of young David here." William, who has been dead for one hundred years, is David's mentor, who acts as a master of ceremonies. Other spirits have spoken in direct voice during the séance; namely, Quentin Crisp and Louis Armstrong, who likes to sing "Hello Dolly." Sir Arthur Conan and Mahatma Gandhi have also made appearances on occasion.

When the light came on, I was surprised to see that David was still shackled in his chair, right in front of me. Somehow the guides had levitated him, chair and all, 12 feet. If that wasn't enough, they had managed to turn his sweater inside out and backward. According to our Reverend Newman, in order to do this, the spirits have to dematerialize and rematerialize David's sweater.

While we heard the footsteps and voices of spirit, it was difficult to see spirit in complete blackout. However, the spirit did move objects and touch us. For example, at the second séance we attended, Timmy, the little spirit child, went around the room and touched each of us on the knee with the drumsticks. In order to do so, he asked in direct voice for Reverend Newman to hand him a set of drumsticks. When the minister opened the bag with toys, Timmy took the drumsticks in his spirit hands and started drumming. Then he asked if we would like to feel the spirit. Of course everyone said, "Yes." He then proceeded to tap each of the forty sitters on the knee!

Orbs over Unity Church in Santa Fe, New Mexico.
Photographer: Elaine M. Kuzmeskus.

CHAPTER 14

The Medium and the Scientist

If you wish to upset the law that all crows are black,
you mustn't seek to show that no crows are;
it is enough if you prove one single crow to be white.

—Professor William James

Ever since Moses, mediums have been a potent force in society. The leader of the Israelites demonstrated clairvoyance, clairaudience, and spirit writing. For example, he saw Jehovah in the burning bush on Mount Horeb, heard voices when he leaned over the Ark of the Covenant, and received the Ten Commandments through precipitated writing.

Still, the majority of psychologists regard mediums as hysterical, deranged people. *The Diagnostic and Statistical Manual V* lists auditory and visual hallucinations as indicators of schizophrenia and does not account for the possibility of benign hallucination or mystical experiences that populate the literature of mediums, mystics, and saints. With few exceptions, psychic research has been largely ignored by social scientists and poorly supported by universities.

Only a few scientists such as Sir William Crookes, Sir Oliver Lodge, Professor William James, Baron von Schrenck-Notzing, Professor Charles Richet, Dr. Gustave Geley, Professor W. J. Crawford, Professor William McDougall, Professor Hans Bender, Dr. Gary E. Schwartz, and Dr. Stephen E. Braude have been willing to investigate mediumship in the laboratory. In 1882, a number of British scientists founded the Society for Psychical Research (SPR) for the scientific investigation of Spiritualist and paranormal phenomena. Early SPR members included chemist William Crookes, physicist Sir Oliver Lodge, Nobel laureate Charles Richet, and psychologist William James. Crookes (1832–1919), a pioneer of vacuum tubes, became its president in 1896.

Between 1870 and 1874, Crookes conducted experiments on the young medium Florence Cook, known for materializing the spirit of Katie King. He even supervised photographic experiments in which several photos were taken of Katie in the spring of 1874. In order to avoid the shock of a flash, Florence would lie on the floor with her face covered by a shawl. According to Crookes, "I frequently drew the curtain on one side when Katie was standing near[,] and it was a common thing for the seven or eight of us in the laboratory to see Miss Cook and Katie at the same time under the full blaze of the electric light. We did not on these occasions actually see the face of the medium, because of the shawl, but we saw her hands and feet; we saw her move uneasily under the influence of the intense light and we heard her moan occasionally. I have one photograph of the two together, but Katie is seated in front of Miss Cook's head."[1] After all of his research, Sir William Crookes remained steadfast in his belief in the hereafter. He issued this statement shortly before his death: "I have never had any occasion to change my mind on the subject. I am perfectly satisfied with what I have said in earlier days. It is quite true that a connection has been set up between this world and the next."[2]

In 1901, another famous physicist, Sir Oliver Lodge (1851–1940), creator of the wireless telegraph, became president of the Society for Psychical Research. In 1909, he published the book *Survival of Man*, which articulated his belief in human survival as demonstrated by mediumship. Later, in 1915, his research became personal when he received a telegram that his son Raymond was killed in action on September 17, 1915. Lady Lodge arranged a sitting with Gladys Osborne Leonard. "Raymond communicated and sent this message: 'Tell Father I have met some friends of his.'" On asking their names, Frederick Myers was mentioned. "On December 3, 1915, Mrs. Leonard brought through a message from Raymond, which gave a detailed description of a photograph taken shortly before his death. "He described himself as sitting on the ground, with a fellow officer placing his hand on Raymond's shoulder. On December 7, 1915, the photograph arrived and corresponded with [sic] the description, given four days earlier, in every detail."[3] The following year, Lodge published a book on his séance experiences titled *Raymond: Or Life and Death*.

Professor William James echoed the sentiments of Crookes and Lodge. The American psychologist was one of the most prestigious parapsychology researchers. He was especially interested in trance mediums and found Lenore Piper (1857– 1950) to be the most evidential of those he studied. William and Alice James visited the medium shortly after the death of their son, Jack. When in trance, Mrs. Piper was under the control of the spirit Dr. Phinuit.

Later, one of James's friends, psychical researcher Richard Hodgson, came in to relay messages from the other side. "James would go to attend séances with Piper for thirteen years, and conclude that she offered the 'dramatic possibility' that her mediumship was real."[4] He gave this report on sittings with Lenore Piper to the American Society for Psychical Research: "Of five of the sittings we have verbatim stenographic reports. Twelve of the sitters, who in most cases sat singly, got nothing from the medium but unknown names or trivial talk. . . . Fifteen of the sitters were surprised at the communications they received, names and facts being mentioned at the first interview which it seemed improbable should have been known to the medium in a normal way."[5]

The Harvard professor soon became convinced of the medium's rare ability to contact the dead. He declared, "If you wish to upset the law that all crows are black, it is enough if you prove that one crow is white. My white crow is Mrs. Piper." Later, in 1901 and 1902, he lectured on religion and mysticism, in particular the neglect of academic study of religion. While he did not give an explanation, he stated that "the definitive philosophy of her trances is yet to be found."[6]

In 1902, these lectures became the book *The Varieties of Religious Experience*. The book provides descriptions of altered states of consciousness—everything from drug-induced states to the deep trance of the mystic. Shortly before his death, James also presented a paper on mediumship to the American Psychological Association. However, his collected works, published after his death, omit his research.

While William James focused on mental mediumship, Baron von Schrenck-Notzinger (1862–1929) researched physical phenomena of mediums. He published the book *Phenomena of Materialization* (English translation, 1920), which included photographs of ectoplasm. The Munich physician even analyzed the ectoplasm emanating from the medium's body.

He found the substance to be composed of protein, fat, and other organic substances. During materialization, it is taken from the bodies of the medium and the sitters. He later examined the phenomena of Willi and Rudi Schneider under very strict scientific control. "An electrical system of control made the phenomena fraud-proof. The best evidence of this is the statement of a hundred profoundly skeptical, often hostile scientists who witnessed the phenomena in 1922 and declared themselves completely convinced of the reality of telekinesis and ectoplasm."[7]

It was Charles Robert Richet (1850–1935) who first coined the term "ectoplasm." The Nobel Prize winner devoted many years to studying paranormal and spiritual phenomena. The renowned French scientist and Dr. Gustave Geley, the director of the International Metaphysical Institute Paris, carried out work with Franek Kluski, a well-bred Warsaw medium who produced not only ectoplasm but also amazing materializations.

During November and December 1920, they were able to make plaster molds of materialized hands and feet by placing a bowl of soft paraffin wax near the medium. The materialized "entity" is asked to plunge a hand, foot, or even part of a face into the paraffin several times. "A closely fitting envelope is thus formed, which sets at once in air or by being dipped into another bowl of cold water. This envelope or 'glove' is then freed by dematerialization of the member. Plaster can be poured at leisure into the glove, thus giving a perfect cast of the hand."[8] In total, they made nine molds of hands, one foot, and one mouth and chin. "In completing our investigations, we have verified that the lines of the hands have nothing in common with those of the medium," Geley wrote, mentioning that observation even though the hands were all smaller than Kluski's. He still had them examined by M. Bayle, a criminologist at the Paris police department, to confirm they had nothing in common.[9]

Dr. Geley replicated the experiment in 1922, in which scientists were able to observe spirit hands dipping into paraffin. According to Geley, "We had the great pleasure of seeing the hands dipping into the paraffin. They were luminous, bearing points of light at the finger-tips. They passed slowly before our eyes, dipped into the wax, moved in it for a few seconds, came out, still luminous, and deposited the glove against the hand of one of us."[10]

Dr. William Jackson Crawford, a lecturer in mechanical engineering at Queen's College, Belfast, Ireland, contributed much to the understanding of the dynamics of ectoplasm. He investigated the physical phenomena produced by Kathleen Goligher, a sixteen-year-old medium. The researcher first witnessed a table "floating," and he suspected that members of her family were touching the table. Soon Crawford realized the raps were genuine and varied in their communication: "They soon become louder and stronger and occur right out in the circle space, on the table, and on the chairs of the sitters. Their magnitude varies in intensity from the slightest audible ticks to blows which might well be produced by a sledge-hammer, the latter really being awe-inspiring and easily heard two stories below and even outside the house. The loud blows perceptibly shake the floor and chairs. Sometimes the raps keep time to hymns sung by members of the circle; sometimes they tap out themselves complicated tunes and dances on top of the table or on the floor."[11]

Once he was certain that was not the case, he put his engineering mind to work. He decided that an ectoplasmic rod projecting from the medium's body had caused the table or other objects to be levitated and then moved upward. He also studied the mysterious raps in the séance room. When he placed Kathleen on a weighing machine, the scientist discovered that her weight loss was proportional to the intensity of the raps. He discovered that the rods were solid and close to the medium's body outward: "From a distance only a few inches from its extremity right up to the body of the medium, all appearance of solidity vanished and nothing could be felt in the line of the structure but a flow of cold, spore-like particles." However, even though the rod was made up mostly of a "gaseous body," it "operated exactly as if it were wholly solid from the body of the medium outwards."[12] He detailed his eighty-seven sittings with the Goligher Circle in his research in four books: *The Reality of Psychic Phenomena* (1918), *Hints and Observations for Those Investigating the Phenomena of Spiritualism* (1918), *Experiments in Psychical Science* (1919), and *The Psychic Structure of the Goligher Circle* (1921).

When Dr. LeRoi Crandon read *The Reality of Psychic Phenomena*, he became fascinated by the idea of psychic research. He decided to invite four friends to his Beacon Hill home to try table tipping. He even had a carpenter construct a round wooden table without nails, as specified by Dr. Crawford. On May 27, 1923, Dr. and Mrs. Crandon; Kitty Brown and her husband, Dr. Edison Brown; and Frederick Adler all gently placed their fingertips on the round wooden table. "Suddenly there was a motion. Instantly all attention was on the wooden table before them. It slid laterally, very slightly but perceptively. Then it rose on two legs and fell to the ground with a crash."[13] Suspecting that one of the six was a medium, Dr. Crandon had each member of the group leave the room one at a time. Kitty Brown left first, then Dr. Brown, Adler, Cross, and Dr. Crandon. The table continued to tip. Finally, when Mina left the room, the table was immobile."[14]

British researcher J. Malcolm Bird wrote a book, *Margery the Medium*, that described her physical phenomena. Harvard professor Dr. William McDougall decided to investigate the medium. When he attended a séance on July 1, 1923, Margery demonstrated automatic writing. During the summer, communications were "in good French, bad German, and ideographic Chinese, in Swedish, Dutch, Greek and English."[15]

While the communications were impressive, the professor preferred to focus on Margery's physical phenomena—breezes, raps, movement of objects, and independent voice materializations, as well as the production of paraffin gloves and fingerprints. Even under strict laboratory conditions, everyone could hear Walter, who spoke in direct voice conversing with sitters. McDougall remained wary. When his assistant, Harry Helson, found a piece of string about 8 inches in length, the professor confronted Margery. "He summoned Margery into his office and told her that they had caught her out at last: the movement of the objects in the séances, they now knew, had been committed by attaching string to them, which an accomplisher could tug through a ventilator in the wall."[16] Margery laughed at his suggestions, since the ventilator had been blocked up for years!

Dr. Lawrence LeShan studied a contemporary of Margery Crandon, Eileen Garrett. He devoted some five hundred hours to testing the famous psychic, who was trained by J. Hewat McKenzie at the British College of Psychic Science in the late 1960s. During the 1920s and 1930s, Garrett had worked in London with a psychic investigator, Hereward Carrington, who came to her in a dream. According to the medium, "Carrington came again into my bedroom, very angry. He said he had told me his wife needed me and I had done nothing about it. He then kicked me out of bed, and I woke up on the floor."[17] After much research, they located Mrs. Carrington in England and detached a constable to check on her. The elderly lady had fallen and broken a hip. When they found her, she had been on the floor unable to move for several days. Fortunately their help had arrived in the nick of time.[18]

Mrs. Garrett also had the ability to do physical mediumship—much to her surprise. When Dr. LeShan asked her to participate in an experiment in psychic photography, "she answered, rather angrily, 'All right, I'll influence films 1, 3, 5, and 7.'"[19] When the photos were developed, only four numbers, 1, 3, 5, and 7, had "white circles ranging in diameter from an eighth to a half inch."[20]

In Europe, Dr. Hans Bender, a professor of psychology at Freiburg University, began lectures on parapsychology as part of his academic teaching duties. He soon became known as the "spook professor." Among the visitors who came to his office were mediums, astrologers, and healers, as well as charlatans and psychotics. He tested the Dutch sensitive Gerard Croiset (March 10, 1909–July 20, 1980), a parapsychologist and psychic, who frequently helped police detectives trace missing persons.

Other scientists who took an interest in life after death include Dr. Elizabeth Kübler-Ross (1926–2004). In her book *Wheel of Life*, Dr. Kübler-Ross describes her own psychic encounter. About a year after her patient "Mrs. Schwartz" died, Dr. Kübler-Ross was thinking about leaving University Hospital, where she had been conducting studies on death and dying. To her surprise, the spirit of Mrs. Schwarz materialized. She came back to bring a message to the physician: "Dr. Ross, I had to come back for two reasons. One, to thank you and Reverend Gaines . . . (He was a beautiful black minister with whom I had a super, ideal symbiosis) to thank you and him for what you did for me. But the other reason I had to come back is that you cannot stop this work on death and dying, not yet."[21]

Upon Dr. Kübler-Ross's request, the spirit even wrote a letter to Reverend Gaines and signed her name—which matched the hospital records.

In recent times, few scientists have explored materializations and other physical phenomena. There are several reasons for this: One, there are only a dozen or so mediums who can do materialization. Often they prefer small circles with no publicity. Those who do public work are usually not at their best in a laboratory setting. Second, the issue of fraud always exists. While physical mediumship is very difficult to achieve, it is relatively easy to fake in a darkened séance room with gullible sitters. On May 1, 2016, Nic Whitham smuggled a night-vision video camera into a séance room at the Banyan Retreat. He was able to film physical medium Gary Mannion leaving his "cabinet" to act out phenomena—not the spirits.[22] To his credit, Mannion produced direct voice and materialization while gagged and tied to a chair at séance I attended in February 2022 (see page 165).

Tom and Lisa Butler, directors of the ATransC, have experienced David Thompson's mediumship and have been impressed by his séances. They are both educated and experienced researchers—Tom Butler has an electronics engineering degree and Lisa has a degree in psychology. During a séance in Australia in 2019, the spirit of Konstantin Raudive, a pioneer in EVP, materialized and spoke directly to the couple: "Raudive spoke to us for seven minutes! It is a comfort to know that our pioneers are still interested in we who are learning to communicate via technology."[23]

While the Butlers have conducted much research on electronic voice phenomena, scientists are just beginning to examine the top physical mediums—notably Kai Muegge. In May 2013, Professor Stephen Braude and a team of scientists observed him. During the course of the séance, the medium apported a materialized Indian statuette while Muegge's four limbs were bound in the chair placed in the spirit cabinet. The apport was viewed under bright-red light. "The trance personality spoke and announced the arrival of an apported gift to Donna James, who did the medium control during the session. Suddenly the medium started to breathe heavily and moan, when in front of everybody's eyes an object fell to the ground: a typical apport as it has happened many times before with Kai."[24] While attending the Felix Circle with Kai Muegge in Germany, Braude filmed a séance in which a table was levitated and ectoplasm was produced by the medium. However, Muegge's mediumship is not without controversy—Kai admitted to cheating by using an LED light to produce "spirit lights." Still, Braude believes that "some of Kai's phenomena seem quite clearly to be genuine."[25]

Kai, along with Eben Alexander, author of *Proof of Heaven*, and Jock Brocas, author of *Dearly Departed*, are working toward higher standards and scientific testing conditions for physical mediums. They have joined forces with Robin Foy, who pioneered the Scole Experiment. In recent years, Foy has expanded his efforts for standards in mediumship to found the American Society for Standards in Mediumship and Psychical Investigation (ASSMPI).

While the ASSMPI is commendable, the current polarization between believers and skeptics may not easily be resolved. On one hand, there are the true believers of the Spiritualist faith, and on the other hand, skeptical researchers who dismiss any evidence at face value. As we go into the next decade, it is likely more scientists such as Dr. Gary E. Schwartz will undertake the study of physical phenomena. When Dr. Schwartz, director of the Laboratory for Advances in Consciousness and Health, has investigated mediums such as John Edward, Anne Gehman, Suzanne Northrup, and Allison DuBois at the University of Arizona, he has found them to be credible. For example, "Schwartz says his experiments with DuBois included a reading for celebrity physician and author Deepak Chopra following the death of his father that Chopra characterized as 77% accurate."[26]

Research on physical mediums, however, is still rare, primarily because there are so few mediums who have this ability. Often, those who possess the gifts of trumpet mediumship, direct voice, and materialization shun publicity. They know the dangers involved working with the public, since materialization mediums have been severely injured when sitters unexpectedly touched ectoplasmic form. At present, most physical mediums prefer to give private séances held in Spiritualist centers, where the sitters can be screened.

When mediums such as Daniel Dunglas Home are successfully tested in the laboratory, the results are often met with skepticism. "While Home has the distinction of never being implicated in any attempts at fraudulent mediumship, Sir William Crookes's reports of his physical phenomena were not received with approval by his colleagues at the Royal Society. Home's phenomena did not comply with Newton's laws, nor did Home's reliance on an alleged spirit 'control' who aided him in his feats impress the advocates of scientific materialism."

After over a hundred years of research, scientists and mediums remain wary of each group's influence. Material scientists focus on disproving phenomena, while evidential mediums work hard to produce observable phenomena of spirit pictures, voices, and apports. As William Blake observed two centuries ago, "Both read the Bible day and night, but thou read'st black where I read white."

Dr. William James

Travels with Spirit

Kindness is the light that dissolves all walls between souls, families, and nations.

—Paramahansa Yogananda

Sometimes truth is stranger than fiction. When Gladys Custance told me the story of her grandmother's spirit playing the harp over forty years ago, I hardly knew what to believe. My curiosity, however, was piqued. Since then, research on physical phenomena has taken me to spiritual centers in the United States, India, England, and Brazil.

My first international trip was to India. Ever since I read *Autobiography of a Yogi* as a student at the University of Massachusetts, I have been fascinated by India and its saints. The author, Paramahansa Yogananda (1893–1952), is considered one of the preeminent spiritual figures of modern times. Luther Burbank, George Eastman, and Leopold Stokowski were among the 100,000 students of this great yogi. While no longer in the body, Yogananda promised to continue to work for the deliverance of the world.

Yogananda's message "Kindness is the light that dissolves all walls between souls, families, and nations" is similar to the philosophy of Sai Baba. The modern Hindu who many believe to be an Avatar preaches, "Love all, serve all." I became aware of Sai Baba quite by chance when I was teaching a parapsychology class at Asnuntuck Community College in Connecticut in 1990. I had invited Boyce Batey to do a past life regression session for the group. At the end of the class, Boyce casually mentioned that there was a guru in India that many considered an avatarSoon I was attending meetings at the local Sai Baba Center, and in the summer of 1992, I made my first of three trips to India. The trip had a profound effect on my inner life. I witnessed him producing vibuthi and producing amrit, a golden nectar that he showered on a group of Israeli men. Everyone felt uplifted by being in Baba's presence. It is believed in the East that just the sight of an avatar can reduce karma.

Another book that greatly influenced my work was *The Sleeping Prophet* by Jess Stearn. Earlier, Margueritte Harmon Bro had written an article for *Coronet Magazine*, "Miracle Man of Virginia Beach," which brought a deluge of inquiries to Edgar Cayce. The author's son, Dr. Bro, knew Cayce and his family well, since he lived with them in his youth. He and his wife, June, were dedicated to helping others in their retirement. The couple visited the back wards of mental hospitals to offer creative therapy to patients shut away from the world.

I've attended many Edgar Cayce conferences in Boston and Virginia Beach. My favorite was the one I attended early in my mediumship career. Kevin Ryerson was the main speaker. He is a trance channeler who works in the tradition of Edgar Cayce. The author of *Spirit Communication* was later featured in Shirley MacLaine's book *Out on a Limb*. His guide, Athun Re, acted as a master of ceremonies. The guide's message was peppered with his characteristic good humor.

A few years later, in December 1989, just days after the fall of the Berlin Wall, I attended a channeling by Jach Pursel in Braintree, Massachusetts. Since I was going through a crisis of my own at that time, I quietly crept into the corner of the Sheraton ballroom during the group. Within minutes, I heard the voice of Lazaris, Pursel's guide, call out to the lady in the corner with her hands over her solar plexus: "Remember, nothing changes until you do." Sure enough, I realized that the message was for me when I glanced down at my stomach and saw my hands tightly clasped together over my solar plexus. If I had any doubts about the validity of Pursel's channeling, they quickly vanished.

In 1998, I made my first trip to Lily Dale Assembly to see James Van Praagh. The Los Angeles medium was the feature speaker at Lily Dale that year. The Spiritualist camp, located in Cassadaga, New York, is one of several surviving camps, which include Camp Chesterfield in Indiana and Camp Cassadaga in Florida. Rev. Gladys Custance and Rev. Kenneth Custance maintained a winter residence in Cassadaga, so I was familiar with the camp. Both ministers loved to travel and made it a point to visit Camp Chesterfield, which was known for its physical mediumship. Many years ago, Mrs. Custance was thrilled to see her grandmother appear during a Chesterfield materialization séance. The Custances also served Lily Dale Assembly, so I was aware of its fine reputation for mediums, such as Rev. Arthur Ford. Both enthusiastically enjoyed Rev. Arthur Ford's mediumship and invited him to serve as a guest medium at the First Spiritualist Church of Onset, Massachusetts.

Later, when I read Ford's biography, I was also impressed by his ability to communicate with spirits such as Harry Houdini. On January 7, 1929, he brought through several evidential messages from the magician to his widow, Bess Houdini, which she validated. Later he conducted séances for Rev. Sun Myung Moon, who was amazed by the medium's ability to bring through first and last names of the deceased: "In a sitting in November 1964, Ford said Fletcher mentioned Pieter Alexander, who had learned about Sun Myung Moon's ideas on spiritual growth."[1] Later, Arthur Ford conducted the first televised network séance when he made contact with the dead son of Bishop Pike in 1967.

Whenever I visit Lily Dale Assembly, I make it a point to take a photograph of Arthur Ford's old home, which is now the residence of Dr. Lauren Thibideau. Lily Dale has been home to many fine exceptional mediums, including Jack Kelly, who was Mae West's psychic. He was known for driving blindfolded as well as giving evidential messages. Other noted mediums included Pierre L. O. A. Keeler, the great slate medium; Hazel Riddle, a trumpet medium extraordinaire; and the famous Campbell brothers, known for the precipitated paintings of spirit guide Ashur and Abraham Lincoln in the lobby of Maplewood Hotel. More recently, direct-voice medium Betty Putnam conducted services at Lily Dale. According to Rev. John Sullivan, spirit voices speaking were heard emanating from both sides of the pulpit when Betty Putnam presented at Lily Dale.

It is always exciting to go to Lily Dale, whether as a presenter or a visitor. First, as you enter the gates, there is a feeling of peace and spiritual protection. No wonder, since spirit can be seen clairvoyantly all over the grounds. On several trips, students from the New England School of Metaphysics have brought their cameras to capture orb photos. Where else would so many spirits be present?

The Lily Dale Museum is a favorite spot for orb photos, especially at night. The curator, Ron Nagy, is known for his spoon-bending classes as well as the ability to point out details found in the many precipitated paintings housed in the museum. According to Ron, "No one knows exactly how, or under what circumstances, precipitated spirit paintings started, but as in most instances the first phenomena occurred with the medium unaware of what was happening or why. The first recorded demonstration of precipitated spirit painting was in the year 1894 by the Bangs Sisters."[2] Nagy is also an author of two books on mediumship: *Precipitated Paintings* and *Slate Writing: Invisible Intelligences.*

Of course, the hotels and halls are filled with spirits. Assembly Hall, where guest mediums stay, is especially haunted. For example, my husband woke up to a playful spirit one night in 2009. In a jovial mood, Ron picked up an antique copper trumpet and placed it at the foot of our bed, just as we were retiring for the evening. "Maybe it will float during the night," he said. I just laughed at the thought. Sure enough, that evening in room 2, the trumpet was active. Ron was awakened in the middle of the night by the sound of the trumpet moving and voices streaming forth!

I have had my own share of remarkable experiences at Lily Dale while we were staying at Assembly Hall. One particular event stands out. One night, I stepped out on the porch to take pictures of the Maplewood Hotel and Lake Cassadaga, hoping to get a few orb photos. Instead of orbs, I photographed hieroglyphic-like symbols over the hotel. Intuitively, I felt that these were from otherworldly intelligence—most probably UFOs. But how could I ever prove this? I received my evidence the next day when Ron unwrapped a new shirt. As he took it from out of the shrink-wrap, there were the very symbols I had photographed. The white symbols remained on his new blue shirt until we pulled into our driveway in Suffield, where they disappeared just as mysteriously as they had appeared!

Another desirable spiritual destination is a visit to Camp Chesterfield in Indiana. It is about a ten-hour car ride from Connecticut, which makes for a good road trip. In April 2005 I visited Camp Chesterfield to take a class titled "Introduction to the Séance Room" with Rev. Suzanne Greer. I was most interested in attending, since the class ended with a trumpet séance. Rev. Greer, who is of Hungarian ancestry, is passionate about mediumship. She suggested that we all read *101 Questions and Answers* by Peggy Barnes. Susie, a trance and trumpet medium at the camp for over thirty years, was an invaluable source of information. She shared stories of materialization medium Pansy and past camp president Mamie Schultz Brown—both of whom she felt were genuine.

The highlight of the class is the last session, in which Reverend Suzanne Greer conducts a trumpet séance. She had sat in a mediumship circle for fifteen years to become a trumpet medium and was well versed in the art of mediumship. She cautioned the class that no matter who their spirit guide was, they were to remain vigilant. "Remember," Susie said, "you are in control of spirit."

The trumpet séance took place in the completely black basement séance room. The medium took her place in a spirit cabinet to prepare herself for the dead trance necessary to conduct the trumpet séance. Meanwhile, the students asked to sing several songs to lift the vibration. As we sang songs such as "Jingle Bells," a favorite of her spirit guide, Penny, the energy in the room seemed thick with ectoplasm. Within minutes of being seated, I was fortunate to witness the trumpet lift and act as a megaphone to the spirit world. The trumpet floated around the room effortlessly; everyone present could hear the voices of their loved ones emanating from the trumpet as it floated in midair. Suzanne even lowered the trumpet, so we could all feel it tap us on our toes!

In 2005, there were several other trumpet mediums at Camp Chesterfield. I attended an Ascended Master séance with Rev. Louise Irvine. She gave a wonderful two-hour demonstration of an Ascended Master who spoke directly through two trumpets in the séance room. While the philosophy was wonderful, no personal messages were given. I was deeply touched to hear the voice of Morya speak. He told us about his ashram located over Darjeeling, India.

Another highlight of my first trip to Camp Chesterfield was taking a meditation class with Rev. Patricia Kennedy in the Hett Auditorium. Pat Kennedy had many fine pointers on the art of meditation, as well as on her amazing life, which included a career in the Air Force, a job as a clown, and her gifts as a Spiritualist medium. The class was given in the Hett Museum, which houses the precipitated paintings of the Bangs sisters. It was amazing to see the pictures, which still retain their vibrant colors more than a hundred years later. If for no other reason, the precipitated paintings are worth a trip to Camp Chesterfield.

Fortunately this art of precipitation has not been lost, since Camp Chesterfield resident Rev. Hoyt Robinette continues to do spirit card séances. While we were at Camp Chesterfield in 2007, Rev. Robinette agreed to do a private séance for us and three students. That evening, eight people assembled for the séance. At the beginning of the séance at Camp Chesterfield, Ron asked if he could have a picture of his spirit guide, Ashtar. Hoyt spoke to his guide Dr. Kenner, who said, "No, your card has already been made." Apparently as soon as we sign up for a spirit card séance, the guides begin the process of making the images. At our next spirit card séance we attended, Ron did receive a picture of Ashtar. By the way, the cards we received that night were created by spirit in a very thick "paint." It took two days for our cards to dry!

In January 2010, I made my first trip to another Spiritualist camp, Camp Cassadaga in Florida. George P. Colby (1848–1933) established it as a southern Spiritualist camp in 1884. In its heyday, Cassadaga attracted stellar mediums such as the famous physical medium Mabel Riffle. Her Sunday evening séances brought the largest audience ever recorded at Cassadaga. No wonder, since Rev. Riffle was known for her ability to give name after name of deceased loved ones in her platform mediumship, which delighted the audience and confounded her critics. As Cassadaga grew in popularity in the 1920s, people were drawn to the Spiritualist camp from all walks of life. In 1926, Anna Fletcher, the wife of Florida senator Duncan Fletcher, defended Spiritualism before a House sub-committee and later in 1926 published a book on the subject, *Death Unveiled*.

With such a rich history, Ron and I were excited at the prospect of attending the Saturday night orb tour. The highlight of the tour was a visit to Colby Temple, which houses a séance room that the old-time mediums used for physical phenomena. While only physical mediums were allowed in the room, tourists were allowed to take photographs from the doorway. Shivers went up my spine as we peered in. Apparently Ron and I were not alone, as seen this series of photographs showing an 8-foot column of white ectoplasm in the center of the séance room. The column literally is moving across the room, as you can see from this photograph.

After our trip to Camp Cassadaga, my interest in physical mediumship intensified. Soon Ron and I were making trips to Lily Dale to see Kai Muegge, Warren Caylor, and Mychael Shane, and later to New Mexico to attend séances with David Thompson, which I chronicled earlier in the book. However, I did not mention the role that spirit played in helping with the research. I had been interested in attending a séance with David Thompson for some time—but had put the idea of seeing the New Zealand medium aside. Then, one July night in 2018, I heard a spirit voice say, "Check on David Thompson," so I googled David Thompson, U.S.A. Sure enough, the noted physical medium was coming to Santa Fe in September—three months away. I immediately contacted the séance organizer, Rev. Thomas Newman. Luck (and spirit) was with me, since there was one spot left in the September 19 séance. When I asked Rev. Newman to let me know if there were any can-cellations, so Ron could attend, he said he agreed to do so. Before the week was out, I received this email from Tom: "I just got an opening for the September 19th séance and have put Ron in that spot. Yeah! Don't you love the way the Universe works?" Yes, I do love the way the universe works!

Recently, I traveled to Schenectady, New York to attend a Gary Mannion séance on February 15, 2022. The highlight of the evening was a materialization. While Gary was securely tied to a chair placed in a spirit cabinet, I saw low clouds of ectoplasm drift into the center of the room. Then I observed the white ectoplasm reach a width of about two to two and half feet and a height of approximately six feet. Within three minutes a solid white-robed form materialized clearly up to the spirit's shoulder. When I looked down at the robe and saw the bare slender male foot peeking out from under the hem. Later, asked the name of the master, Guy replied. "The same one that came last night—Saint Germain".

"There is only one thing in this Universe that can surround you with limitation, and that is accepting the outer appearance instead of the Mighty, Active Presence of God in you." —Saint Germaine

Energy vortex appeared in a Spiritualist church séance room.
Photographer: Ronald Kuzmeskus.

Author and husband, Ronald Kuzmeskus, at Camp Chesterfield in Indiana

Glossary

apports: Objects such as flowers, jewelry, and old coins that materialize in the presence of a medium

aura: An energy field that emanates from all living things. Auras may vary in size, color, and patterns.

aura colors: The colors contained in the aura that reveal the basic nature of the soul, the emotions, or, in auric healing, the nature of any dysfunctions taking place within the individual

They include

Red: Vitality, physical strength. Too much red: anger.

Orange: Confidence, pride. Too much orange: very sensual.

Yellow: Intelligence, reason, sense of humor. Pale yellow: timid.

Green: Harmony, healing, kind. Slime green: jealous.

Blue: Idealistic, spiritual. Too much blue: reclusive.

Dark blue: Conservative, responsible. Too much dark blue: overwhelmed by responsibility.

Black: Negative or depressed. Depression often shows up by dark energy over the forehead.

White: Pure at heart

Gray: Doubt

Brown: Materially minded

cabinet: An enclosed space with a curtain in front. The medium sits in the cabinet for the purposes of gathering ectoplasm use in physical phenomena.

chakras: Energy centers located on the crown of the head, the area of the third eye, the throat, the heart center, the solar plexus, just below the navel, and at the base of the spine. The seven chakras relate to the seven planes of existence. In addition to the seven major chakras, there are twenty-one minor ones.

channeling: A form of deep-trance mediumship in which a medium is used as a vehicle for different levels of spirits who speak directly through the medium

circle: Spiritualist term for a group of like-minded people who sit in a circle for the purpose of communicating with the spirit world

clairaudience: Psychic ability to hear spirit voices with the inner-ear or fifth chakra

clairgustance: Psychic ability to taste or smell through the inner senses

clairsentience: Psychic ability to sense spirit through the solar plexus or third chakra

clairvoyance: Psychic ability to see spirit through the third-eye or sixth chakra

dharma: Path of fulfilling one's spiritual destiny in this life

direct voice: The voice of spirit manifesting directly in the séance room, so everyone in the room can hear spirit speaking. This is also known as "independent voice."

ectoplasm: A cloudy substance extracted from the solar plexus for the purposes of physical mediumship. It has a musky smell and can vary in composition from a gas to a solid state.

electronic voice phenomena (EVP): The recorded sounds of spirit voices, raps, and snaps

guides: Spirits of deceased loved ones, master teachers, and angels who offer assistance and support to the medium as well as control trance state. Types of guides can vary:

—angels**:** Loving and positive spiritual beings who have never incarnated

—Ascended Masters: Perfected beings such as Jesus, Saint Germaine, and Mora who work for humanity

—gatekeepers: Spirits who come to keep order in the séance room

—joy guides: Spirit children and lighthearted spirits who try to lift our mood

—loved ones: Spirits of departed parents, grandparents, children, aunts, uncles, and other relatives as well as departed friends

—master teachers: Highly evolved master souls who wish to teach philosophy

—protectors: Spirits such as Native Americans or religious guides who come in for protection

—spirit chemists: Spirit doctors who help to adjust the chemistry of the medium for spirit communication

—spirit workers: Guides who attracted by occupation and hobbies of the medium

—temporary guides: Those spirits who come in on an emergency basis

intuition: Immediate inner knowledge

materialization: Ability of spirit to form in the séance room in a manner that can be seen by all

meditation: Method of focusing and quieting the mind

medium: A person who is sensitive to the vibrations from the other side of life and can communicate with the spirit world

mental mediumship: A sensitive who uses inner senses of clairsentience, clairaudience, and clairvoyance to communicate with the spirit world

orbs: Energy circles of various sizes and colors that indicate the presence of spirit

physical mediumship: Mediumship in which physical phenomena are produced

precipitated pictures: A rare form of mediumship in which images literally appear or "precipitate" onto paper or 3-by-5-inch cards

psychic: A person who receives information through clairsentience or intuition

psychic photography: Spirit photographs of orbs, mists, rods, spirit faces, or full figures

psychometry: The ability to provide readings by touching objects or pictures

séance: French word for sitting, which is used to denote a session with a medium

spirit art: Images or portraits produced through a spirit guide or a medium's own clairvoyance

spirit cards: Cards on which spirit has drawn or precipitated names and pictures

spirit guides: Ethereal beings who assist a person on their path in life. Guides can be the spirits of deceased loved ones, master teachers, and angels who offer assistance and support to the medium. *See* **guides**.

Spiritualism: Science, philosophy, or religion that believes in communication with the dead

table tipping: The ability to tip or turn a table by using unseen hands or psychokinesis (PK)

trance: An altered state of consciousness that can range from relaxation to the unconscious state

trumpet: An aluminum cone approximately 3 feet in length that is used in trumpet séances

trumpet séance: A séance in which the medium goes into a deep trance and spirit guides speak directly through a levitated trumpet

white noise: Background sound used to produce EVPs

Bibliography

Alexander, Stewart. *An Extraordinary Journey: The Memoirs of a Physical Medium.* Guildford, UK: White Crow Books, 2020. www.whitecrowbooks.

Babbitt, Elwood. *Talks with Christ.* Flagstaff, AZ: Light Technology, 1981.

Babbitt, Elwood. *Testament of the Vishnu.* Flagstaff, AZ: Light Technology, 1982.

Bias, Clifford. *Trumpet Mediumship and Its Development.* Agawam, MA: Modern American Spiritualism Publishing, 1945.

Bird, Malcolm. *Margery the Medium.* Boston: Small, Maynard, 1925.

Brealey, Gena. *Two Worlds of Helen Duncan.* Guildford, UK: Saturday Night Press, 2008.

Brown, Salter. *The Heyday of Spiritualism.* New York: Pocket Books, 1972.

Buckland, Raymond. *Buckland's Book of Spirit Communications.* Saint Paul, MN: Llewellyn Books, 2004.

Chaney, Robert. *Mediums and the Development of Mediumship.* Whitefish, MT: Kessinger, 2010. Originally published in 1946 (Eaton Rapids, MI: Psychic Books).

Crawford, W. J. *The Reality of Psychic Phenomena.* www.forgotten books, 2018. Originally published in 1916 (London: John M. Watkins).

Crossley, Alan. *The Helen Duncan Story.* 2nd ed. Greenford, UK: Con-Psy, 1999.

Doyle, Arthur Conan. *The History of Spiritualism.* Vol. 1. Newcastle upon Tyne, UK: Cambridge Scholars, 2000.

Eynden, Rose Vanden. *So You Want to Be a Medium.* Woodbury, MN: Llewellyn Books, 2006.

Findlay, Arthur. *On the Edge of the Etheric.* Book Tree, 2010. www.thebooktree.com.

Flint, Leslie. *Voices in the Dark.* Rev. ed. London: Leslie Flint Trust, 2020. www.leslieflint.com.

Fodor, Nandor. *Encyclopedia of Psychic Science.* London: Arthurs, 1933.

Ford, Arthur. *Unknown but Known.* New York: Harper and Row, 1968.

Garrett, Eileen. *Many Voices.* New York: Dell Books, 1969.

Geley, Gustave. *Clairvoyance and Materialization.* New York: George H. Doran, 1927.

Glendinning, Andrew. *The Veil Lifted: Modern Developments in Spirit Photography.* Sacramento, CA: Creative Media Partners, 2018.

Grant, Solomon. *The Scole Experiment: Scientific Evidence for Life after Death.* Victoria, Australia: Campion Books, 2006.

Grosso, Michael. *The Man Who Could Fly.* Lanham, MD: Rowman & Littlefield, 2015.

Guiley, Rosemary Ellen. *Harper's Encyclopedia of Mystical and Paranormal Experience.* San

Francisco: Harper, 1991.

Hapgood, Charles. *Voices of Spirit*. New York: Delacorte, 1975.

Harlow, S. Ralph. *Life after Death*. Garden City, NY: Doubleday, 1961.

Harris, Louie. *Alec Harris: The Full Story of His Remarkable Physical Mediumship*. Guildford, UK: Saturday Night, 2009.

Harris, Louie. *They Walked among Us*. London: Psychic Press, 1980.

Harrison, Tom. *Life after Death: Living Proof*. Guildford, UK: Saturday Night, 2009.

Heagerty, N. Riley. *The Direct Voice: The Mediumship of Elizabeth Blake*. Morrisville, NC: Lulu, 2017. www.Lulu.com.

Heagerty, N. Riley. *The Phenomena of Spirit Materialization: The Transcendent Wonder of the Ages*. Morrisville, NC: Lulu, 2021. www.Lulu.com.

Heagerty, N. Riley. *Portraits from Beyond: The Mediumship of the Bangs Sisters*. Guildford, UK: White Crow Books, 2016. www.whitecrowbooks.

Heagerty, N. Riley. *Spectral Evidence*. 2 vols. Morrisville, NC: Lulu, 2017–2018.

Holzer, Hans. *Psychic Photography: The Visual Proof*. New York: Black Dog & Leventhal, 2012.

Inglis, Brian. *The Paranormal Encyclopedia of Psychic Phenomena*. Glasgow, Scotland: Grafton Books, 1985.

Jefts, Lena Barnes. *Lo, I Am with You Always*. Ephrata, PA: Camp Silver Belle Publishing, 1950.

Jolly, Martyn. *Faces of the Living Dead*. London: British Library, 2006.

Keller, Joyce. *Seven Steps to Heaven: How to Communicate with Your Departed Loved Ones in Seven Easy Steps*. New York: Atria Books, 2003.

Kuzmeskus, Elaine. *The Art of Mediumship*. Atglen, PA: Schiffer, 2012.

Kuzmeskus, Elaine. *The Medium Who Baffled Houdini*. Chula Vista, CA: Aventine, 2015.

Kuzmeskus, Elaine. *Séance 101: Physical Mediumship*. Atglen, PA: Schiffer, 2007.

Lally, Teresa. *Table Tipping for Beginners*. Woodbury, MN: Llewellyn, 2012.

Lamont, Peter. *The First Psychic*. London: Little Brown, 2006.

LeShan, Lawrence. *A New Science of the Paranormal: The Promise of Psychical Research*. Wheaton, IL: Quest Books, 2009.

Lord-Drake, Maud. *Psychic Light: The Continuity of Law and Life*. Kansas City, MO: Frank T. Riley, 1904.

Meilleur, Maxine. *Great Moment of Modern Mediumship*. 2 vols. Guildford, UK: Saturday Night, 2018.

Moore, William Usborne. *The Voices*. Guildford, UK: White Crow Books, 2011.

Nagy, Ron. *Precipitated Spirit Painting*. Guildford, UK: Saturday Night, 2018.

Nagy, Ron. *Slate Writing: Invisible Intelligence*. Lakeville, MN: Galde, 2014.

Nielsen, Einer. *Solid Proofs of Survival*. London: Psychic Book Club, 1950.

Notzing, Baron von Schrenck. *Phenomena of Materialisation*. www.kindle.com, 2016.

O'Hara, Gerald. *Ethel Post Parrish: Mediumship in America*. Amazon Publishing, 2020.

Olcott, Henry Steel. *People from the Other World*. Hartford, CT: American Publishing, 1875.

Pilkington, Rosemarie. *The Spirit of Dr. Bindelof: The Enigma of Séance Phenomena*. San Antonio, TX: Anomalist Books, 2006. www.anomalistbooks.com.

Post-Parrish, Ethel. *A Treatise on Physical Phenomena*. AfterlifeLibrary, 1943. https://afterlifelibrary.com.

Smith, Susy. *Confessions of a Psychic*. New York: Macmillan, 1972.

Solomon, Grant. *The Scole Experiment: Scientific Evidence for Life after Death*. Victoria, Australia: Campion Books, 2006.

Steele, Henry. *People from the Other World*. Cambridge, UK: Cambridge University Press, 2011. Originally published in 1875.

Stemman, Roy. *Spirit Communication*. London: Piatkus Books, 2011.

Strack-Zanghi, Jeanette. *I Walked with Spirits: Gerda Slater's Proof of Life after Death*. CreateSpace, Kindle edition, 2010.

Tietze, Thomas R. *Margery*. New York: Harper & Row, 1973.

Tymn, Michael. *The Pioneers of Psychical Research*. Guildford, UK: White Crow Books, 2011. www.whitecrowbooks.

Vandersande, Jan W. *Life after Death*. Denver, CO: Outskirts, 2008.

Weaver, Zofia. *Other Realities? The Enigma of Franek Kluski's Mediumship*. Guildford, UK: White Crow Books, 2015. www.whitecrowbooks, 2015.

Yogananda, Paramahansa. *Autobiography of a Yogi*. Los Angeles: Self Realization Fellowship, 2007.

Endnotes

CHAPTER 1

1. http://esotericbooks.deds.nl/index.php/content/campchesterfield.
2. http://www.campchesterfield.net/Camp_Chesterfield_A_Spiritual_Center_of_Light/____The_Middle.
3. Robert G. Chaney, *Mediums and the Development of Mediumship* (Eaton Rapids, MI: Psychic Books, 1946), 59.
4. Ibid., 60.
5. Ibid., 55.
6. Ibid., 30.
7. Ibid., 202.
8. Ibid., 202.
9. http://en.wikipedia.org/wiki/Camp_Chesterfield.
10. https://lostaddress.wordpress.com/the-psychic-mafia/the-psychic-mafia-part-3/.
11. Ibid.

CHAPTER 2

1. http://www.psychictruth.info/Medium_Andrew_Jackson_D.
2. http://www.survivalafterdeath.info/library/fodor/chapter8.
3. http://www.psychictruth.info/Medium_Andrew_Jackson_D.
4. http://whitecrowbooks.com/features/page/does_free_will_exist_by_silver_birch.
5. Ibid.
6. http://www.spiritualpathspiritualist-church.org/grace-cooke-physical-trance-medium/.
7. Rev. Glenda Cadarette, May 19, 2017, interview with Normandi Ellis, https://www.youtube.com/watch?v=N_LDC_gqbDU.
8. Dr. Joshua David Stone, "The Psychic Life of Madam Blavatsky and the Theosophical Society."
9. Henry S. Olcott, *Old Diary Leaves: The True Story of the Theosophical Society*, vol. 1, *(1874–1878)* (New York: G. P. Putnam's Sons, 1895).
10. https://theosophy.net/profiles/blogs/what-everyone-should-know.
11. Olcott, *Old Diary Leaves*, 1:377, 379–81.
12. http://www.edgarcayce.org/about-us/blog/blog-posts/the-little-prophetess-from-the-cayce-readings.
13. Edgar Cayce reading 2156-2.
14. Ibid.

15. Ibid.

16. J. Malcolm Bird, *Margery the Medium* (Boston: Small, Maynard, 1925), 430.

17. http://www.unexplainedstuff.com/Mediums-and-Mystics/Mediums-and-Channelers-Eileen-garrett-1893-1970.html.

18. "Airships: R101 Interior," Airship Heritage Trust via Airshipsonline.com, retrieved August 27, 2010.

19. "R101 Passenger List," Airship Heritage Trust via Airshipsonline.com, retrieved August 27, 2010.

20. https://www.theosophical.org/publications/quest-magazine/3038.

21. Milbourne Christopher, *Mediums, Mystics, and the Occult* (New York: Thomas Y. Crowell, 1975), 122–30.

22. http://psychictruth.info/Medium_Arthur_Augustus_Ford.htm.

23. http://psychictruth.info/Medium_Arthur_Augustus_Ford.htm.

24. http://www.nytimes.com/1971/01/05/archives/rev-arthur-a-ford-dead-at-75-medium-who-aided-bishop-pike.html.

25. Elwood Babbitt, *Perfect Health: Accept No Substitutes*, Kindle Edition (Flagstaff, AZ: Light Technology, 1993), Kindle locations 1941–46.

26. J. Z. Knight, *White Book* (Yelm, WA: JZK, 2004).

27. http//mychaelshand.com/theascendedmasters.

28. http//www.angelfire/com/ok/silverbirth/death.html/

29. Séance with Kai Muegge, Cassadaga NY, August 15, 2014.

CHAPTER 3

1. http://www.occultopedia.com/p/psychometry.htm.

2. http://fst.org/buchanan.htm.

3. https://www.amazon.com/Winged-Pharaoh-Far-Memory-Books/dp/158567886.

4. https://mara-gamiel.blogspot.com/2009/01/word-on-psychometry.htm.

5. https://www.survivalafterdeath.info/mediums/ossowiecki.htm.

6. https://www.survivalafterdeath.info/mediums/ossowiecki.htm, Baron Schrenck-Notzing.

7. https://www.scribd.com/document/108715754/

Scientific-Evidence-for-Survival-1-0.

8. https://www.llewellyn.com/journal/article/1133.

9. http://www.intuitive-connections.net/issue2/tomorrow.htm.

10. www.lakeandsumterstyle.com/medium.

11. http://unsolvedmysteries.wikia.com/wiki/Jake_and_Dora_Cohn.

12. Ibid.

13. Tom and Lisa Butler, published in the Fall 2010 *AA-EVP News Journal*.

14. Joseph Rinn, *Sixty Years of Psychical Research: Houdini and I among the Spiritualists* (New York: Truth Seeker, 1950), 576.

CHAPTER 4

1. https://encyclopedia2.thefreedictio-nary.com/Table+Tipping.
2. Colin Wilson, *The Occult* (New York: Random House, 1971), 466–67.
3. http://seteantigoshepta.blogspot.com/2009/08/daniel-doug-las-home-paranormal- mais.html.
4. Arthur Conan Doyle, *The History of Spiritualism*, vol. 1 (Cambridge, UK: Cambridge University Press, 1926), 196–97. Reprinted in 2000 (Newcastle upon Tyne, UK: Cambridge Scholars).
5. William Crookes, "Notes of Séances with D. D. Home," *PSPR* 6, Pt. XV (1889): 107–08, 116.
6. Ibid.
7. http://www.survivalafterdeath.info/mediums/eglinton.htm.
8. Brian Inglis, *The Paranormal: An Encyclopedia of Psychic Phenomena* (Glasgow, Scotland: Grafton Books, 1985), 146.
9. Maxine Meilleur, *Great Moment of Modern Mediumship*, vol. 2 (Guildford, UK: Saturday Night, 2018), 115–16.
10. Bird, *Margery the Medium*, 35.
11. Ralph S. Harlow, *Life after Death* (Garden City, NY: Doubleday, 1961), 59.
12. https://www.survivalafterdeath.info/mediums/schneider.htm.
13. Ibid.
14. Ibid.
15. https://www.encyclopedia.com/science/encyclopedias-alma-nacs-transcripts-and-maps/schneider-brothers-willi-1903-1971-and-rudi-1908-1957.

CHAPTER 5

1. Kenneth R. Andrew, *Nook Farm: Mark Twain's Hartford Circle* (Seattle: University of Washington Press, 1950), 56.
2. Susy Smith, *Confessions of a Psychic* (New York: Macmillan, 1972).
3. http://whitecrowbooks.com/michaeltymn/feature/the_mystery_of_patience_worth.
4. Raymond Buckland, *Buckland's Book of Spirit Communications*, Kindle Edition (Saint Paul, MN: Llewellyn Books, 2004), Kindle locations 1922–25.
5. Ibid.
6. http://www.spiritwritings.com/williameglinton.html.
7. Ibid.
8. http://psychictruth.info/Medium_William_Eglinton.htm.
9. Ibid.
10. Ibid.
11. https://www.csicop.org/sb/show/abraham_lincoln_an_instance_of_alleged_spirit_ writing.
12. Arthur Conan Doyle, *Our American Adventure* (London: Hodder & Stoughton, 1924), 144–45.
13. Ibid.
14. J. J. Owen, *Psychography: Marvelous*

Manifestations of Psychic Power Given through the Mediumship of Fred P. Evans (San Francisco: Hicks-Judd, 1893).

15. http://people.wku.edu/charles.smith/wallace/zOwen1893Psychography.pdf.

16. Ibid.

17. https://encyclopedia2.thefreedictionary.com/Writing%2c+Slate.

18. Ibid.

19. Edward Abdill, *Masters of Wisdom: The Mahatmas, Their Letters, and the Path*, Kindle Edition (New York: Jeremy P. Tarcher, 2015), xxii.

20. Abdill, *Masters of Wisdom*, 56–57.

CHAPTER 6

1. http://www.psychictruth.info/Medium_Bangs_Sisters.htm

2. Ibid.

3. Ibid.

4. Miss May Bangs, wrote in a letter to Mr. James Coates, 17 September, 1910

5. http://whitecrowbooks.com/michaeltymn/entry/the_amazing_bangs_sisters

6. Heagerty, N. Riley. Portraits From Beyond: The Mediumship of the Bangs Sisters (Kindle Locations 507-511). White Crow Productions Ltd.. Kindle Edition.

7. Heagerty, N. Riley. Portraits From Beyond: The Mediumship of the Bangs Sisters (Kindle Locations 2346-2350). White Crow Productions Ltd.. Kindle Edition.

8. Heagerty, N. Riley. Portraits From Beyond: The Mediumship of the Bangs Sisters (Kindle Locations 2395-2396). White Crow Productions Ltd.. Kindle Edition.

9. http://ronnagy.net/rons-blog/2011/03/azur-the-helper-unusual-photos/

10. Ibid.

11. https://www.ggspiritualistchurch.org/reverend%20becker.pdf

12. https://www.ggspiritualistchurch.org/reverend%20becker.pdf

13. Ibid.

14. Ibid.

CHAPTER 7

1. http://www.edgarcayce.org.

2. http://www.victorzammit.com/evidence/directvoicemediums.htm.

3. http://www.psychictruth.info/Medium_Emily_S_French.htm.

4. http://www.psychictruth.info/Medium_Elizabeth_Blake.htm.

5. N. Riley Heagerty, *The Direct Voice: The Mediumship of Elizabeth Blake* (Morrisville, NC: Lulu, 2017), 10.

6. https://www.encyclopedia.com/science/encyclopedias-almanacs-transcripts-and-maps/lord-maud-e-1852-1924.

7. Maud Lord-Drake, *Psychic Light: The Continuity of Law and Life* (Kansas City, MO: Frank T. Riley, 1904).

8. *The Voices*, William Usborne Moore, White Crow Books, Guildford England, 2011, pp. 324-5

9. http://whitecrowbooks.com/michaeltymn/entry/titanic_victim_reported_on_after-death_experiences.

10. www.psychictruth.info/Medium_Etta_Wriedt.htm

11. William Usborne Moore, *The Voices* (Guildford, UK: White Crow Books, 2011), 324–25.

12. http://www.thegreatquestion.com/books/On_the_Edge_of_Etheric.pdf, 23.

13. http://www.thegreatquestion.com/books/On_the_Edge_of_Etheric.pdf, 24.

14. J. Malcolm Bird, *My Psychic Adventures* (New York: Scientific American, 1923), 66–67.

15. Ibid., 78.

16. Bird, *Margery the Medium*, 118.

17. Ibid., 129.

18. Ibid., 127–31.

19. Ibid., 139.

20. http://www.fst.org/margery.htm.

21. http://psychictruth.info/Medium_George_Valiantine.htm.

22. http://psychictruth.info/Medium_George_Valiantine.htm.

23. http://psychictruth.info/Medium_George_Valiantine.htm.

24. http://adcguides.com/whymant.htm.

25. www.leslieflint.com/tv-interview-1976.

26. *Psychic News*, August 3, 1940

27. Ibid.

28. Ibid.

29. https://archive.org/details/ValentinoDec15th1962.

30. Ibid.

CHAPTER 8

1. https://www.thoughtco.com/all-about-electronic-voice-phenomena-evp-2594007.

2. Sheila Ostrander and Lynn Schroeder, *Handbook of Psychic Discoveries* (New York Berkeley, 1975), 226.

3. https://atransc.org/konstantin-raudive.

4. http://www.worlditc.org/h_07_meek_by_macy.htm.

5. http://www.worlditc.org/h_07_meek_by_macy.htm.

6. Martha Copeland, *I'm Still Here*, Kindle Edition (Reno, NV: AA-EVP, 2005), 731.

7. Ibid., 795.

8. Ibid., 812.

9. Ibid., 1034.

10. afterlifeinstitute.org/sonia-rinaldi-gets-messages-nicola-tesla/.

11. Sonia Rinaldi, "TESLA IS BACK: Voice Communication from the Invetor [*sic*] Nikola Tesla via ITC," *IPATI* (E-magazine), book 3 (2017): 13 (Kindle edition).

CHAPTER 9

1. Kaplan, Louis (2008). *The Strange Case of William Mumler*. University of Minnesota Press. p. 304.
2. .http://www.historynet.com/the-ghost-and-mr-mumler.htm
3. *One Hundred Years of Spirit Photography*, Tom Patterson, Regency Books, London, England, 1965, page 12.
4. Melvyn Willin, in his book *Ghosts Caught on Film*.
5. Boese, Alex. "William Mumler's Spirit Photography". Retrieved 2008-05-04.
6. http://www.historynet.com/the-ghost-and-mr-mumler.htm
7. *Psychic Photography, Light, Vol. XXII*, January 4, 1902, Letter dated December 3, 1901
8. www.psychictruth.info/Medium_Edward_Wyllie.htm
9. Ibid.
10. Ibid.
11 Pattrerson, 23
12. https://ghostaugustine.com/2011/03/12/william-mumler-spirit-photographer-or-hoax/
13. Pattrerson, 34.
14. http://www.survivalafterdeath.info/mediums/deane.htm
15. Martyn Jolly, *Faces of the Living Dead* (2006)
16. I M. Barbanell, He Walks in Two Worlds (London: Herbert Jenkins, 1964) p 5.
17. http://psychictruth.info/Medium_John_Myers.htm
18. M. Barbanell, He Walks in Two Worlds (London: Herbert Jenkins, 1964) p 24
19. http://psychictruth.info/Medium_John_Myers.htm
20. M. Barbanell, He Walks in Two Worlds (London: Herbert Jenkins, 1964) p 157
21. https://www.thescoleexperiment.com/paranormal-apports-phenomena.html
22. The Scole Investigation: A Study in Critical Analysis of Paranormal Physical Phenomena1 (MONTAGUE KEEN, Journal of Scientific Exploration, Vol. 15, No. 2, pp. 167–182, 2001 0892-3310/01 © 2001 Society for Scientific Exploration)
23 https://www.thescoleexperiment.com/paranormal-apports-phenomena.html

CHAPTER 10

1 www.corarichmondooks.com
2. http://www.victorzammit.com/evidence/transfiguration.htm
3. WWW.psychictruth.info/Medium_Queenie_Nixon.htm
4. Diana Palm, *Mediumship Scrying & Transfiguration for Beginners: A Guide to Spirit*, Llewelyn Publishers, Minneapolis, MN, page 137
5. Ibid., 138

CHAPTER 11

1. occult-world.com/mediumship/ectoplasm/.

Maud Lord-Drake, *Psychic Light*, 363.

2. Ibid.

3. Ibid.

4. Ibid., 371.

5. William James, *Essays in Psychical Research*, ed. Frederick Burkhardt and Fredson Bowers (Cambridge, MA: Harvard University Press, 1986), 14.

6. http://the-voicebox.com/aberrysistersseance.htm.

7. Ibid.

8. Meilleur, *Great Moment of Modern Mediumship*, 2:146.

9. http://www.fst.org/cook2.htm.

10. Ibid.

11. https://infogalactic.com.

12. Doyle, *The History of Spiritualism*, 1:235–40.

13. https://infogalactic.com/info/Trevor_H._Hall.

14. William Hodson Brock, *William Crookes (1832–1919) and the Commercialization of Science* (Aldershot, UK: Ashgate. 2008), 184–85.

15. https://www.unexplained-mysteries.com/forum/topic/70991-carlos-mirabelli-the-medium/.

16. http://www.psychictruth.info/Medium_Carmine_Carlos_Mirabelli.htm.

17. Ibid.

18. Ibid.

19. E. J. Dingwall, "An Amazing Case: The Mediumship of Carlos Mirabelli," *Journal of the American Society for Psychical Research* 24 (1930): 26.

20. www.unexplainedstuff.com/Mediums-and-Mystics/Mediums-and-Channelers-Carlos-mirabelli-1889-1951.htm.

21. Dingwall, "An Amazing Case," 26.

22. Nandor Fodor, *Encyclopedia of Psychic Science* (London: Arthurs, 1933).

23. http://www.spiritualisttv/spiritualism/history/vol1chapter12html.

24. http://sanctusgermanus.org/ebooks/Old%20Diary%20Leaves%20Chapter%201.pdf.

25. http://psychictruth.info/Medium_Franek_Kluski.htm.

26. Weaver, *Other Realities?*, Kindle locations 1064–69.

27. Pawlowski, "The Mediumship of Franek Kluski of Warsaw."

28. Weaver, *Other Realities?*, Kindle locations 1064–69.

29. Ibid., Kindle locations 1658–60.

30. Ibid., Kindle locations 1962–69.

31. "Introduction" in the Camp Silver Belle Booklet.

32. Strong, "Materialization Extraordinary: Ethel Post-Parrish Carried from the Cabinet while in Trance."

33. Ibid.

34. Ibid.

35. Strack-Zanghi, *I Walked with Spirits*, 336.

36. Ibid., 37–38.

37. Ibid., 54.

38. Keller, *Seven Steps to Heaven*.

39. Edmunds, *Spiritualism*, 137–44.
40. http://www.victorzammit.com/book/4thedition/chapter11.html.
41. Ibid.
42. Ibid.
43. Harris, *Alec Harris*, Kindle locations 899–901.
44. Ibid., Kindle locations 903–04.

45. Ibid., Kindle locations 931–32.
46. Ibid.
47. Ibid., Kindle locations 1019–21.
48. Ibid., Kindle locations 1279–80.
49. Ibid., Kindle locations 1584–86.
50. Ibid., Kindle locations 2161–66.
51. Ibid., Kindle locations 2043–50.
52. Ibid., Kindle locations 1631–32.

CHAPTER 12

1. http://www.spiritualpathspiritualist-church.org/noteworthy.
2. Holy Bible, Ezekiel 2:9–10.
3. Holy Bible, Mark 6:40–42.
4. https://www.themystica.com/apports/.
5. http://www.spiritualpathspiritualist-church.org/noteworthy-apports/.
6. Bird, *Psychic Adventures*, 90–91, 232–33.
7. Bird, *Margery the Medium*, 129.
8. Ibid., 127–31.
9. Ibid., 165.
10. http://the-voicebox.com/apportsandasports.htm.
11. http://www.spiritualpathspiritualist-church.org/noteworthy-apports/.
12. http://zerdinisworld.com/?p=204.
13. Ibid.

14. Ibid.
15. http://victorzammit.com/book/4thedition/chapter08.html.
16. https://leo-bonomo.com/robin-foy-the-scole-experiments-part-2/.
17. Solomon, *The Scole Experiment*, Kindle locations 803–07.
18. Ibid., Kindle locations 811–13.
19. https://leo-bonomo.com/robin-foy-the-scole-experiments-part-2/.
20. Solomon, *The Scole Experiment*, Kindle locations 551–53.
21. Ibid., Kindle locations 1297–99.
22. Ibid., Kindle locations 1328–31.
23. http://www.psychictruth.info/Medium_Ethel_Post_Parrish.htm.
24. Ibid.

CHAPTER 13

1. Noah's Ark Society for Physical Mediumship, May 23, 2000, http://home.clara.net/noahsark/ind1.htm.
2. Ibid.
3. Ibid.

4. http://atransc.org/circle/stewart_alexander.htm.
5. Ibid.
6. http://www.scsad.afterlifeinstitute.org/articles/mediums/crossley-returns.html.

7. Ibid.
8. Warren Caylor, *Walking Two Worlds*, Kindle Edition (Morrisville, NC: Lulu, 2014), Kindle locations 691–97.
9. Ibid., Kindle locations 855–58.
10. Ibid., Kindle location 852.

11. http://webtalkradio.net/internet-talk-radio/the-message-and-the-masters.
12. http://mychaelshane.com/faqs/.
13. Ibid.
14. https://www.youtube.com/watch?v=7NjFgGn_xm.

CHAPTER 14

1. http://www.fst.org/cook2.htm.
2. William Crookes, *Researches in the Phenomena of Spiritualism* (London: J. Burns, 1874), reprinted from the *Quarterly Journal of Science*, n.s. 1 (July 1871).
3. http://fst.org/lodge.htm.
4. Ibid.
5. https://www.csicop.org/specialarticles/show/william_james_and_the_psychics.
6. William James, "Report of the Committee on Mediumistic Phenomena," *Proceedings of the American Society for Psychical Research* 1, no. 2 (1886): 103.
7. Statement made in 1907 letter by Henry James, The Complete Letters of Henry James, vol. 2 (1920), p. 287.
8. http://www.survivalafterdeath.info/researchers/notzing.htm.
9. https://atlantisrisingmagazine.com/article/the-paraffin-mold-experiments/.
10. Ibid.
11. Geley, *Clairvoyance and Materialization*, 234.
12. http://whitecrowbooks.com/michaeltymn/entry/dr._william_j._crawford_discusses_his_mediumship_research.
13. Rosemarie Pilkington, *The Spirit of Dr. Bindelof: The Enigma of Séance Phenomena*, Kindle Edition (San Antonio, TX: Anomalist Books, 2006), 131–32.
14. Thomas R. Tietze, *Margery* (New York: Harper & Row, 1973), 18.
15. Ibid.
16. Ibid., 23.
17. Brian Inglis, *Science and Parascience: A History of the Paranormal, 1914–1939* (London: Hodder and Stoughton, 1984), 161.
18. Lawrence LeShan, *A New Science of the Paranormal: The Promise of Psychical Research*, Kindle Edition (Wheaton, IL: Quest Books, 2009).
19. Ibid.
20. Ibid.
21. Ibid.
22. http://griefandmourning.com/kubler-ross-schwarz.
23. https://thesearchforlifeafterdeath.com/2016/06/26/physical-medium-gary-mannion-exposed-committing-fraud/.
24. https://atransc.org/

david_thompson_seance.

25. FEG blog, elixcircle.blogspot. com/2012/09/amazing-demonstra-tions-at-gordon.html.

26. Stephen E. Braude, "Follow-Up Investigation of the Felix Circle," *Journal of Scientific Exploration* 30, no. 1 (2016): 27–55.

27. Carla McClain, "Varied Readings on Arizona Psychic," *Arizona Daily Star,* January 17, 2005, archived from the original on May 16, 2007, and retrieved on December 10, 2009.

28. https://www.brainyquote.com/authors/william_blake.

EPILOGUE

1. Arthur Ford, *Known but Unknown: My Adventure into the Meditative Dimension* (New York: New American Library, 1972).

Appendix

I attended several séances with Rev. Hoyt Robinette, Kai Muegge, Warren Caylor, and Mychael Shane, and one with Scott Mulligan. Notes from these séances would fill another volume; however, here are my notes from those séances that were the most memorable.

REV. HOYT ROBINETTE, MEDIUM FROM CHESTERFIELD, INDIANA

Spirit Photography on Silk Séance

Medium: Rev. Hoyt Robinette

Jessup, Maryland

April 26, .2012

Séance conditions: total darkness

Materials: 6-inch white silk squares and pots of black ink

Rev. Robinette had piles of silk squares and a dozen or so small bottles of black ink similar to those used for ink pads on the table of the séance room. He removed the lids and left them on the table near the stack of silks. "These," he said, pointing to the ink pots, "are the source of ink that would be used for the images on the silks just as the pens and crayons in the basket were used as the source of color for the spirit cards."

After Rev. Robinette said a brief prayer, each person was handed a sheet of construction paper, which we placed on our laps. Then he gave us a silk square, which was, we were told, to place on the sheet of construction paper. The silk squares were to remain in place during the séance. The lights were turned off and the singing began. During the meditation, spirits precipitated pictures on silk. At the end of the séance, we were told to roll up our silk squares in the construction paper and to keep them in a dark place for 24 hours to develop. When I opened mine the next day, I was pleased to see many faces, including one of my godmother, Aunt Ruth, who had died in 1953!

Trumpet Séance

Medium: Rev. Hoyt Robinette

Agawam, Massachusetts

April 13, 2013, 6:30 p.m.–8:30 p.m.

Séance conditions: total darkness

Materials: two aluminum trumpets

Rev. Hoyt Robinette began with a billet séance. Before the séance I had written a question regarding a book that I was researching on the Boston medium Margery Crandon. This is the question that I wrote on my billet April 13, 2013.

Next Rev. Robinette took two aluminum trumpets, placing one upright and the other trumpet horizontal. Spirit voices came through immediately. Rev. Clifford Bias gave me this message in direct voice: "Writing is the thing that last. You have been dragging feet on Margery book [which was true]. It's going to be a good publisher."

Ron Kuzmeskus was given the message "Saint Francis is close to you. You are a diamond in the rough. Good with animals, kind, and nonjudgmental."

Then we could hear the rattle of apports coming down the trumpet. Everyone received a stone. We all received various apports:

—Ron and I both received almost identical light-blue stones.

—Our hostess, Sylvia, received a red heart-shaped stone.

—Faith, a devotee of Sai Baba, received an onyx stone from Sai Baba.

—Louise was told that she would receive a stone that "came from a long distance." Apparently she had prayed for a stone from beyond this world!

Note: Spirit also told us that White Cloud (Elaine's guide) and Wild Rose (Ron's guide) were working together. I was also told that D. D. Home had helped create the spirit slate drawing that the group had received earlier in February that year.

Spirit Card Séance

Medium: Rev. Hoyt Robinette

Agawam, Massachusetts, 6:30 p.m.–8:30 p.m.

March 19, 2015

Séance conditions: total darkness

Materials: cobra basket, colored pens and pencils with caps on, and 3-by-5-inch white index cards sealed in package.

Billet Readings

I wrote this question on my billet: "Who are my guides for my next book?" During the billet séance, I received my answer: "Kathryn Kuhlman" [later I wrote *Healing with Spirit*]. Message from Rev. Robinette: "I would call my name but then you would be calling your own name. Eleanor Hoffman. Dr. Oswaldo Cruz on your card. You and Ron are going to Brazil. [We did not make this trip that year, since John of God came to the United States.]

Everyone received beautiful precipitated pictures on their cards. Spirit precipitated a picture of Dr. Oswaldo Cruz on mine. On the other side were these names:

—Gladys Strohme

—Clifford Bias

—Gladys Custance

—Kenneth Custance

—Peebles

—Dr. Oswaldo Cruz

—Ethel Post Parrish

—Crazy Horse

—Mom

—Eleanor Hoffman*

*A year ago, I received a spirit flame card from Gail with the name Eleanor Hoffman. When I went to make a copy to mail to Gail, the name disappeared!

Ron's message from Rev. Hoyt Robinette: "Joseph, Gerald, Tony here, Wild Rose, Archangel Raphael. You are going to same place as Elaine—Brazil. You will feel better."

Ron's Spirit Card had an image of Wild Rose in later years (Ron's joy guide).

These names were on the front of Ron's Spirit Card:

—Joe Kuzmeskus (deceased brother)

—Gerald Kuzmeskus (deceased brother)

—Dad

—Wild Rose

—Saint Francis

—Saint John

—Jesus

—Ashtar

Spirit Card Séance

Medium: Rev. Hoyt Robinette

Agawam, Massachusetts, 6:30 p.m.–8:30 p.m.

March 29, 2017

Séance conditions: total darkness

Materials: cobra basket, colored pens and pencils with caps on, and 3-by-5 white index cards sealed in package.

First card that Rev. Gail Hicks received was a picture of Our Lady of Guadalupe. In 2017, she received a picture of Nicodemus taking the body of Jesus, which she shared with us.

Next, Rev. Robinette conducted a billet message séance. He gave me this message: "You cannot put the pen down. Once you finish one book, you will start another. [There will be] someone else to represent you in publishing."

Kenneth Custance was on the card with mediums from the National Association of Spiritualist Churches (NASC). There were indeed six spirit faces of older gentlemen on the card. Within the year, the History Press asked if I was interested in writing a book about Connecticut and Spiritualism. I was interested and wrote a book titled *Connecticut in the Golden Age of Spiritualism*.

Here are the names spirits on the other side of the card:

—Margery

—Dorothea

—Carl

—Clifford Bias

—Elwood Babbitt

—Gladys and Kenneth

—Edgar Cayce

—Yogananda

Ron was told that his great-grandfather's picture would be on the back of the card, which it was. On the front were these names:

—Joe

—Tiger (his father's nickname)

—Al and Frank (two uncles)

—Ann and Joe (his aunt and uncle)

—Buck

His message from spirit: "You have plenty of us to work with."

Spirit Card Séance

Medium: Rev. Hoyt Robinette

May 13, 2019, 6:30 p.m.–8:30 p.m.

New London, Connecticut

Séance conditions: total darkness

Materials: cobra basket, colored pens and pencils with caps on, 3-by-5 white index cards sealed in package.

Rev. Robinette gave me this message: "Rod Sterling, Bias; Dorothy Lynde Baba. We are here together. Margery is here with you. Gladys Strohme is here. You have lots of people that are beckoning to you—D. D. Home is here. D. D. Home wants you to know that some of the best things come in small packages. Going to show you a likeness of myself. I was not a large person. So show a picture of someone who looks small. That is going to be good, and I am the one who is going to help her. It is going to take place swiftly." [I had asked a question regarding a book on physical mediumship.]

I was most pleased to see that the picture on the card was indeed a likeness of the medium Daniel Dunglas Home! By the way, this was not the first spirit card with Home's image. I had received his picture in séance a few years before. The spirit of Rev. Carl Hewitt came through Rev. Robinette to give the message "My image will be on your card. My hair color has changed a bit." Rev. Carl Hewitt had owned a beauty salon before becoming a medium, so the message had some significance. However, when I saw the card there was indeed a brunette gentleman on it [Carl had light-brown hair]. The image was definitely not Carl, but that of D. D. Home—the great physical medium. Carl, the pastor of the Gifts of the Spirit Church, had been very interested in physical phenomena before his death in 2005, so it would make sense that he would contact Home on my behalf.

Warren Caylor, Medium from England
Physical Phenomena Séance

Medium: Warren Caylor

Cassadaga, New York, 7:00 p.m.–9:30 p.m.

October 27, 2016

Séance conditions: total darkness

Materials: spirit cabinet, aluminum trumpet, candle, drumsticks with florescent paint on knobs

We were excited to attend our first Warren Caylor séance. The invitation from Dr. Neal Rzepkowski stated: "Once this Medium is searched/secured/bound/gagged, he will then enter a trance state within a *completely darkened setting*, which will bring through the Spirit team that works with him. You will experience independent sounds and lights in the room, as well as touches from spirit[-]materialized forms and more. Séance objects will levitate, move around, and be interacted with by Spirit directly. Apportation is a common element within Warren's séances that you will likely experience. You will also have a chance, in either candle or red light, to see ectoplasm that is generated by the spirit team, and well as materialized forms that come from that ectoplasm."

The spirits were alive and well at Warren Caylor's séance that night! The spirit of Winston Churchill came through and spoke to the group within the cabinet, and then his spirit stepped 4 feet out from the cabinet and spoke again to the group in a very loud voice—even my husband, Ron, with his hearing loss could hear him!

The most interesting phenomena that occurred included a 5-inch crystal apport in Warren's mouth, which he gave to a one of the sitters.

The trumpets flew around the room. They hit the ceiling so forcefully that one broke into parts—the largest segment was dented. Drumsticks, which had florescent paint on the knobs, also levitated as a pair and performed a light show for the group. Tommy, one of the spirit children, materialized and played the flute placed on the floor. At the end, the spirit children took the duct tape on the floor and wrapped it about ten times around Warren—front and back. They even wrapped his right wrist about twenty times. When we turned the lights on, they had managed to take off Warren's hoodie!

Physical Phenomena Séance

Warren Caylor Séance

Glastonbury, Connecticut

Feb 15, 2017, 7:00 p.m.

Séance conditions: total darkness, with a candle lit on command

Materials: two metal trumpets, markers in a package, two black cardboard trumpets, two black ties, two slates tied together by rubber band, wood plank, drumsticks with florescent paint on their knobs

Instructions:

—No jewelry was allowed in séance room

—People wearing contact lens were examined for hidden camera in their contacts.

—You could not cross your legs or arms during the séance.

—You could not ask spirit how they died. [This is a sensitive question.]

Silence for one song, then we sang songs such as "YMCA" and "Respect" by Aretha Franklin, among other popular tunes. In about five minutes we could hear raps. Then we saw lights move in time to music.

Luther, a tall Nubian, came though, speaking in his deep voice. Also we heard Winston Churchill speak in his characteristic British accent. Next, seven-year-old Tommy spoke in a high-pitched voice. Then Tommy play the drumstick on a wood plank in time to music. The spirit asked in his-high pitched voice, "Who wants the trumpet?" Ron called out his name. The trumpet, which was made of black cardboard, flew over to Ron, tapping on his chest several times. [I felt Ron was being given a healing.]

Next the spirit children tied Warren up with one of the ties and took his hoodie off. They also used black tape to tie him to the chair.

I observed the following phenomena.

—raps

—drumstick levitated and played by invisible hands

—Spirit children drew with green marker. Happy Valentines' Day on one side and stick figure with Priscilla on the other side.

—lights circling and also forming a heart

—Luther, Yellow Feather, Winston Churchill, and Tommy spoke in direct voice.

—phenomena of matter through matter

—medium's hoodie removed and reversed

—spirit children taping Warren to the chair with duct tape

Physical Phenomena Séance

Medium: Warren Caylor Séance

Glastonbury, Connecticut

Feb 18, 2017, 7:00 p.m.

Séance conditions: total darkness, with a candle lit on command

Materials: two metal trumpets, markers in a package, two black cardboard trumpets, two black ties that were put together, two slates tied together by rubber band, wood plank, drumsticks with florescent paint on their knobs

Warren explained the séance protocol and gave the names of his guides: Luther, Yellow

Feather (Chief Massasoit), Tommy, and Winston Churchill. He explained that they would talk to us in direct voice.

Lights were turned off. Tommy played the harmonica and kazoo. Also, white chair with a glow-in-the-dark star levitated, and we could see the star move across the room and up. Spirit took a marker and wrote in blue ink heart of #12, who was a police officer.

In the middle of séance, he coughed up two rings, one with citrine, which he gave to Sylvia, and one cubic zirconia, which he gave to woman who was afraid of the dark, Susan. Also told Sylvia to wear it with a string around her neck and put it under the full moon.

I sat next to Kristen, who was next to cabinet. Saw Luther's big hand materialize next to white plaque that had levitated. Before the séance, Warren had people tie him up with five zip ties, so there was no way that he could have manipulated the 8-inch-square plaque. During the séance, all of the zip ties were untied and two placed on sitter's arms. Also, spirit took Warren's coat off and Tommy took the black duct tape and taped it around Warren in his chair several times.

Physical Mediumship Séance

Medium: Warren Caylor

Date: May 12, 2017, 6:30 p.m.

Location: Suffield, Connecticut

Séance conditions: total darkness, with a candle lit on command

Invitation stated: This is like no other séance you have experienced. During the session, Warren will be placed in a cabinet with his arms and legs taped to the chair, and his mouth gagged. Participants will witness levitation, direct voice of Warren's guides, and even apports.

Comments on Warren's May 12, 201, Séance:

The séance began with a beautiful 5-inch crystal apport that formed in Warren's mouth. Warren had just sat down in the cabinet and was not yet in trance. All of the sudden he seemed to be gagging on something in his mouth. His cabinet attendant placed a towel under him. He opened his mouth, where a crystal was literally forming. Within a minute, he forcefully expelled the crystal unto the towel. Understandably, Warren needed a moment to recover from the spontaneous apportation.

When the séance commenced, Yellow Feather, Luther, Winston Churchill, and little Tommy all came through and spoke so everyone in the room could hear them. The trumpet levitated and rapped so loudly on the ceiling, it broke apart. To everyone's delight, the wooden drumsticks with florescent knobs levitated as a pair and performed a light show for the group. At the end, the spirit children took the duct tape on the floor and wrapped it about twenty times around Warren, front and back! All these events took place while the medium was in trance—tied and gagged in the cabinet.

Physical Mediumship Séance

Medium: Warren Caylor

Date: July 24 at 6:30 p.m.

Location: Suffield, Connecticut

Séance conditions: total darkness, with a candle lit on command

During the session, Warren will be placed in a cabinet, with his arms and legs taped to the chair and his mouth gagged. Participants will witness levitation, direct voice of Warren's guides, and apports.

Three contraindications:

—One: Porch was light on, and had to stop the séance to put dark sheets up to cover the light. [Someone had switched it on just before the séance, to my dismay!]

—Two: Need florescent tabs for the CD player, as hard to adjust in the dark

—Three: Stern warning from Yellow Feather about listening carefully for full instructions

Yellow Feather said, "Open the cabinet," then paused, and I went do so, and he said, "Do you want to kill young Warren?" The only light that is safe is a candle, which Yellow Feather allowed to be lit at times. "However," the guide explained, "it is vital to count from 1 to 10 first." Séance about lasted two hours: 7:00–9:15.

As requested, I began the séance with a prayer. Then we started off with singing and a few jokes from Yellow Feather. When Yellow Feather saw that there was light coming though the blackout curtain, he stopped the séance. It seems someone had put the porch light on. We scrambled to put up a green sheet with duct tape.

The spirit children rang the bells, and the trumpet moved about. Winston Churchill came in and spoke to the group in his own voice [direct-voice phenomena]. He allowed questions. I asked how we can increase our spirituality. He gave an eloquent answer emphasizing understanding others and where they are in the world.

Ron asked a question regarding healing. Winston Churchill suggested working on ourselves first. He also emphasized praying for ourselves as well as others.

Then Yellow Feather was able to produce ectoplasm, which he extruded from Warren's nose. What did it look like? Well, it looked a bit like cotton candy but with cheesecloth texture. Yellow Feather stretched it into sheets. Warren is a very gifted physical medium. He is coming back to the United States to do a program at Lily Dale in September. We look forward to a return visit. He came through and produced ectoplasm, including an ectoplasmic hand, which came out of the cabinet; the hand just poked through the cabinet.

There were several powerful demonstrations of ectoplasm, which looked a bit like gossamer cheesecloth. It was stretched into sheets. At the last demonstration we were allowed to pull back the curtains and saw Warren sitting in the cabinet with ectoplasm extruded from his nose while he was in trance. Then Sylvia was allowed to come up and touch it. She said it felt like sticky cotton candy.

I sensed that there was a lot of healing that went on during the séance. I felt waves of healing over my breasts. I closed with a prayer.

The group was very energized and stayed until 10 or so. One of the guests shared his psychic photos, which included spirits, angels, and Ascended Masters.

Physical Phenomena Séance
Physical Mediumship Séance

Medium: Warren Caylor

Date: July 25 at 6:30 p.m.

Location: Suffield, Connecticut

Séance conditions: total darkness, with a candle lit on command

We had more control tonight, though top sheet was off the cabinet. It was very dark with no lights in the séance room. We also had better control with the music, as Steve was in charge of the CD player. At one point there seem to be static. It was Tommy—he said impishly, "I was playing with the stereo." Yellow Feather, who was a bit impatient, requested an MP3 player. The spirit children came out and rang the bell and played the drumsticks. Tommy (8-year-old spirit boy) picked up the drumsticks with the florescent tips and played a beat on the floor with such verve, you would have thought he was a professional drummer!

The trumpets levitated and whizzed through the air. At one point, there were three trumpets up in the air! The energy was incredible.

The spirit of Winston Churchill came through in his own voice with great nobility. He spoke in his own voice directly in the room. Warren, of course, was gagged. He also knew about our trip to a local Chinese restaurant that had seen better days. He commented that the chicken was not chicken, implying it might have been from a lesser animal. (I thought I will never eat there again!)

Then Luther (the tall Nubian spirit) came and allowed four people to go up to sit in the chair placed in front of the cabinet. While seated, each felt Luther's spirit hands touch them on the head and shoulders. There was a great mass of ectoplasm—even a spirit hand fully materialized, which went around the room. Steve, a parapsychology student, was allowed to touch it, and he said it was solid and felt just like a human hand. Warren was cut from the ties, and while in trance he walked over to me with about 2 feet of ectoplasm extruded from his nostrils. Yellow Feather led Warren over to me, and I was allowed to touch the ectoplasm. It felt like cotton candy with a rougher or netlike texture.

As always, there was so much energy present that I did not go to bed till midnight. When I fell asleep, I slept like a baby. There was so much healing in the room—I feel great today!

Physical Phenomena Séance
Physical Mediumship Séance
Medium: Warren Caylor
Date: September 8 2017, 6:45 p.m.
Location: Glastonbury, Connecticut
Séance conditions: total darkness, with a candle lit on command

Warren went into trance easily (about three minutes). Winston Churchill came through first. He spoke in direct voice so everyone in the room could hear his comments: "You may call me friend." Then the spirit commented on President Trump's wall: "You just taken down one wall, and now you are building another. You [humanity] hasn't learned very much!" When a scientist analyzed Winston Churchill's voice, comparing it with old WWII news clips, there was a 97% match.

Tommy, the 8-year-old spirit child, played the flute, using Warren's lungs. Spirits do not have organs, so Tommy had to use Warren's lungs! The spirit of Tommy, a boy about 8, played the flute and also used the drumsticks. His enthusiastic demonstration was visible since the knob had fluorescent paint.

Jeffry, a man about 40, sat next to me, and he was asked to go up and sit in the chair outside the cabinet. He felt a large male hand (Luther) on his shoulder and a tiny touch from a small hand (Jessica, a 3-year-old spirit child).

Next, the spirit of Yellow Cloud materialized to take Warren's left hand out of ties and left his right hand in. I saw ectoplasm like white ribbon from outside the cabinet.

Physical Mediumship Séance
Medium: Warren Caylor
Date: September 9, 2017, 6:45 p.m.
Location: Glastonbury, Connecticut
Séance conditions: total darkness, with a candle lit on command

The trumpet flew across the séance room again Saturday night in Glastonbury, Connecticut. International medium Warren Caylor went easily into trance and brought through the spirit of Winston Churchill. He spoke clearly and loud enough for all to hear in direct voice. Winston Churchill told the group, "Look up, not down. Look forward, not backward," in his distinct British accent.

This time the spirit of little Tommy played a folk tune on the harmonica, as he tried to follow along with the music. Then he made some lively music of his own, as he seized the drumsticks and loudly hammered out a tune, which all could hear. He finished by twirling the drumsticks so their fluorescent knob produced a light show.

There was a wonderful demonstration of ectoplasm. Yellow Feather explained the milky substance extruded from the medium is three-dimensional. He also stretched it into a triangle with a 3-foot base. It was truly an amazing sight!

The highlight of the evening came when Yellow Feather coaxed the spirit of a famous singer to come out. Yellow Feather said, "He's taking awhile to come through. Then we heard the singer speak in very soft voice, saying, "Good evening" two times. The singer then snapped his fingers and sang "Hold My Hand." Finally, a Louis Armstrong song came on, "You've Got a Friend." It was all so deeply moving!

Priscilla, who had placed a piece of chocolate brownie on top of the spirit cabinet for Luther, checked to see if the spirit had eaten it. Sure enough, it was gone at the end of the séance. Luther loves chocolate!

Physical Mediumship Séance

Medium: Warren Caylor
Date: March 23, 2018, 6:45 p.m.
Location: Glastonbury, Connecticut
Séance conditions: total darkness, with a candle lit on command

Warren Caylor gave a spectacular séance that night. The medium went into trance easily (about 3 minutes). Then spirit brought through blessings and physical evidence for life after death. The séance began with apports—about 20 formed in Warren's mouth. Some were from Ascended Masters and others from relatives. One woman received a stone from her father, "James," another gentleman received a stone from his American Indian guide, and another received a gemstone from the Buddha with a personal message. I was called up to pick out two rose quartz stones—one heart-shaped one for my husband, Ron, to put under his pillow for healing, and a smaller one for my benefit. There was so much healing energy in the room that I believe everyone received some benefit just by sitting in the circle!

Winston Churchill came in to greet "young Elaine," and asked how I was doing. He spoke in direct voice. The spirit of eight-year-old Tommy giggled and stepped out of the cabinet to play the drumsticks with florescent knobs. What a show—the lively beat of the drums—followed by a light show with the florescent knobs in a dark séance room! Tommy even managed to take the magic marker out of its package to write a message on a small canvas, "love you, XXX."

Christmas Tree Séance

Medium: Warren Caylor
Date: November 18, 2019, 7:00 p.m.
Location: Glastonbury, Connecticut
Séance conditions: total darkness, with a candle lit on command
Materials: a bare Christmas tree, toys supplied by sitters, two metal trumpets, markers in a package, two black ties that were put together with wood plank, drumsticks with fluorescent paint, wooden spirit cabinet

Séance instructions were as follows: "Please bring an unwrapped toy for under the tree.

During the session, Warren will be in a cabinet (enclosed space) with arms taped to a chair and his mouth gagged." We were told to expect levitation of objects, ectoplasm, direct voice, teleportation of objects, and the materialization of spirit children. They would be unwrapping and playing with toys.

Christmas certainly came early with English medium Warren Caylor's Christmas Tree Séance. Warren sat in a spirit cabinet, with his arms taped to a chair and his mouth gagged. Everyone held hands, so no one but the spirits could move the objects. When the spirit children came in, we could hear the sounds of toys being torn from their wrapping paper, to the delight of the children. One even took out the toy dog I had donated and pressed the button on the toy's leg to make barking sounds. Too cool!

Warren's guides orchestrated the event. Luther, Yellow Feather, Winston Churchill, and Tommy, who did a spectacular light show with the drumsticks and trumpet. Priscilla received a message, "Merry Christmas, XXX," with magic markers and white board shrink-wrapped

Kai Muegge, Medium from Frankfurt, Germany
Physical Phenomena Séance

Medium: Kai Muegge

Dates: Thursday, August 15, and Saturday, August 17th, about 9:00 p.m.

Location: Cassadaga, New York

Séance conditions: complete darkness, candle lit on command

Everyone (about 23 sitters) arrived at 7:30 p.m. His spirit cabinet was stung together with black cloth and a hula hoop. We were told to remove all jewelry. Men were also told to remove their belts. Next, Kai explained the rules:

—One: No one allowed beyond the tape, which marked about 2 feet in front of the cabinet, as it was a force field

—Two: When Julia said "Chain," we were to link hands. When she said "Silence," we were to cease talking.

—Three: It was important that everyone sang or hummed to the music, as the singing helped to raise the energy in the room.

Kai works in the tradition of Rudi Schneider. His main guide is Professor Hans Bender, who sounds like a kindly old man. While the United States was more involved in Spiritualism, Germany focused on parapsychology. Kai then explained the three phases of the séance that evening:

—Phase 1: complete darkness

—Phase 2: Some florescent light from a ping-pong ball, tile, and trumpet, which had been sprayed with florescent paint.

—Phase 3: Red light allowed

Then Ron volunteered to watch Kai undress for séance, to be sure he was completely naked under the séance garb.

Another volunteer was selected to hold Kai's left hand and knee. Julia held Kai's right hand and knee when in chain. The medium held in control by Julia on his right and another female sitter on the left.

—First sensation: I was startled by spirit hitting me in the chest when the room was completely dark. Not wishing to stop the phenomena, I said, "Welcome spirit."

—Then we heard taps on the ceiling—a sign that the spirits were present and ready to begin the séance. Julia shouted "Chain," the command to sit in control by linking hands.

Our host, Neal, had a tape with Beatles songs, "Let It Be," "Imagine," and "My Sweet Lord," as well as favorites "Row, Row, Row Your Boat, "You Are My Sunshine," and "I've Been Working on the Railroad." As the energy in the room built, spirit responded with more taps, and we could hear rattles!

In the second phase, there was some light from the items that Julia sprayed, including three ping-pong balls to illuminate them. We saw ping-pong balls rise off the bucket/table to go to the floor, then 8-inch tile, as invisible hands juggled the balls. Then we saw spirit hand a form on another illuminated 8-inch tile placed on the séance room floor. First, three spirit fingers formed, then four fingers appeared. On Saturday, I was in a better position and saw two fingers and a thumb form on the 8-inch tile in the middle of the room.

Next, the trumpet quickly rose and began darting around the room. It hit Ron in the chest several times with a staccato beat, and on the bridge of his glasses. Then the trumpet hit me on the left side, then the right, and then on the bridge of my glasses.

While Kai was in the cabinet, bright white lights crisscrossed the room. Both Ron and I saw white lights spontaneously appear and crisscross the room. Ron saw a very small green light chased by a red light.

The third phase was held in red light. Professor Hans Bender came in and talked about human consciousness. He explained that alien consciousness began being mixed with humans about 6,000 years ago. The first group was quite humanistic. The second mixing, the group was more materialistic. "Don't worry about your dead relatives; they have just taken an early exit off the highway. You will catch up with them later."

He was upset with dust on the floor left over from shaman, and said it would be detrimental to the medium. The two attendants opened the cabinet carefully, as ectoplasm can stick to the curtain. There was Kai covered with ectoplasmic cobwebs over his face and chest and some at his feet. In the center was a 10-inch oval photograph of a brunette middle-aged woman. After some prodding from the spirit of Professor Hans Bender, a gentleman said it looked like the face of his friend Barbara, who had died recently. Then an ectoplasmic hand appeared at the base of the cabinet and waved playfully to us.

We were energized and very wide awake when the séance ended about 1:30 a.m., and we went out for breakfast at Denny's!

Summary of Phenomena

—sound of taps on the ceiling

—sound of rattles rattling

—ping-pong ball glide to group

—hand with three fingers forms on tile

—trumpets rise and float around the room

—Both of us were hit forcefully by trumpet multiple times.

Medium: Mychael Shane explained the rules to the twenty-five sitters. Everyone was to remain seated unless told to move. No one was to touch him while he was in trance, nor were we to speak his name, "Mychael," as he would be likely to return from the trance state prematurely, putting an end to the séance.

Medium: Mychael

Ascended Master séance medium: Rev. Mychael Shane

Location: Cassadaga, New York

In 2017 and 2018, I was able to sit with another medium famous for apport—Seattle medium Mychael Shane. As a child he had psychic gifts—receiving his first apport, a gem, as a child. Still, he was reluctant to follow the path of physical mediumship even though his mother was a member Keith Rhinehart's Seattle church. Instead, he had a varied career, from the military to rock music.

Ascended Master Séance

Medium: Rev. Mychael Shane

Date: July 27, 2017, 7:30 p.m.

Location: Cassadaga, New York

Séance conditions: total darkness with red light upon request

My husband and I attended Thursday night's "Q&A with Lady Nada and St. Germaine." After a brief introduction, Mychael went into the spirit cabinet and closed the curtains. In a few minutes, he was in deep trance. The red light was shut off, and the séance was in complete darkness. There was a trumpet, which levitated so the spirit voices could speak through the séance trumpet. There was also a bell at the top of the cabinet. When spirit rang the bell attached to the cabinet, we knew that they had materialized in the room. The spirits drew open the curtains of the cabinet. Several spirits spoke in direct voice, so everyone in the room could hear them. When Lady Nada came through, we were given the opportunity to ask her a question. My question was "How can I become a physical medium?" Lady Nada answered in her characteristic high-pitched voice: "Are you sure that is what you want?" I said, "Yes." She then gave some encouraging advice.

Ascended Master Healing Séance

Medium: Rev. Mychael Shane

July 29, 2017, 7:30 p.m.

Location: Cassadaga, New York

Séance conditions: total darkness with red light upon request

We also attended Saturday night, July 29, a hands-on healing event with partial or full materialization of one of the masters. The person lies on a massage table, and materialized hands will perform the healing. That evening, twelve people were selected for healing. Ron was one of those chosen. The healing was in red light. I saw him go up to the chair in front of the cabinet. Spirit took his glasses off and sent healing to his eyes and the top of this head. When they were finished, spirit hands put his glasses back on!

Mychael aported about 40 faceted crystal stones of various sizes and gave us each one crystal with a personal message. Ours was from Lord Maitreya. Others received stones from archangel Michael and other Ascended Masters. We both received apports in the form of small crystal triangles. We were given this message: "You have worked hard for others. Now more leisure time."

We were then given the opportunity to choose one or two for others. Ron picked one for his brother David, who has been ill. I picked a heart-shaped oval for our daughter Kimberly, who needed more abundance.

Dr. Neal Rzepkowski, president of Lily Dale Assembly, later commented, "I know, hard to believe. But I have even larger apports that have been gifted to me by other 'materialization mediums.'"

Materialization Séance

Medium: David Thompson

Date: September 26, 2019

Location: Santa Fe, New Mexico

Séance conditions: total darkness, with a candle lit on command

Ron and I attended materialization séances with David Thompson. I went to three on September 26, 27, and 29—Ron attended two on Thursday the 26th and Sunday the 29th.

The séance began after everyone was searched and seated. I was placed directly opposite David Thompson—about 20 feet from the cabinet. David was tied to a chair and gagged.

Two people examined him to be sure his gag and zip ties were secure. Steve watched as they did so. Before the séance began, Rev. Thomas Newman explained the rules:

One: We had to be quiet during the séance and hold hands if requested. Should we let go of a hand (for any reason), we were to let Tom know immediately. Since the ectoplasm is attached to David, we were not to touch it or put our feet out, as we could kick it. This would cause a shock to the medium—and could even burn his internal organs.

I sat a few chairs away from Ron, next to Mary, a mediumship student from camp. During our brief conversation, it turned out that she knew a mutual acquaintance, Rev.

Suzanne Greer. I sensed the cordial presence of Rev. Susie Greer as were asked to sing happy tunes such as the Black Eyed Peas song "It's Going to Be a Good Night" and the standard "Somewhere over the Rainbow."

In about ten minutes, William came through. We could all hear his booming resonant British accent to welcome us. He opened the séance up for questions for discussion.

Tom suggested describing the seven planes. Steve suggested William talk about the relationship of soul, spirit, and God. William chose Steve's topic and gave a very erudite talk on philosophy.

William mentioned that even Jesus ate meat—he materialized the bread and fishes for the multitude. "It is OK to kill animals for our sustenance, but not otherwise," said William. He next discussed war. "Killing another person is an abomination," William said emphatically. He added, "We are all part of God and should treat each other as brothers and sisters."

After a twenty-minute discussion, William opened the room up for a second question.

I asked, "Do extraterrestrials work with David and physical mediums?" William replied, "No."

Then he asked Steve if he worked with extraterrestrials, and he said, "No."

William spoke about how important it was to be evidential—not just say, "I have a grandfather's vibration." He said, "Philip, who was called Phil, came in to speak to his grandson." No one said a word. Later, a middle-aged brunette man said, "My grandfather's same was Philip, but I never knew him." William said his grandfather was with him. The spirit of the man's grandfather walked about 20 feet from the cabinet and stood directly in front of him to speak in direct voice. Grandfather said, "Look, learn, understand. You have my blood, and it is only natural to want to help a blood relative."

Next, the spirit of Andrea, who died two years ago at 41, materialized to talk to her parents, David and Sue, members of the Saratoga Church. William announced, "Someone very special is here." Andrea even took off her mother's pink baseball cap and kissed her on the head and held her father's hand.

It was so poignant that William did not wish to have the trumpet phenomena or hear Louis Armstrong sing, as it could not compare with the love in the room. He ended the séance by requesting the song "Music of the Night from *The Phantom of the Opera*. We all felt spirits around us. I sensed the spirits of Margery Crandon and Dry Prince in the room, as well as my grandmother and grandfather Gladys and Kenneth Custance. It was a grand finale!

Materialization Séance
Medium: David Thompson
Date: September 28, 2019

Location: Santa Fe, New Mexico

Séance conditions: total darkness, with a candle lit on command

I attended this séance alone. Rev. Tom Newman said during his opening remarks that last year, Abraham Lincoln had materialized and said, "God bless America" five times. Four years ago at the Masonic Hall, spirit had transported David some 40 feet. He also told the group about another séance where David was tied to the chair and put upside down and passed by spirit around the room, so people could pat his bald head! (Intuitively, I believed this to be true.)

William spoke for 20 minutes or more about the need to take care of ourselves before we take care of others. [Intuitively, I heard the name "Roberts."] Later, William said a Mr. Roberts was here to talk to his grandson. Then an English man with his wife answered, "My grandfather's last name was Roberts." The materialized spirit of his grandfather went over to him and asked, "Why are you here?" He said, "I am here on holiday with my wife." Grandfather said, "Nice to meet you" to the man's wife. She said, "I am a medium and have a séance circle." Grandfather then asked, "Does Michael attend?" She answered, "No." Grandfather quipped, "Maybe he should."

Then the spirit of Bob came to talk to his mother. He urged her not to be so sad. They exchanged some personal information, which brought tears to his mother.

Next, the spirit boy Timmy, materialized and did a light show, using drumsticks with florescent knobs. It was spectacular and lightened the mood.

Finally, we heard the voice of Louis Armstrong, who sang "Hello Dolly." He was very lively. We thanked him, and he said in direct voice, "My pleasure." David started songs by the Black Eyed Peas, "It's Going to Be a Good Night," and ended with "Love Is Like a Boat."

When the lights came on, David's sweater was in inside out and backward!

Materialization Séance

Medium: David Thompson

Date: September 29, 2019

Location: Santa Fe, New Mexico

Séance conditions: total darkness, with a candle lit on command

I was excited to attend the Sunday séance, as William, David's guide, promised to bring through a special guest. Both Ron and I attended the séance. I took orb photos after the event as well. There were many orbs over the United Church that night!

William came through and spoke in direct voice very clearly so all could hear. He said that he had been with David since he took his first breath. William then took questions. One woman asked about planes after birth, and William answered, "The first place that you go after birth is very much like earthly home."

Louis Armstrong came in to sing "Hello Dolly." Then "the special guest" arrived. It was none other than the spirit of the great Native American chief Sitting Bull. He spoke in direct voice. He said that he waited five years to be able to come through David. Sitting Bull added, "Some here can see me and will do a spirit picture." [I felt the message was for me, as I had been thinking of taking art classes to do spirit portraits.] After the séance, a medium from Florida approached me. She said, "I think that you could do a picture of Sitting Bull." [Her spontaneous comment confirmed my intuition!]

Scott Mulligan, Medium from England

In February 2019, the *We Don't Die* podcast sponsored Scott Mulligan, one of the world's top physical mediums. I knew Sandra Champlain, the founder of the podcast, as I had been on her program twice—once to discuss *The Medium Who Baffled Houdini* and another time for *Séance 101: Physical Mediumship*.

Materialization Séance

Medium: Scott Mulligan

Date: February 21, 2019

Location: Quincy, Massachusetts

Séance conditions: total darkness, with a candle lit on command

I drew the number 130, so my seat was directly opposite the medium. About 3 feet away were an array of toys for the spirit children. These included a drum, drumsticks, shoelaces, rattles, a whistle, and other musical toys. [This, by the way, was a perfect position for observation, as I was directly across from Scott and had a full view of the room.]

After Scott went into trance, we listened to three songs played on the iPad and then sang along to tunes such as "What Do You Do with a Drunken Sailor," "Nick Knack Paddy Whack, Give a Dog a Bone," "You Are My Sunshine," and "Jingle Bells." The singing was loud and enthusiastic.

The sound of the singing was pierced by the sound of a very loud whistle. Then we heard the sounds of a group of spirit children playing with the toys. Eventually, one played on the drum in time with our singing. Impressive!

The spirit of Daniel spoke to the group at length as he tried to place two young girls, one who died from a blood illness and another in an accident. This took about 15 minutes, as two women said, "I understand."

Finally the young girl came through and sang "The Star Spangled Banner." Immediately, her mother knew it was her daughter, Ashley, as she had been practicing that song before she died.

Scott remained in deep trance for the séance, which lasted about an hour. Toward the end, we heard a distinctly British voice. A few sitters recognized it as that of the spirit of Bram Rogers, the partner of the late medium Leslie Flint. Bram spoke briefly about love. Everyone in the large ballroom heard him and was touched by his message. Apparently he has come through before. Scott on occasion has had the spirit of Judy Garland come in. When she does, she prefers to be called by her real name, Frances Gumm. However, Frances did not come in this evening.

Eric Robert Johnson did make an appearance. When he spoke in direct voice, he sounded like an elderly English gentleman from another age and gave a philosophical talk. He spoke through Scott in a loud and clear voice. He ended with messages of hope and that we don't die but live on in the hearts of loved ones.

Finally, at the end of the evening we all heard a loud thump. It was so loud we were momentarily startled. When the lights were turned on, there was Scott in a heavy oak chair about 5 feet outside the cabinet, with his back to us. The spirits had moved his chair and all outside the cabinet in trance and turned the chair and Scott around!

After the séance, I picked up the oak Morris chair, which Sandra had brought from her home. It must have weighed a good 50 pounds—Scott is about 5 feet, 11 inches tall and 185 lb. or so in weight. To think that spirit energy could lift over 200 pound is truly amazing!

Index

Elaine M. Kuzmeskus, director of the New England School of Metaphysics, is a nationally known Spiritualist medium. During her many years of mediumship, she has conducted several well-publicized séances, including the official Houdini séance as well as séances at the Mark Twain House and Long Wharf Theater. She is the author of nine books on metaphysics including *The Art of Mediumship*, *The Medium Who Baffled Houdini*, and her biography, *The Making of a Medium*. She has also written articles for *Fate Magazine*. For the past 20 years, Elaine has been a popular guest on radio programs such as *Coast to Coast with George Noory*, *We Don't Die*, and *The Paranormal View*, as well as television programs, including *Better Connecticut*, *Practical Talk Time*, and the PBS special, "*Things That Go Bump in the Night.*"